THOMAS GRAY, SCHOLAR

G. B. Bosio dir.   L. Rados inc.

Tommaso Gray

A LATE EIGHTEENTH-CENTURY ITALIAN PRINT OF GRAY

Thomas Gray, Scholar

The True Tragedy of an
Eighteenth-Century Gentleman

With two youthful notebooks now published for the
first time from the Original Manuscripts in
the Morgan Library, New York City

BY

WILLIAM POWELL JONES

New York
RUSSELL & RUSSELL
1965

To

MY FATHER AND MOTHER

WHO DEPRIVED THEMSELVES OF COMFORTS TO

EDUCATE THEIR CHILDREN

THIS BOOK IS LOVINGLY DEDICATED

PREFACE

THE reputation of Thomas Gray as a poet is secure. His poetical works, slight enough to be mistaken, he feared, for those of an insect, have been reprinted and praised in countless new editions and anthologies. Only a few critics, notably the great Dr. Johnson, have ventured to disturb the encomiums of Gray's poetry, and even they have gladly bowed to the universal appeal of the *Elegy*.

The world has been justly curious about a poet who could gain such a name for himself by writing so little. Gray's contemporaries were no exception. After his death they eagerly read his letters and talked about him. They began to learn, even before Mason printed the letters in his biography of Gray, that he was not only poet but scholar as well. In March 1772, less than a year after the poet's death, the *London Magazine* printed a sketch of him by the Reverend William Johnson Temple, who knew a great deal about him through Norton Nicholls. As John Mitford afterwards pointed out, Temple did justice neither to Gray's poetic imagination nor to his sense of humor. At the same time he gave so good an account of the variety and extent of the poet's scholarly pursuits that Mason printed it with a few additions in his memoir of Gray (1775), and Johnson adopted it six years later for his notorious critique of Gray in the *Lives of the Poets*.

Temple's account of Gray's learning is concise but revealing:

Perhaps he was the most learned man in Europe. He was equally acquainted with the elegant and profound parts of science, and that not superficially but thoroughly. He knew every branch of history, both natural and civil; had read all the original historians of England, France, and Italy; and was a great antiquarian. Criticism, metaphysics, morals, politics made a principal part of his plan of study; voyages and travels of all sorts were his favourite amusement; and he had a fine taste in painting, prints, architecture, and gardening.

Such was Gray's reputation as a scholar shortly after his death. Many of his friends, curious about his learning, borrowed some of his notebooks from Mason and concluded that Temple's estimate was not grossly exaggerated. Not until 1814 did the reading public get a sample of the poet's erudition, in the second volume of T. J. Mathias' expensive edition of Gray's works. This was in the form of comparatively few excerpts from the voluminous Commonplace Book, newly acquired by Pembroke College (Cambridge) as a bequest from Richard Stonhewer. The meager and garbled versions of Mathias have been reprinted from time to time [1] and have been generally accepted by critics without reference to the original notebooks. John Mitford, a very industrious editor, left, in his letters and notebooks,[2] a great deal of unused material relating to Gray, some of which was printed by Duncan C. Tovey in *Gray and His Friends* (1890). Gray's notes have been described at times, notably in the catalogues of sales in 1845 at Evans' and in 1851 at Sotheby's. The present work is the first attempt to give a complete account of Gray's learning and a critical estimate of its importance in his life.

My book was ready for the printer when early in 1935 I saw for the first time two works of M. Roger Martin, *Maître de Conférences* at Montpellier University, concerning Gray. The smaller, *Chronologie de la vie et de l'œuvre de Thomas Gray* (London, Oxford University Press), is valuable chiefly for its critical history of writings on Gray and for its publication of excerpts from the Commonplace Book, particularly the essay, "Cambri," in full. The more ambitious *Essai sur Thomas Gray* (London: Oxford University Press, 1934), in spite of its title, is a noteworthy book, the best study of Gray's personality yet attempted. In 1933 M. Martin very kindly sent me a rough outline of the proposed *Essai* and a few proof sheets from the *Chronologie*. The latter, he explained, was at that time printed and deposited at the Sorbonne, but no copies of it could be had, since it would not be published until his degree was granted.

---

[1] Notably by Edmund Gosse, *The Works of Thomas Gray* (London, 1884), vol. IV, and by C. S. Northup, *Essays and Criticism by Thomas Gray* (Boston, 1911).

[2] The notebooks are now in the British Museum, the letters relating to Gray in the Harvard Library.

Martin has divided his *Essai* into four parts: physical and moral character, feelings, intellectual activity, and poetry. This very extensiveness is the weakness of the book, for not all parts of it are equally good. The last part, for example, may be essential to Martin's scheme, but it contributes little that is new or important to an English reader who is already familiar with the work of many critics of Gray's poetry. The first part, on the other hand, is brilliantly conceived and executed. Using the methods of modern psychiatry, Martin has traced in the poet's personality the germs of his melancholy and sterility. Gray inherited a frail body and an anxious temperament, so that he was always enchained by actual pain or fear of pain.[3] Add to this inheritance the environment of Cambridge, Stoke Poges, and London, and the character of Gray is completely described.

In the second part of his *Essai,* Martin has depicted with great accuracy Gray's relations with his friends, first at Eton with Walpole, West, and Ashton, next in mature life with Wharton, Mason, Brown, and others, finally with the young men at Cambridge. He has analyzed Gray's love for young Victor de Bonstetten with merciless exactitude. He ends the second part with a discussion of Gray's interest in the fine arts and in natural history, which belongs more logically to the third part — Gray's intellectual activity. The third part treats, in a sketchy but very stimulating manner, the subject I have taken. Martin holds the theory that all of Gray's study was but a revival of the past, and parades his examples in a bewildering array to prove his point. To me, the sequence of Gray's scholarly activity seems much less logical, and at the same time of more consequence, both to his own circle and to the world at large, than Martin's theories allow.

Martin should find two classes of enthusiastic readers: scholars for his array of new material, and students in his own country for his translations into French of many poems and letters. The English reader will not be able to detect, in French dress, the informal charm of Gray's letters. The parts of my book which necessarily

[3] That Martin has leaned heavily upon the scientific diagnoses of Professor A. Hesnard strengthens rather than minimizes the findings.

duplicate Martin's work will, therefore, have the additional excuse of presenting the arguments to English readers in Gray's own
words. The new material I have presented speaks for itself.

Shortly after the publication of Martin's essay on Gray, the
Clarendon Press at Oxford brought out the long-expected defini-
tive edition of Gray's correspondence, begun by the late Paget
Toynbee and completed by Mr. Leonard Whibley. This work
contains not only the best available texts of the letters but also a
wealth of new illustrative material that makes it a Gray encyclo-
pedia. Mr. R. W. Ketton-Cremer's recent biography of Gray in
the " Great Lives " series would have profited from this new material, yet it holds a place with all lovers of Gray because of its
simplicity and its charming style.

My indebtedness for help in this work is too great to allow
mention of more than a few outstanding examples. I wish especially to acknowledge the aid of the late Paget Toynbee and of
Mr. Leonard Whibley in finding scattered Gray material in England; of the Master and Fellows of Pembroke College, Cambridge,
for permission to use the Commonplace Book; of their genial
librarian, the late Mr. A. L. Attwater, for much assistance; of Sir
John Murray and Mr. Geoffrey Howard for making it possible for
me to use the Gray notebooks in their possession; and of the Trustees of the Pierpont Morgan Library for permission to publish
their Gray notebooks. I am indebted to the Trustees of the Henry
E. Huntington Library for permission to reproduce the frontispiece. Designed by G. B. Bosio (c. 1780) and engraved by Luigi
Rados (1773–1840), the likeness appears to have been adapted
from the Basire engraving in Mason's life of Gray (1775); the
idealized figure, taller and thinner than Gray is said to have been,
is from Bosio's imagination. This print, not listed in Hans Singer's
Allgemeiner Bildniskatalog or in the British Museum catalogue
of British portraits, is here reproduced from a copy bound in a
Huntington Library volume (HM 12550–3).

I wish also to thank the many librarians, especially those at
the British Museum, the Morgan Library, Eton College, and Harvard University, who have made my research easier and more

pleasant. My work in England was made possible through the generosity of the Dexter Fund at Harvard University. My book has fewer errors because of the criticism of my colleagues, Professors Holly Hanford, Benjamin Bourland, and Finley Foster. My whole scheme has been made possible by the encouragement and assistance of Professor George Lyman Kittredge, to whom I again pay a small part of my debt of homage.

W. P. J.

CLEVELAND, OHIO

JUNE 19, 1937

CONTENTS

I. FASTIDIOUS LITTLE GENTLEMAN 3

II. THE EVOLUTION OF A BOOKWORM 30

III. THE HERITAGE OF GREECE AND ROME 49

IV. THE ROAD TO CATHAY 70

V. NOTES FOR THE FIRST HISTORY OF ENGLISH POETRY . . . 84

VI. PROFESSOR OF MODERN HISTORY 108

VII. THE DISCIPLE OF LINNAEUS 125

VIII. SCHOLAR AND POET 142

ADDENDA

TEXT OF GRAY NOTEBOOKS IN PIERPONT MORGAN LIBRARY . . . 151

1. GRAY'S EARLY CATALOGUE OF HIS LIBRARY 151

2. NOTES ON LEARNED JOURNALS 164

REGISTER OF GRAY AUTOGRAPH MANUSCRIPTS 175

INDEX 183

ABBREVIATIONS OF BOOKS AND MANUSCRIPTS FREQUENTLY CITED

CPB.................... Gray's MS. Commonplace Book, 3 vols. folio, now in the care of the Master and Fellows, Pembroke College, Cambridge.

Gray's Linnaeus .... Interleaved *Systema naturae*, 2 vols. (10th ed., Stockholm, 1758–1759), now in Harvard University Library.

Martin, *Chronologie* .... Roger Martin, *Chronologie de la vie et de l'œuvre de Thomas Gray.*

Martin, *Essai* .... Roger Martin, *Essai sur Thomas Gray.*

Mathias .... *The Works of Thomas Gray*, 2 vols. (London, 1814), ed. by T. J. Mathias.

Mitford MS. .... The Notebooks of John Mitford in the British Museum. Volumes III and IV consist of transcripts from Gray MSS. then (1845–1851) in the possession of G. J. Penn. Add. MSS. 32561–62. Volume III is in two parts, with fresh pagination from p. 121.

Register .... Register of Gray Autograph MSS. at end of this volume.

Tovey .... *The Letters of Thomas Gray*, 3 vols. (London, 1900–1912), ed. by D. C. Tovey.

Toynbee .... *The Correspondence of Gray, Walpole, West, and Ashton, 1734–1771*, 2 vols. (Oxford, 1915), ed. by Paget Toynbee.

Whibley .... *Correspondence of Thomas Gray*, 3 vols. (Oxford, Clarendon Press, 1935), ed. by the late Paget Toynbee, and Leonard Whibley.

THOMAS GRAY, SCHOLAR

CHAPTER I

FASTIDIOUS LITTLE GENTLEMAN

Thomas Gray was by temperament a student in that he cared a great deal more for the mind of man than for active participation in human affairs. His reflective nature was encouraged by the circumstances of his daily life to such an extent that he sought refuge and found consolation within himself. He took learning as his mistress to ward off boredom, and she became his wife, leading him with soothing hands from poetry into the world of books. By the time of his death, although he was only in his fifty-fifth year, he had become so erudite that even Dr. Johnson, who did not appreciate his poetry, was willing to accept Temple's estimate of him as " perhaps the most learned man in Europe."

To the world at large he was still " Mr. Gray the Poet," for his famous churchyard elegy had in a few years after its publication charmed all England, and his two Pindaric odes from the Strawberry Hill Press had created much excitement even if they were not understood. The entire body of his verse, reprinted from time to time in Dodsley's popular miscellanies, was notably meager. Three years before his death Gray himself collected his poetical works for publication in London and in Glasgow, and, lest for their leanness they be taken for the works of a flea or a pismire, added "about two ounces of stuff" from his files. In spite of his slim output, however, Gray had at his death the general reputation of being an outstanding poet, while to those who knew him best his greatest achievement lay perhaps in the line of scholarly research in many fields of learning, even to the point of virtuosity in English history and in entomology.

With all his erudition Gray was far from being " the most learned man in Europe." Voltaire comes nearer that description; and even in England, several antiquarians, notably his friend William Cole, surpassed Gray in collecting odd facts. But surely Temple had good reasons for making an estimate that seems extravagant in the light of modern scholarship and yet was acceptable to his contemporaries.

The purpose of the present work is to evaluate Gray's reputation as a scholar and to show the overwhelming role that learning played in his life. This can be done only by a careful study of numerous unpublished relics of his research. As a prelude to such study, let us see how the more important events in his career conspired with his temperament to make him more scholar than poet.

I

Gray cannot have had a very happy childhood in London. Born in Cornhill the day after Christmas 1716, the fifth of twelve children, and the only one who lived to grow up, he himself was saved at birth, it is said, only by his mother's bravery in opening one of his veins with her own hand to prevent suffocation. Whether apocryphal or not, the story is typical of much of the boy's relation to his family. His father indolently and selfishly depleted the small fortune he had inherited, treating his wife with such extreme cruelty that in 1734 she left his house for a time and contemplated legal action against him. Gray's mother, with her sister, kept a millinery shop, the profits from which went to buy her clothes and even the furniture of the house, " almost providing everything for her son, whilst at Eton school, and now he is at Peter-House at Cambridge." [1] What little home life there may have been amid such domestic quarreling would have been trying to any child, and torture itself to one so sensitive as Thomas.

Fortunately the boy escaped while still young. His mother saw to that, sending him when he was about ten to Eton, where two of her brothers, Robert and William Antrobus, were teaching. He must have got a great deal from the classical training of Eton and especially from the personal interest of his uncles. Robert Antrobus, by avocation a naturalist, taught his nephew the rudiments of botany, and bequeathed him, at his death in 1730, his

---

[1] The whole case, which Dorothy Gray submitted to her lawyer in 1735, was first printed by John Mitford, *Poems of Thomas Gray* (London, 1814), pp. lxxxvii ff.

scientific books. Most important of all to young Thomas Gray, Eton gave him companionship with other boys, especially with boys who shared his love of books and poetry. Gray became part of an intimate " Quadruple Alliance " that had for its other members Thomas Ashton, Horace Walpole, son of England's prime minister, and Richard West, son of Ireland's lord chancellor and grandson of the famous Bishop Burnet. Such highborn companions as Walpole and West, far from frightening the unfortunate milliner's son from Cornhill, seem to have brought out in him his gayest and most poetical sides. Walpole often paid tribute to Gray's mature judgment even when young by saying that " Gray was never a boy," but the recently discovered youthful letters show that this is not wholly true. In writing to Walpole Gray revealed a playful humor that is gay almost to the point of frivolity. To West, on the other hand, he laid bare his more sincere poetical nature, bringing to the surface of his letters depths of imagination and emotion. Even as a lad Gray had many sides, which he displayed in the banter of youthful sophistication, in the love of literature, or in the first budding of his poetical genius.

In 1734 he enrolled as a fellow commoner at Peterhouse, Cambridge, where he studied for four years without taking a degree, though he held two scholarships and acquired a reputation for the composition of Latin poetry. He hated the mathematics and metaphysics of the university curriculum, and sought consolation in more intimate acquaintance with his " classical companions." His fastidious temperament began to assert itself, and he acquired among the more robust undergraduates the nickname of " Miss Gray." Like the genuine introvert of any age he made few friends outside his books, but he never seemed to miss human companionship so long as he could read more Latin and Greek literature, learn Italian " like any dragon," go to London occasionally to see a new play or opera, and write enthusiastically to West at Oxford about his latest acquisition or the tyrannical stupidity of university life at Cambridge. Obviously no match for the rougher element, he found refuge and consolation in his books and in himself. Before he was twenty Gray was showing plainly the temperament which goes to make the poet or the scholar, or, as with him and with John Milton before him, both the scholar and the poet.

West left Oxford in April 1738 in order to study law at the Inner Temple. Gray wanted to join him, and in September left Cambridge to do so, happy at the change but disturbed by the confusion of moving, by "the dust, the old boxes, the bedsteads, and tutors that are about my ears." Of that next winter in London we know nothing, but we can imagine many evenings by the fireside when he and West talked about the great things of the world and made ambitious plans for themselves. Horace Walpole startled their poetic dreams with his plans to make the Grand Tour of the continent, as befitted a prime minister's son. He invited Gray to become his companion, to travel without expense to Paris, and south into the glory of ancient Rome. Gray's love of the romance of distant lands joined with his passion for classical literature to make him accept Walpole's offer and forget for the time being the things which tied him to England.

Gray has left us in his letters and journals a lively description of his two years in France and Italy. At times he reveals an enthusiastic enjoyment of new scenes, only to break into a homesick longing for the company of West. The constantly varying sights interest him: the streets and people of Paris, more fascinating by far than the English expatriates who herd together and continually call on Walpole; the romantic grandeur of nature up the steep road to the monastery of the Grande Chartreuse; or the wealth of art in a hundred Italian churches and palaces. The only drawback lay in the difference in temperament between the two young travelers. Walpole loved company and because of his rank and connections never lacked the society and entertainment of Englishmen and foreigners alike. Gray wanted to see things and read about them, much preferring a visit to an art collection or a stroll in the streets to attendance at the fashionable gaming parties of Rheims or a dinner with my lord this or that. He was keenly appreciative of the consideration that Walpole constantly gave him, but could never quite forget that fate had put him in a state of dependence upon his friend both in wealth and in rank.

After three interesting months in Paris and three tedious months of dallying at Rheims, the two young men set out for the south, going by way of Dijon, Lyons, Grenoble, across the Alps to Turin, and finally by way of Bologna to Florence in time to settle there for the winter. In March 1740 they set out for Rome upon the death of Pope Clement XII, hoping to see the coronation of a new pope. The antiquities and churches of Rome and the beauty of the country around Naples were enough to keep them interested until July, when upon finding still no prospect of a papal election they returned to Florence, where they remained until the end of the following April. They finally set out for Venice, but at Reggio they quarreled, going on separately to Venice, whence Gray returned alone to England.[2]

Much has been written about this quarrel, as if it were some great enigma. Walpole magnanimously took upon himself the blame but left us no details as to its occurrence. In my opinion, the circumstances of the actual quarrel represent only the culmination of the little misunderstandings that two years of fairly intimate association can produce. The forced companionship of travel accentuated the essential differences between the two men, which in ordinary life would have melted easily into their many common interests. Gray felt so dependent upon Walpole that his consciousness of their relation gradually festered in his mind until its dull dissatisfaction became open rebellion. He could not help feeling at the same time that the friend who really understood him was in England. He wrote West long letters at every opportunity and impatiently sent messages by Ashton, chiding West for not writing him more often. Long before he left Italy he complained to West of the emptiness of his life in Florence: " I have struck a medal upon myself: the device is thus O, and the motto *Nihilissimo,* which I take in the most concise manner to contain a full account of my person, sentiments, occupations, and late glorious successes." [3] He was not altogether bored with Florence, for he was studying music and collecting engravings,

[2] See Mr. Leonard Whibley's very interesting account of this whole journey in *Blackwood's Magazine,* CCXXVII (1930), 813–827.
[3] Tovey, I, 79; Whibley, I, 172.

but he was homesick for West and for some steady work to allay the tedium that was already creeping on him. On leaving Florence he penned for West a portrait of himself that in places touches the real man: "You must add then, to your former idea, two years of age, reasonable quantity of dullness, a great deal of silence, and something that rather resembles, than is, thinking; a confused notion of many strange and fine things that have swum before my eyes for some time, a want of love for general society, indeed an inability to it." [4] He was no longer impressed by the many strange and fine things he had greeted so eagerly two years before. On his way home he wrote in the book at the Grande Chartreuse a Latin ode full of his feelings of weariness with the vulgar tumult of the world of action.

Gray arrived at last in London, September 1, 1741, but the peace he had prayed for in the Chartreuse ode did not last long. The death of his father two months later probably did not disturb him emotionally so much as it added to his responsibilities. The greatest blow of all came the next spring when West fell ill. Gray wrote him long letters, trying to nurse him back to health with laughter and with literary gossip about a new novel called *Joseph Andrews,* or about the proper kind of language to use in poetry. He even composed an English poem to vary the succession of Latin verses he had been sending him, but West never saw it, for he was dead when Gray's letter containing the *Ode to Spring* arrived. Characteristically Gray wrote in English a stilted sonnet on West's death and put his genuine feelings into the Latin verses that he appended to his philosophical fragment, *De principiis cogitandi.* Not enough of a romantic to wear his heart on his sleeve, he concealed his emotions in classical Latin until they came out years later, thoroughly fused with the common sorrow of the world, in the *Elegy Written in a Country Churchyard.*[5]

Gray had no reason to stay in London after West's death; and so in the fall of 1742 he went back to Cambridge to study law. He evidently thought he ought to enter some profession, and what

[4] Tovey, I, 86; Whibley, I, 181.
[5] See Odell Shepard, "A Youth to Fortune and to Fame Unknown," *Modern Philology,* XX (1923), 347–373.

was more suitable than that which he had once planned to take up with West? At any rate he must have pursued his study faithfully, for in December 1743 he took his degree of bachelor of laws at Cambridge.[6]

Instead of beginning the practice of law, however, he continued in residence at Peterhouse, delving at random into whatever line of study interested him. He has left us no reasons for staying at Cambridge; circumstances and his own temperament made it almost inevitable. He had a modest income from his father's estate. His mother was comfortably settled with her sister at Stoke. He was interested in law as a branch of learning, but scarcely enough to justify spending his life at it. With a passion for reading in many fields of knowledge, he stayed on at Cambridge, where libraries were convenient and comfortable living quarters cheap enough for his small income. No wonder he could twelve years later look upon his removal a few hundred feet to Pembroke "as a sort of æra in a life so barren of events as mine."

Gray never tired of ridiculing the emptiness of university life, perhaps as compensation for his own unwillingness to take his place in the active world. He laughed at its foibles, but inwardly he loved it and honored its air of learning. West was dead, moreover, and with him had gone all youthful enthusiasm for writing poetry. The glorious world Gray shared with West had burst like a bubble and left him staring at the necessity of making the best of a prosaic substitute. In order to keep on living with any degree of happiness he must find something to do. He loved Cambridge in spite of himself, because it offered him the materials of learning to occupy his mind and thereby ward off tedium.

Gray also found friends in Cambridge, a few choice souls who saw beneath the fastidious exterior and warmed to him. The closest friends of his mature life came from relations in the university town among them Thomas Wharton, Richard Stonhewer, William Mason, Richard Hurd, James Brown, and Norton Nicholls. Many of them moved on into the world of affairs, but they never forgot him, feeling themselves honored by his friendship.

[6] See Whibley, App. F, for the facts of Gray's legal studies.

As he grew older he made new friends among the younger men, always few and carefully chosen.[7]

Gray found his friends valuable for more than congeniality. Acquaintance with the fellows of various colleges made it easy for him to borrow books from their libraries. This situation is most evident from his contact with Pembroke Hall, conveniently located across the street from his residence at Peterhouse. From Pembroke he borrowed numerous books in the names of James Brown and other fellows, often recording the loan and its return in his own handwriting in the library register.[8] He had access to other libraries at Cambridge, including the University or "Publick Library" and several college collections, notably those of Emmanuel, Trinity, Gonville and Caius, and St. John's.[9] He bought from time to time a number of books for his personal use but continually depended upon college libraries for expensive works of reference, learned journals, collections of travel or natural history, and, of course, for manuscripts.[10]

As he was not ambitious, Gray took the easier way and stayed on at Cambridge with congenial friends and accessible books. He was well aware of what he was doing in 1744 and was able to laugh at himself and the indolence of university life, describing in a letter to his friend Thomas Wharton the spirit that holds everyone at Cambridge under her sway, " our sovereign Lady &

[7] See Martin, *Essai,* pp. 90–124, for the best account of Gray and his friends.

[8] The register is still preserved in Pembroke Library. The items begin about 1743 and become quite frequent long before Gray himself took up his residence at Pembroke.

[9] Richard Hurd, who was fellow of Emmanuel from 1742 to 1757, also borrowed frequently from Pembroke *c.* 1748–1749. At Trinity Gray could get books through Conyers Middleton until his death in 1750, and afterwards through L. Brockett (cf. Tovey, II, 1). At St. John's Gray was intimately acquainted at different times with William Heberden and George Ashby.

[10] Gray investigated manuscripts at Cambridge containing early English poetry. About 1755 he transcribed in his Commonplace Book an unpublished poem of Lydgate from a manuscript in the university library (printed in Mathias, II, 76–80). Gray wrote to Walpole, September 2, 1760, sending information for *Anecdotes on Painting*: "Be assured, that Occleve's portrait of Chaucer is not, nor ever was in S[t] John's Library: they have a Mss of the Troilus & Cressida without illuminations, & no other part of his works. In the University Library indeed there is a large volume with most of his works on vellum" (Tovey, III, 325; Toynbee, II, 187; Whibley, II, 696).

Mistress, the President of Presidents, & Head of Heads (if I may be permitted to pronounce her Name, that ineffable Octogrammaton) the Power of LAZINESS." He had so pleased this august power at the outset that she had promoted him over the heads of her old servants to the honorable office of "Grand Picker of Straws, & Push-Pin-Player in ordinary to her Supinity."[11] That very year he began taking notes on the most erudite of the learned journals of Europe and working up an elaborate bibliographical notebook which laid emphasis upon the best editions and reference books for the study of the classics, history, and travel. At the same time he was comparing modern travel accounts of the Mediterranean countries with those of the ancient world found in Strabo. Such were the straws he was picking in the service of laziness.

Gray did not lose touch with the world by choosing to stay at Cambridge. He continued to spend his summers at Stoke with his mother. He visited friends: Lady Cobham at Stoke House, Walpole after a reconciliation in 1745, John Chute at the Vine in Hampshire, and many others. He often went to London, where he continued to haunt the opera and the theater. He frankly enjoyed "flaunting about at publick Places of all kinds" in the fall of 1746 with Chute and young Francis Whithed, just back from Italy. He confessed to Wharton on his return from this jaunt to the solitary life at Cambridge that the world still attracted him, "& agreeable well-meaning People of Sense (thank Heaven there are so few of them) are my peculiar Magnet." But the world and society were not for a man in his circumstances: "It is a foolish Thing, that one can't only not live as one pleases, but where & with whom one pleases, without Money."[12] His stocks were particularly low at the time, and he was asking Wharton for a small loan to pay off an old debt, yet his words reveal a constant factor in his melancholy. They remind us of his quarrel with Walpole in Italy, and also of what Richard Hurd said of him after his death: "If he had been more at ease in his circumstances, and a little

[11] Tovey, I, 118; Whibley, I, 223.
[12] Tovey, I, 149; Whibley, I, 255.

higher in rank, he would have been, not more estimable, but more happy." [13] Gray had the tastes of an eighteenth-century landed gentleman, and with more wealth would gladly have become one, but he was much too sane a philosopher to waste his time on futile regrets. He became a literary gentleman instead, disdaining to be looked upon as a professional writer. The very month he returned from his holiday in London with his two wealthy friends, December 1746, he launched into his first scholarly project — a thorough survey of ancient Greek civilization as seen through its philosophers, poets, orators, historians, and geographers.

He began with Diogenes Laertius, whose lives of the ancient philosophers led him after much meandering to years of intimate contact with Plato. As a side interest he continued to supplement Strabo's descriptions of the ancient world with the accounts of modern travelers, until he found himself in Cathay and Japan, having meanwhile become an expert in Oriental history and geography. These two lines of study — classical literature and travel books — took years of concentrated effort, running in almost parallel lines from 1746 to about 1754. Such tragic waste of creative energy appalls the critic who observes that these were the years in which the *Elegy* was perfected, and wishes with all his heart that more such poems had been written. But the cold interpretation of fact is more valuable in this case than regret or surmise. The point to be remembered is that after 1742 Gray was more scholar than poet; he valued the peace of mind that came to him from steady work more than the doubtful glory of public acclaim for authorship. What brought about this momentous change? To answer this question is, I believe, to find the reasons for Gray's "sterility." At any rate Gray wrote little poetry after 1742, for West was no longer alive to prod his reticent muse.

The summer of 1742 was a period of brilliant poetical composition, coming as a climax of the years of apprenticeship of Latin poems written under the incentive of West's friendship.

[13] *Correspondence of Richard Hurd and William Mason* (Cambridge University Press, 1932), ed. by Leonard Whibley, p. 104.

The promise Gray had shown up to that time was warmed by the depth of his feeling at the loss of his friend, until it blossomed into the *Ode on Adversity,* the *Ode on a Distant Prospect of Eton College,* and the touching memorial verses to West. Poetical genius was abundant in him at Stoke that summer in preparation for the universal lament of the *Elegy.* After 1742, however, his composition of poetry was sporadic: in 1747 an ingenious trifle on Mr. Walpole's cat as a relief from his study of Athenaeus and Pausanias; in 1748 some interesting lines on liberty in government as a companion of true education, probably inspired by his study of Isocrates; in 1750 a *jeu d'esprit* called *A Long Story,* written for Lady Cobham and Miss Henrietta Speed; and sometime before 1751 the famous *Elegy,* emotionally at least a part of that memorable summer of 1742. Obviously poetry meant very little to him after the death of West. To occupy his fertile mind, he took that which was nearest at hand and most congenial to his taste. He gradually built up his philosophy of happiness, basing it on the simple maxim, "Have something to do." With him, staying busy meant more than the discursive reading of a dilettante; it meant concentrated study on a definite branch of learning until he had mastered it to his satisfaction. Since scholarship was for his own personal happiness, however, he seldom thought of publishing his results, copying them instead into his notebooks until he was ready for the sake of variety to turn to a new subject.

After the publication of the *Elegy* in February 1751, Gray found himself suddenly and unwillingly famous. Before the end of the year the *Elegy* had appeared in at least five regular quarto editions and four widely circulated magazines. Gray had regretted its unusual popularity before publication. When he went to town for a month in 1750, he found that people were saying such superlative things about his verses that he could not repeat them to Wharton. "I should have been glad," he said, sincerely one feels, "that you & two or three more People had liked them, wch would have satisfied my Ambition on this Head amply." [14]

[14] Whibley, I, 335.

In 1753 six of Gray's poems were reprinted in an elaborate volume, in which the designs of Richard Bentley played a prominent part. Gray showed a great deal of interest in the project but insisted from the beginning that his verses be printed only as explanations of the engravings. He flatly refused to allow his own portrait to be included, and dictated the title of the work to publisher Dodsley, " Designs by Mr. R. Bentley for six poems of Mr. T. Gray." The notice of the book in the *Monthly Review* showed that the poet's position in the contemporary world of letters was already secure: " With regard to the ingenious author of these poems; to enlarge in his praise, would be impertinence; as his churchyard elegy is in every one's hands, and not more justly than universally admired." [15]

On March 11, 1753, Gray saw his mother die " after a long and painful Struggle for life." He probably loved her even more than he had loved West, since he was the only child, as he said in the simple but beautiful epitaph he wrote, who had " the misfortune to survive her." But where he had felt in the loss of West an aching emptiness that only the moving sense of tragedy could fill, he looked upon the death of his mother as a release for her from the pain that alone made death seem terrible to him. " I know what it is," he wrote Mason shortly afterwards to console him for the loss of his father, " to lose a person that one's eyes and heart have long been used to, and I never desire to part with the remembrance of that loss, nor would wish you should." He was truly a man of deep and genuine emotion who chose to conceal his feelings from the general public he so consistently mistrusted.

After his mother's death Gray went farther afield on his occasional jaunts from Cambridge. He finally made, in 1753, the trip he had long contemplated, a visit to the family estate of the Whartons, Old Park near Durham, which afterwards became his second home to replace the one he had lost at Stoke. He took his time, and found many fine things — cathedrals, country houses, the changes of nature, and, what he genuinely loved, the companionship of congenial folk. In later years his failing health de-

[15] *Monthly Review*, VIII (1753), 477 [Griffiths].

manded many more such excursions, until they became rather the rule than the exception of his summers.

During the winter of 1753–1754 and for a few years afterwards Gray was delving into poetics. He had projected with Mason a history of English poetry and was probably already at work on some phases of it. The backgrounds of English poetry, which must precede any research in the field, would of course take one into Provençal and Italian. From there the trail led straight back to Greece, to Helicon's harmonious springs, and especially to the combination of passion and harmony that was to be found in Pindar. The result is "An Ode in the Greek Manner," since known as *The Progress of Poesy*. Gray had, back in 1747, made a thorough analysis of Pindar's meters, and so he was able to show, as nearly as one could in English verse, what a genuine Pindaric ode should be.

In his search for the origins of English poetry Gray went not only to the Romance field but also to the Germanic ancestors of the English people on the continent, and to their Welsh neighbors in the west. A rumor in Thomas Carte's *History of England* that Edward I had massacred the Welsh bards gave him the idea of portraying the last surviving bard perched on a mountain crag hurling curses upon Edward's army. The theme was sublime, Pindaric, and he made it savage besides, by bringing in the trochaic refrain of an Old Norse poem he had been reading, as well as a hint of the complicated *Gorchest-beirdh* from Welsh prosody. A strict Pindaric ode on such a subject was new and startling, the most original piece of composition he had yet attempted. This poem, afterwards known as *The Bard,* was the direct result of much scholarship, fused to white heat by his own poetic power. It is the most remarkable relic he has left us of his abortive attempt to write a history of English poetry. The rare promise Gray showed in *The Bard* was never realized, however, for the poem was too obscure for the same public which had acclaimed the *Elegy*. And thereby hangs a story.

In spite of his playful bluster in talking about them Gray really was very proud of his two Pindaric odes, especially in the

handsome dress that Walpole gave them in August 1757 as the
first-fruits of his new Strawberry Hill Press. He offered them
willingly and proudly to the public, and even received forty
guineas from Dodsley for the publication rights. Expecting
another such appeal to their emotions as the *Elegy,* the public
bought his *Odes* and then either cried out against their obscure-
ness or ignored them. Gray was frankly annoyed and became
more melancholy, withdrawing into his shell of simulated indifference.[16] He afterwards laughed at the public taste and never
missed an opportunity of ridiculing it, but the fact remains that
he never wrote any more poetry except the Norse and Welsh
imitations, certainly nothing in those years of maturity to equal
The Bard. He never forgot, as he showed when he wrote some
notes for the 1768 collected edition of his works: " The Author
was at first advised (even by his Friends) to subjoin some few
explanatory notes, but had then too much respect for the understanding of his Readers to take that liberty." The veiled sarcasm
of this statement becomes open contempt in the words he first
wrote and then crossed out: " but chose to leave both his writings
and the world to themselves." [17]

When Gray abandoned poetry in 1757 he became even more
wedded to learning. Having by that time wearied of his project
for a history of English poetry, he began in 1758, purely for
amusement, to make a list of all the sights worth seeing in his
own country. This inventory, which afterwards became the basis
for the catalogue in Kearsley's *The Traveller's Companion, in a
tour through England and Wales,* had a more serious corollary in
his antiquarian researches in English church architecture. He
seems nevertheless to have felt the necessity of explaining to Wharton that he was doing this to avoid the tedium of life:

> It is indeed for want of spirits, as you suspect, that my studies lie among
> the Cathedrals, and the Tombs, and the Ruins. To think, though to little
> purpose, has been the chief amusement of my days; and when I would not,

[16] For the whole story of the contemporary reception of the *Odes,* see my
article in *Modern Philology,* XXVIII (1930), 61–82.

[17] From the autograph notes in the margins of his own copy of the *Odes,* now
in the Pierpont Morgan Library.

or cannot think, I dream. At present I find myself able to write a Catalogue, or to read the Peerage book, or Miller's Gardening Dictionary, and am thankful that there are such employments and such authors in the world. Some people, who hold me cheap for this, are doing perhaps what is not half so well worth while. As to posterity, I may ask, (with some body whom I have forgot) what has it ever done to oblige me?[18]

Gray came nearer describing his own feelings in his letters to Wharton than anywhere else, yet even in them he was constantly reproaching himself for his indolence or laughing at his own ineffectiveness. His playful allegiance in 1744 to the sovereign Lady of Cambridge, the Power of Laziness, has by 1758 turned to melancholy and serious apology. In such gradual change lies much of the secret of his life, for he turned less and less to writing poetry as scholarship became more and more the essential factor in his thoughts. He realized that the inertia of his own introspective nature, aided by the sweet, reluctant, amorous delays of his mistress, Learning, was gradually engulfing him. In order to defend himself he blamed the indolence of Cambridge. In 1749, for example, he playfully linked his own discontent with the inertia of university life. Time would reconcile him to "Ennuy" as a languid companion and leave him in obscurity: "Brandy will finish what Port begun; & a Month after the Time you will see in some Corner of a London Even:ng Post, Yesterday, died the Revnd Mr John Grey, Senior-Fellow of Clare-Hall, a facetious Companion, & well-respected by all that knew him."[19] The fame of the *Elegy* soothed his conscience for a few years, giving him a spurt of creative activity, but about 1755 his already frail body began to give way under attacks of the gout.

No one can say just how great a part poor health played in his growing discontent. He was never very strong and probably suffered many slight attacks before his condition became acute enough to warrant medical attention. Even though we have come to look upon melancholy as a symptom of the eighteenth century, we can easily see in Gray's listlessness and "leucocholy"

[18] Tovey, II, 24; Whibley, II, 565.
[19] Tovey, I, 196; Whibley, I, 318.

the results of indigestion and insomnia. Whether his poor health was the cause or result of his ennui is a matter of speculation, even for the psychologists.[20] At any rate the two seem to go together, reaching an acute stage for the first time during the summer of 1755. Since Gray kept notes on his health in his pocket diary for that year, we can follow day by day his symptoms, treatment, and results, obtaining from the modest Latin of his descriptions a moving account of what he must often have suffered in later life.[21]

Long before the disease became acute, Gray spent many sleepless nights, and many days when dyspepsia disturbed him with attendant headaches and general listlessness. When the gout attacked him, he could not even bear at times the weight of the bedclothes upon his legs. He tried dieting as well as drugs, eating gruel with milk and drinking only pure water. He believed acidity to be the cause of his disorders, but when the mulberries and figs ripened at Stoke in September he ate them and again fell ill. Short intervals of health and seeming vigor deceived him into breaking down his regimen. He had, for example, felt strong enough to take a twelve-mile walk just the day before he ate too much fresh fruit. He spent the last fortnight in July with his friend Chute in Hampshire, where, he confesses, he drank a little wine every day and indulged so freely in rich food that he suffered afterwards from torpor and insomnia. The diary goes on to record the intimate details of his daily health, revealing his suffering and his desires in a way that no amount of public utterance can do. Many heroic souls have conquered physical afflictions, but few have been able to rise far above the daily martyrdom of chronic dyspepsia.

Gray was obviously depressed by the attacks of gout that came more often after 1755. He showed it plainly in August 1757, when his worries over his recently published *Odes* aggravated a light

[20] Martin has an excellent chapter on the sources of Gray's melancholy (*Essai*, pp. 8-19).

[21] These notes were published in *Gentleman's Magazine*, n. s. XXIV (1845), 229 ff., and in Martin, *Chronologie*, pp. 151 ff. The original is now in Pembroke College Library.

attack. To ward off his low spirits and gloomy thoughts he bought the two latest volumes of the French *Encyclopédie* and read straight through them.[22] Lady Cobham, Miss Speed, and the David Garricks tried vainly to amuse him. He explained his list-lessness and ennui to Richard Hurd as due to poor health, which is " no great malady, but several little ones, that seem brewing no good to me." [23]

In the spring of 1759 Gray suffered three attacks of the gout within three months, but by that time he had become reconciled to it enough to speak of it calmly and almost humorously in his letters.[24] During this illness he developed the indoor amusement of comparing thermometers and weather conditions with Wharton, who had gone to Old Park to live. He was in London at the time, and as soon as he could walk he went to see the new British Museum, just opened to the public. He must have been impressed with its treasures, for he took residence in Southampton Row nearby and for nearly two years studied the manuscripts of the famous Cottonian and Harleian collections.

Gray managed to pass the time while he was sick by reading anything that came to hand, but in the periods of comparative vigor that followed the attacks he did some of his most concentrated work in the field of learning. From 1758 to 1761, for example, he became an expert in English history by delving into the original sources of information that he found in the manuscripts of the British Museum and in the architecture and funeral monuments of England. He became an expert in heraldry in order to interpret the history of noble families from the crests he found on tombs and in stained-glass windows. He became familiar with the chronological development of English ecclesiastical architecture — the Norman style that he tolerated and the Gothic that he loved — for he wisely held that the changes in English cathedrals and abbeys reflected the artistic, and to a certain extent

[22] Tovey, I, 345; Whibley, II, 518.

[23] Tovey, I, 347; Whibley, II, 520. Hurd obviously attributes Gray's condition to too much study. See his reply in *Correspondence of Hurd and Mason,* p. 38: " You must abstain from books for the present, and use all the exercise you can."

[24] Tovey, II, 78, 81, 84; Whibley, II, 617, 618, 624.

the political, development of his country. How was he able to accomplish so much? Why did he not succumb to his discomfort and nurse the melancholy which came at the slightest nod? He had to keep busy in order to be happy. Since it was not in his nature to find one all-consuming interest, he studied like a gentleman in the several fields of learning that he liked.[25]

Gray had early taken to learning because he had no taste for professional life, whether in the practice of law or in authorship. By 1757 he had built up from his own experience a philosophy of happiness: "To be employed is to be happy," as he expressed it to Hurd.[26] He congratulated Walpole on being busy: "The receipt is obvious: it is only, Have something to do; but how few can apply it!"[27] Although he usually added that he himself was not able to put his philosophy into practice, the idea of staying busy was unquestionably the guiding principle of his life. He had demonstrated it well by 1760 when he wrote Wharton:

> To find oneself business (I am persuaded) is the great art of life; & I am never so angry, as when I hear my acquaintance wishing they had been bred to some poking profession, or employ'd in some office of drudgery, as if it were pleasanter to be at the command of other People, than at one's own; & as if they could not go, unless they were wound up. yet I know and feel, what they mean by this complaint: it proves, that some spirit, something of Genius (more than common) is required to teach a Man how to employ himself.[28]

Women, he goes on to say, find a multitude of little things to fill up the void, but men have to search diligently to avoid the distemper of boredom. Gray himself seems to have come so naturally by his series of scholarly projects that one can scarcely imagine he ever had to think up subjects to occupy his time.

In 1761 Gray returned from London and the British Museum to his rooms in Cambridge. He stayed in the university town for the remaining ten years of his life, except for the succession of

---

[25] Martin (*Essai*, p. 19) concludes that Gray suffered from an inherited psychic disorder that gradually crushed him by ruining his will power.

[26] Tovey, I, 347; Whibley, II, 520.

[27] Tovey, I, 340; Whibley, II, 508.

[28] Tovey, II, 132; Whibley, II, 666.

summer expeditions in search of health. He did not read quite so much as was his custom, for he had acquired a social maturity that allowed him to spend more time in the company of his friends. His chief intellectual amusement during those ten years was natural history, a subject which was then undergoing great changes through the epoch-making work of the Swedish scientist Linnaeus. As usual Gray learned all he could about the subject from the most recent books, then started out for himself in the English field. He found Cambridge congenial to his scientific studies, for among the younger men he knew and liked in the university town were such enthusiastic botanists as Israel Lyons, Thomas Martyn, Michael Tyson, and Charles Miller. He began to collect specimens, mostly of insects because they were easily handled. He had a microscope and lenses, with which he delved into the secrets of the smaller creatures and discovered much about the metamorphoses of gnats and flies. He found it convenient and interesting to study the insects, birds, fishes, and plants of the places he visited on his summer trips, at Old Park and the neighboring Hartlepool, at Southampton, at various places in Kent, even in the Lake District and the highlands of Scotland. He discovered and catalogued many specimens not described by Linnaeus, adding their characteristics in his terse Latin to his own interleaved and much enlarged copy of the *Systema Naturae*. In short, he became one of England's best naturalists in the generation that came just before Thomas Pennant. He undoubtedly knew more about English insects than any one before him, and although he did not bother to publish his findings, he probably influenced some of the younger scientists who contributed to the history of biology.

In spite of his temperate habits and the activity of the summer trips, Gray could not fight off indefinitely the attacks on his constantly weakening body. In 1768 he became professor of modern history at Cambridge, but with all his desire to reform the office he was forced by ill-health to forego lectures. He told Mason in 1770 that he was ready in despair to resign his professorship. He must have suffered a great deal during those last years. Although he felt temporarily relieved after the bodily exercise of the summer expeditions, he hated the necessity for such a regimen, as we see in his letter to the poet James Beattie in 1770: "That forced dissipation and exercise we are obliged to fly to as a remedy, when this frail machine goes wrong, is often almost as bad as the distemper we would cure." [29]

In 1770 he went to Wales with Nicholls and was well for a short time. All that winter he complained of a cough which would not leave him. He had planned to go in the summer of 1771 to Switzerland to see Bonstetten, but by May writes Wharton that he will probably get no further than Old Park, " for travel I must, or cease to exist. till this year I hardly knew what (mechanical) low-spirits were: but now I even tremble at an east-wind." [30] A month later he found his spirits much oppressed, " & the more so, as I foresee a new complaint, that may tie me down perhaps to my bed, & expose me to the operations of a Surgeon." [31] Not long afterwards the frail machine gave way and he died of " gout of the stomach " at eleven on the night of July 30, 1771.

II

The events of Gray's life, we see, were not dramatic or exciting. After the quarrel with Walpole he successfully avoided emotional crises, even though he could not escape the death of loved ones. It is small wonder that he could look upon his removal from Peterhouse across the street to Pembrock " as a sort of Æra in a life so barren of events as mine." The drama of Gray's life lies not in the chronicles of everyday events but rather in the exciting quality of his mind. Behind the books and the neatly penned notebooks, behind the fastidious excellence of his letters, behind the universal sorrow of his *Elegy* — in short, behind all those relics that testify to his fertile brain lies the drama of the mental conflict between the creative artist and the antiquarian.

This book is the story of that mind and its conflict, of the final

[29] Tovey, III, 287; Whibley, III, 1140.
[30] Tovey, III, 320; Whibley, III, 1189.
[31] Tovey, III, 321; Whibley, III, 1191.

triumph of the scholar over the poet. I have already set the scene, and now, before the drama unrolls, I must more clearly show the chief character himself, both as the world saw him and as his best friends knew him. There are conflicting reports that must be reconciled, for some say he was an effeminate recluse, morose and uncompanionable, others that he was polite, affable, and, while inclined to fastidiousness, very genial. We know that at one time he feared the pranks of rough Cambridge undergraduates, and yet he was on such intimate terms with the Wharton children as to inquire about their tricks between visits:

has Miss Wh: served her time yet as a Bride-maid? I hope it may prove a good omen to her! does Miss Peggy rival Claude Lorraine yet, & when does she go to York? do Debo & Betty tend their Chrysalises, & their samplers? is Kee's mouth as pretty as ever? does Robin read like a Doctor, dance like a Fairy, & bow like a Courtier? does Dicky kick up his heels, & study Geography? please to answer me as to all these particulars.[32]

To the world at large, especially to the undergraduate body at Cambridge, Gray was fastidious to the point of being finical and effeminate. Certainly he did nothing to counteract this reputation, affecting a contempt for the general run of humanity. Perfume, wigs, breeches, stockings, and handkerchiefs are prominent items in the expense accounts of his trips to town. Contemporary gossip gives an idea of his reputation: "After his return from his travels, he commonly wore a muff, an object of no small derision with the university-lads! If he went to a coffee-house, he would tell the waiter, in a tone the most effeminate, to give him 'that silly paper-book.' The Gentleman's Magazine this was, and, sometimes, very likely, the Review." [33] The fear of fire that led him to install a rope ladder in his room at Peterhouse caused some of the college boys to set up a false alarm in order to see him use it needlessly. He was never on horseback in an age when that mode of travel was very common. Although he loved wild scenery, he saw only that part of the highlands of Scotland which

[32] Whibley, III, 988.
[33] *Monthly Review*, LIII (1775), 102, from a review of Mason's life of Gray by John Langhorne, who had been student at Clare College, Cambridge, 1759-1761.

lay conveniently near his host's castle at Glamis, and he failed to penetrate into the rougher sections of the English Lake District. Mason, who knew him intimately, admitted in his memoir that Gray affected a delicacy and effeminacy, " that he chose to put on this appearance chiefly before persons whom he did not wish to please." [34]

A recluse of Gray's known fastidiousness, living in a university wholly in male society, may easily get a reputation for effeminacy or among the more outspoken even for homosexuality. No one can deny that most of his friends at Cambridge during the last ten years of his life were among the younger men, Norton Nicholls, Michael Tyson, Victor de Bonstetten, and others.[35] After all, they revered the great poet, and he probably found them much more interesting than most of the stodgy fellows of the various colleges. In fact the finest tributes to Gray's excellent qualities are to be found in his relations with these young friends at Cambridge, in his advice to Nicholls to read Dante and Strabo, in Bonstetten's picture of him dividing his time between Shakespeare and Linnaeus, in Tyson's passionate desire to see his notebooks after his death.

When Norton Nicholls, as an old man, wrote his reminiscences of Gray, he left out one of the best parts, a description of his enthusiasm about their first meeting and " the happiness of drinking Tea with the great Mr Gray." His letter to William Johnson Temple tells, among other things, of Gray's suggesting that he read the Ugolino episode from Dante's *Inferno,* and gives a character sketch of the poet which is far from the usual conception of him: "I did not find him as you found Johnson, surly, morose, Dogmatical, or imperious. But affable, entertaining and polite. He had no other opportunity of shewing his superior abilities but

---

[34] *Memoir of the Life and Writings of Mr. Gray* (York, 1775), p. 403. Sir Egerton Brydges in his character of Gray (Ruminator, no. xxix, *Censura Literaria*, London, 1808, VII, 395 ff.) attributes this to the poet's love of assuming " the character of *the fine gentleman* . . . . He would shrug his shoulders, and distort his voice into fastidious tones; and take upon him the airs of what folly pleased to call *high company*."

[35] Martin describes Gray's relations with Bonstetten as a burning passion, the poet's first love (*Essai*, pp. 116–122).

such as naturally presented itself from the subject of Conversation, which however he never propos'd." Again at the end of the letter he sums up his impression of his new acquaintance: "What I could chiefly observe in him was vast politeness, great Good nature, and the most elegant accuracy of Phrase in the World." [36] Discounting the enthusiasm of the undergraduate meeting for the first time a famous poet, we still have a picture of Gray as a polite and genial man, entertaining in conversation.

In spite of his aversion to general society, Gray was amiable to those he liked, whether at Cambridge or on one of his many summer expeditions. He was very much at home when he visited the Whartons at Old Park. The whole family collected plants and insects for him, and he in turn taught them much about natural history. He was always interested in the doings of the children and often sent them playful messages in his letters. At other places he seems to have been most welcome, at Walpole's Strawberry Hill, at Chute's place in Hampshire, or at Lady Cobham's Stoke House. His expense accounts show that he paid out a good deal in gratuities to servants in houses he visited but never mentioned in his letters. When he went to Scotland it was as the guest of Lord Strathmore, whom he had known as an undergraduate at Cambridge. Two of the most pleasant visits of his life were with the Reverend Billy Robinson at Denton in Kent. He tells us about them in his letters, but the most revealing accounts of his genial relations with this family come from other sources.

According to Sir Egerton Brydges, who married Robinson's daughter, his father-in-law "thought Gray not only a great poet: but exemplarily amiable and virtuous." [37] A letter of Mrs. Robinson's, written June 2, 1766, shows a side of Gray that is seldom seen:

My inclination has over and over again led me to sit down to write to you but I have met with several interruptions partly owing to our having

[36] These excerpts are from the original in the possession of Mr. W. S. Lewis. The entire letter is printed in Whibley, III, 1303 f.

[37] This and the two letters that follow are from material collected by Mitford for his various editions of Gray, beginning about 1812. The two volumes of manuscript letters (from the W. A. Fraser collection) are now in the Harvard Library.

had for almost a fortnight a very agreable Gentleman in the House whose conversation is both instructing and entertaining. After what I have said you will wish to hear his Name, tis Mr Gray who is well known for having wrote several pretty Ellegies, he is also an acquaintance of your friend Mr Rycroft. . . . I wish you could hear the Lectures Mr Gray gives me on Education. He agrees with you that there is no necessity to hasten the Learning her to read, the great business at present shou'd be to form her temper and disposition in order in future time to make her happy to herself and those about her, he fears she is in some danger of being spoil'd. . . . Mrs. Glover has been very ill and seems declining apace notwithstanding that Mr Gray cou'd not help observing how much she was drest.

Gray was obviously willing to talk when the occasion arose, and took pains to be agreeable to his friends. The marvelous sense of humor he showed in his letters must surely have lent spice to much of his talk as well. That he was often very bad company, however, is shown by his general reputation for reserve. When he is portrayed in one of his sulking moods, we are inclined to agree with the opinion of the famous bluestocking, Mrs. Elizabeth Montagu, sister of Mrs. Robinson, who observed in her letter from Denton, December 4, 1766:

I was told Mr Gray was rather reserved when he was in Scotland, tho' they were disposed to pay him great respect. I agree perfectly with him that to endeavour to shine in conversation and to lay out for admiration, is very paltry, the witt of the company next to the Butt of the company is the meanest person in it; but at the same time, when a man of celebrated talents disdains to mix in common conversation, or refuses to talk on ordinary subjects it betrays a latent pride. . . . I shall be very glad to see Mr Gray whenever he will please to do me the favour. I think he is the first Poet of the age, but if he comes to my fireside I will teach him not only to speak prose, but to talk nonsense if occasion be. I would not have a Poet always sit on the proud summit of the forked hill. I have a great respect for Mr Gray as well as a high admiration.[38]

But things were not always so. Gray was certainly good company when he wished to be, that is, I believe, when he felt well enough and when he found people sincere and straightforward. Men, women, and children who knew him well liked him, the

[38] The whole letter was published for the first time by Brydges in *Censura Literaria* (London, 1807), III, 136 ff.

simple as well as the learned. No one could ask a greater tribute than that, let the idle gossip fall where it may. Gray had learned much from Plato, above all the kind of virtue that transcends the petty selfishness of everyday humanity and strives to impart beauty and strength to those who are worthy of them. He could despise the average Cambridge undergraduate and at the same time spend hours on end explaining Shakespeare and Milton and Dante to Nicholls or Bonstetten.

Emotionally Gray was not very stable. He was inclined, especially when young, to be moody, with the alternate phases of elation and depression that are usually associated with the artistic temperament. As he grew older he learned, mainly from the Greek philosophers, to exercise a control over his emotions and to sublimate both high spirits and melancholy in the steady pursuit of learning. He had before him at all times the ideal of the classical gentleman, to curb excess feeling and use moderation in all things. Guided by this philosophy and his own practical maxim, " To be employed is to be happy," he was able to make adjustments in what might otherwise have been a very unhappy life.

Gray never loved any woman except his mother. One feels with Austin Dobson [39] half sorry that he never married Henrietta Jane Speed " with her £30,000, her house in town, and her ' china and old japan infinite,' " but " Gray was not a marrying man." He knew very few women outside his own blood relations, and those only casually. He found congenial surroundings for the first time at Eton, where for about eight years of the most formative period in his life he was entirely surrounded by male companions. He had a rather frail body and a decided love of poetry, a combination that the rougher male element seldom forgives. As a defense he learned to laugh at himself and at the world, developing a distinctly superior sense for burlesque and satire. He was nevertheless intimate only with men. Only a year before he died, he betrayed for Bonstetten the pathetic tenderness of a first love.[40]

[39] *Eighteenth Century Vignettes* (1st ser., London, 1892), p. 144.
[40] Martin, *Essai*, p. 119.

With such a background Gray's fastidious nature grew easily into what the world likes to look upon as effeminacy. On the other hand it contributed to some of the finer qualities in his work. He developed an extremely neat and fine handwriting that makes all of his notebooks beautiful to look upon. In conversation he learned to be silent until he had something to say, when he expressed himself " with an elegant accuracy of phrase." Best of all he composed, especially in the *Elegy,* with a conciseness and simplicity that is the despair of all who try to imitate him. Compressing into a few well-chosen phrases what others had been saying verbosely for centuries, he has left us in the *Elegy* a remarkable triumph of nicety and fastidiousness.

Gray's character, as we have seen, was far from simple, combining as it did his introvert temperament and the conditioning factors of his early surroundings with the noble philosophy that allowed him to make his own adjustments. He learned to be happy in spite of his genuine desire to live as a gentleman with wealth and rank, and in spite of the frail constitution that kept him from living a normal life. He compensated for his poor body by using his excellent mind and for his feeling of inferiority in rank by becoming the sort of gentleman who writes and studies purely as an amateur. That is why he wrote poetry only for himself and his friends, spent most of his time reading in many fields, and refused to become poet laureate or in any way be looked upon as a professional writer.

In the remaining chapters of this book I shall attempt to fill out this picture by describing the high lights of Gray's scholarly activities and showing the effect they had on his life and poetry. I have arranged the various parts in rough chronological sequence, although a separate treatment of each major interest involves a great deal of overlapping and a certain amount of repetition. I have divided the phases of Gray's scholarship into six chapters: (1) preparation and scholarly methods; (2) his first project, a thorough survey of ancient culture; (3) his subsequent study of travel and geography, especially of the Orient; (4) his plans to write a history of English poetry, leading to the beginnings of the Celtic and Scandinavian revivals for the enrichment of Romantic poetry; (5) his research in English history through the study of manuscripts, heraldry, and architecture; and (6) his interest in natural history. The completed picture, I believe, amply explains Gray's " sterility " and his richness; it offers, in short, the critical biography of an eighteenth-century poet who preferred to be known as a " gentleman."

CHAPTER II

THE EVOLUTION OF A BOOKWORM

I

EVEN as a boy Gray was a voracious reader, continually turning to books and to his own thoughts rather than to the active pursuits of the outside world. His remarkable taste led him, with a few notable exceptions, to the greatest writers, and he read their works with all the zest of an explorer of new lands. His love of beauty took him into many strange places where the colorful scenes shifted constantly, from the glory of Vergil and the precision of Pope to the glamor of Ariosto and the worldliness of Restoration comedy. But this browsing is in a way a prophecy of the future scholar, whose learning shows the catholic tastes of an eighteenth-century gentleman. The interests of Gray's youth gradually merged into the erudition and scholarship of his maturity.

At Eton he studied like any other gifted and serious school boy of his time.[1] His chief accomplishment was a thorough grounding in Latin, for he read many of the best Latin writers and wrote poems himself in that language. One of his school exercises, a poem preserved in his Commonplace Book under the title, "Knowledge of Himself, Latin Verses at Eton," shows a certain youthful poetic ability and a mastery of Latin.[2] Although Eton demanded much study of Latin, his own tastes in reading, the encouragement of his uncles,[3] and his association with such

---

[1] See L. Whibley, "Thomas Gray at Eton," *Blackwood's Magazine,* May 1929, CCXXV, 611–623.

[2] The best edition is that given in *The Poetical Works of Thomas Gray* (London, 1891), ed. by John Bradshaw, pp. 124–127.

[3] Robert and William Antrobus were both assistant masters at Eton during the lad's school years. Robert died in 1730 and bequeathed his library to William, directing him to give his nephew, Thomas Gray, all such books as related to the "practice of physick," if he should be educated to that profession (cf. *Notes and Queries,* December 14, 1912, 11th ser., VI, 461). Much more to Gray's taste, however, were books from his uncles that we know he kept in his library — Cicero, Euripides, Horace, and Vergil, the last three probably from Robert's library, as Gray dated them 1731.

friends as Richard West not only introduced him to Latin literature but also gave him an ease of composition in Latin second only to that in his mother tongue.

Gray reveled in the classics during his four undergraduate years at Cambridge. He wrote poems and even a letter in Latin, sending them all lovingly to West at Oxford.[4] He composed a Latin poem for the Cambridge *Gratulatio* in honor of the marriage of the Prince of Wales, much better than the verses of other college bards with " such soft unmeaning stuff about Venus and Cupid, and Peleus and Thetis, and Zephyrs and Dryads." [5] He read Vergil on vacation while sitting under venerable beeches, and he quoted Homer in his letters. He translated and sent to West, among other things, an elegy of Propertius and the description of the discus contest from the sixth book of Statius' *Thebaid*. He was asked by the moderator to make the " Tripos Verses " for the year 1736–1737, and his contribution on the subject, "Luna est habitabilis," was published in *Musae Etonenses*.[6] He handled the fantastic theme with imagination and even with humor, not only showing that the moon was habitable but predicting a future commerce, with England, already mistress of the seas, assuming the supremacy of the air. Latin had indeed become natural to him.

Although the classics were his chief love, Gray found relaxation and enjoyment in other things as well, in French and Italian, in Pope and Milton and Shakespeare, in the actual performances of drama and opera on the stage. His early letters to Walpole, characterized by youthful exuberance, evince a remarkable gift for humor and satire. He inserts phrases from Shakespeare and Restoration comedy, and writes amusingly of the London stage. He tells how he labors through clouds of tobacco smoke at Cambridge " with as much pains, as Milton's poor Devil took, when he travel'd through Chaos." He describes a Plow-Monday custom in the form of a burlesque on the romance *Amadis of Gaul*. He

---

[4] Toynbee, I, 175 ff.

[5] Toynbee, I, 74 f. Ashton writes West: "Master Gray seems to touch upon the Manner of Claudian " (*ibid.*, p. 68).

[6] II, 107. See Toynbee, I, 117, n. 3.

composes a letter in a poetical strain that seems half-Milton and half-Pope.[7] The playfulness of these youthful letters furnishes an excellent antidote for those who think of Gray only as a melancholy recluse. Here are the seeds for the burlesque which he wrote so easily in his *Ode on the Death of a Favourite Cat, Drowned in a Tub of Gold Fishes,* in *A Long Story,* and in the notorious *Jemmy Twicher.* Gray as a student at Eton and at Cambridge was interested in much besides the classics. The theater held a world of delight for him, whether it showed Shakespeare or the latest extravagant opera.[8] He was familiar with Pope and Addison, and doubtless consumed many new romances, whether of Marivaux and Crébillon or of their English counterparts.

One of the best indications of Gray's tastes in reading during his youth is to be found in an unpublished notebook, which seems to be an early catalogue of his library, divided roughly into classes.[9] Many of the books listed appear in the later sales of Gray's books, and others we know that he read. This first notebook of the poet shows better than anything else his youthful tastes in reading and how they foreshadow the later study that dominated his life.

The most interesting list is that headed "Poetry, History, Travels, &c: &c:." The miscellaneous jumble suggests the random reading of a boy, while the large handwriting seems to mark it as the beginning of the catalogue. Of the first five items three have survived with Gray's youthful autograph and such

[7] Toynbee, I, 1–67. See Walpole's comment on the letters, pp. xxxii f.

[8] See his description of Dryden's *King Arthur* with music by Purcell, January 3, 1736, in Toynbee, I, 57 ff.

[9] Now in the Pierpont Morgan Library, Register II. 1. For complete text, see below, p. 151. Gray puts no date to his list, but the entries begin in the large and fairly neat hand of his first letters to Walpole in 1734. (See facsimile of the first letter, in Toynbee, I, 1.) The notebook was probably begun about the time Gray went to Cambridge, or even earlier, and abandoned soon after his return from the Continent. There are no entries of books published after 1742, and the last few items in almost every class are in the small neat hand which begins about 1739, when he took up annotation more or less in earnest. The list bound in the middle of this notebook, headed "Books bought since I came to London, 1760," is in a very much later hand and will be discussed hereafter.

dates as 1729 (Waller), 1731 (Dryden's Vergil), and 1732 (Pope's Homer). A little farther down the list is the eight-volume Dacier translation of Plutarch, dated by Gray in each volume " Januar: 22, 1733." English poetry is represented by Milton (*Paradise Lost* and " Juvenilia "), Waller, Prior, Pope (" Ethic Epistles " and 1729 *Dunciad*), and several collections (mostly from the Restoration) in addition to Dryden's *Miscellanies* in six volumes. In a later hand at the end of the list appear Theobald's Shakespeare (1741)[10] at a guinea, and " Spencer's Works, by Hughes " at eighteen shillings. The prose items run to periodical literature — the *Spectator,* the *Tatler,* the *Guardian,* and the *Intelligencer* (Dublin) — or to romantic fiction, such as " Turkish Tales," " Persian Tales, 3 Vol:," and a collection of novels " containing Prazimene, The Loving Revenge, Cynthia, &c: "[11] with *Don Quixote* in Motteux's translation thrown in to leaven the lump.

Gray lists here his copies of translations of the classics, which include, besides the Homer and Vergil and Plutarch already mentioned, Hughes's Suetonius, Dryden's Juvenal, and Creech's Lucretius. Except for these and a few other miscellaneous items, all the other books are concerned with two of Gray's most lasting loves, plays and travels. The books of plays are a motley assortment: nondescript editions of Congreve, Etherege, Addison, and Steele, and a few quarto volumes of miscellaneous plays whose titles are written out in full, "Shakespeare's Macbeth, Hamlet, and Othello " by the side of many heroic plays. Gray's interest in Oriental fiction finds a substantial counterpart in travel books describing the Levant (Sandys, Baumgarten, Roe) or China (Navarette, Lecomte).

Of the other classes listed in Gray's first notebook none is so revealing as the above. In an equally early hand are recorded what appear to be his textbooks at Eton and at Cambridge — twenty-two items under " Grammarians, Antiquaries, &c:," and twenty-six items under " Moral and Natural Philosophy, Mathe-

---

[10] This book is now in the Folger Library at Washington.

[11] This is probably the same as the "Collection of six delightful Novels," 12mo, 1710, which appears among Gray's books with his mother's name on the title page.

matics, Logick, &c: in several Languages." The former, in addition to Greek, Latin, French, and Italian dictionaries and handbooks, lists four books on geography and a copy of Tallent's *Chronological Tables*. The latter, except for two editions of "Lock on human Understanding," consists of various books on metaphysics and mathematics. These textbooks have naturally not survived. Gray passed judgment on some of them in a letter to West in 1736:

> Must I plunge into metaphysics? Alas, I cannot see in the dark; nature has not furnished me with the optics of a cat. Must I pore upon mathematics? Alas, I cannot see in too much light; I am no eagle. It is very possible that two and two make four, but I would not give four farthings to demonstrate this ever so clearly; and if these be the profits of life, give me the amusements of it.[12]

Gray includes in this early catalogue, although in a slightly later hand and therefore in a more orderly arrangement, a section of "Libri Classici" with seventy-two items, all of which include the editor, publisher if noteworthy, format, place and date of publication, and often the price as well. The first item is a four-volume quarto Livy, whose date (1735) may well mark the beginning of Gray's first interest in bibliography. The next item, a folio Thucydides (1731), appears among the poet's books after his death, as do also eleven of the eighteen following items which are listed as a group "8 vo cum Notis Variorum." Some of these, as well as the Homer, Euripides, Horace, Vergil, and Sophocles listed farther down, were in Gray's possession, as we know, as early as 1733. At least four of the other books in this list have also survived, and it is not at all unlikely that he owned all of them, for the classics represent his first genuine interest along scholarly lines. He evidently prized them very much, for nearly every one of these early books that has survived contains, in addition to his name and often the date, an extract from De Bure and a memorandum of the price. The list offers a fairly comprehensive survey of classical authors, whether in poetry, history, rhetoric, or philosophy, the only notable exceptions being among

---

[12] Tovey, I, 3; Toynbee, I, 112; Whibley, I, 56.

the Greeks; Plato, Aristotle, Aeschylus, and Pindar — all favorites of Gray's in later years — are missing.

Of two other classes written in Gray's large youthful hand, one is an uninspired list of modern Latin writers, the other a selection of French and Italian books on many subjects. Already familiar with French and Latin, Gray found Italian easy to master, as he wrote West in March 1737.[13] He read profusely in the poetry of Tasso, Ariosto, Petrarch, and Dante, and made translations into English verse of some seventy lines from Tasso and of the Ugolino episode from Dante's *Inferno*. The French books he was reading are more numerous and varied than the Italian. The best-known writers, in the order in which they occur in the catalogue, are Boileau, Racine, La Bruyère, Montesquieu, La Rochefoucauld, La Fontaine, Marot, and Madame de Sévigné, while other books of criticism, history, memoirs, travel (four items), and fiction also appear. Although they represent a miscellaneous assortment of subjects, the books in this French and Italian list, sixty-two items in all, show a vivid interest in these two foreign literatures and reëcho thè young student's love of history, travel, and romantic fiction.

This account of Gray's early interests is for the most part the story of the haphazard browsing of an alert youth. The child is father of the man in this case, but the parts which are to fit later into the complete picture lie here in a jumbled heap. Until he left England to tour the Continent with Walpole, Gray read with intelligence and a catholic but discerning taste. The Latin and Greek in his curriculum led him far into classical literature, giving him a love which was soon to turn to passionate scholarship in that field. He learned French and Italian, browsing in them as he had browsed in English, first among the great poets, then among the historians and critics, and finally in the more ephemeral literature of travel and fiction.

Gray was able to poke fun at his random reading. The ingen-

[13] " I learn Italian like any dragon, and in two months am got through the 16th book of Tasso, whom I hold in great admiration" (Toynbee, I, 128). See also Norton Nicholls' " Reminiscences of Gray " in Tovey, II, 286, and Whibley, App. Z.

ious "battle of the books," which he wrote for West, describes the quarrels of authors jumbled on the shelves of his study. Madame de Sévigné's sixth tome is squeezed to death by Aristotle. Her cousin Bussy Rabutin would come to her rescue but finds himself being murdered by Strabo. The whole shelf is a strange mixture, Catullus, La Bruyère, Malebranche, and Gronovius. Locke is heard to say, " Certainly our owner must have very confused ideas, to jumble us so strangely together. He has associated me with Ovid and Ray the Naturalist." Vergil, Henry More, George Cheyne, Euclid, Boileau, and Swift interrupt each other with their speculations, and the vision is finally disturbed by Gray's laughter on hearing his vade mecum saying, " Pshaw! I and the Bible are enough for any one's library." [14]

Gray left his books in 1739 to see the world with Walpole. For two years, unquestionably the most exciting of his whole life, he substituted men and monuments for literature. Although he continued to read, comparing the accounts of the ancients with their remains in Italy, he filled his letters with descriptions of cities and mountains and people. He kept notebooks describing the numerous art collections to which Walpole's influence gave them access. He wrote down his critical impressions of ancient sculpture and Renaissance painting. He collected as many prints and engravings as he could afford to buy, that he might carry back to England some visual evidence of the artistic richness of Italy. He bought, mostly in Rome, fifty books on art and antiquities, profusely illustrated with fine engravings.[15] In short, he became very learned in these phases of the fine arts, chiefly through firsthand observations. This exciting interlude interrupted his reading and gave him his first opportunity for scholarship. He showed during those two years in Italy the curiosity of the true scholar, but not until much later did he again have such

[14] Toynbee, II, 17 ff. Whibley (I, 93, n. 1) argues plausibly for December 1738 (not 1740) as the date of this letter to West.

[15] For the entire list, entered as the last class in his youthful catalogue, see p. 156. At least ten of the fifty items have survived with Gray's assurance that they belong to the stay in Italy. E.g., Bartoli's *Colonna Traiana*: " T. Gray, June, 1740, a Roma; costo 9 scudi."

an opportunity to explore and evaluate for himself the firsthand sources of knowledge, not indeed until he studied manuscripts at the British Museum and insects in the fields of England.

After his return from the Continent and before he went to Cambridge at the end of 1742, Gray again turned to general reading. He enjoyed it at times, but found it often boring without a definite goal.

At one time he describes his jubilant progress from Pliny and Martial to Theocritus, and a fortnight of drinking and singing with Anacreon thrown in; a few weeks later he speaks playfully of the " white Melancholy " which is still " a good easy sort of a state," but " which is apt now and then to give a sort of Ennui." As early as 1742, therefore, Gray rates reading as one of his chief amusements, an occupation that keeps his melancholy from becoming the black variety which already he has " now and then felt." He reads anything and everything: " My life is like Harry the fourth's supper of Hens. 'Poulets a la broche, Poulets en Ragôut, Poulets en Hâchis, Poulets en Fricasées.' Reading here, Reading there; nothing but books with different sauces." [16]

Gray was reading extensively in the classics during that winter in London, varying his diet with such contemporary literature as Pope's *Dunciad* and Fielding's *Joseph Andrews,* not to mention the " paradisaical pleasures " of Marivaux and Crébillon.[17] With such frank enjoyment of books he could not have been very serious in his continuous complaints to West about the insipidity of life. The idea of boredom is present, nevertheless, and it grows until it will not be put off by random reading but must be fed with concentrated study. The tinge of romantic melancholy ends in the necessity for more and more books to fill the voids of life.

Until 1742 Gray read widely and greedily, sampling the offerings of many centuries and many moods. He had the varied tastes of a browser, mixed at times with the antiquarian's industry and

---

[16] Tovey, I, 103; Toynbee, II, 43; Whibley, I, 209 f.

[17] Tovey, I, 96; Toynbee, II, 25; Whibley, I, 191. In the cargo of books, chiefly historical and political, sent to Horace Mann at Florence in July 1742, Gray included Crébillon's *Sofa,* Marivaux's *Marianne,* and a ten-volume collection of plays.

the scholar's desire to penetrate beneath the surface. Sooner or later the browser in him had to give permanent place to the scholar, an event already foreshadowed in his study of Italian art and Roman antiquities.

This evolution from bookworm to scholar was delayed by two years of legal study. The little we know about the period from 1742, when Gray reëntered Peterhouse at Cambridge, to the end of 1743, when he took his degree of bachelor of laws, shows it to be a more or less drab interlude between browsing and scholarship. He was at the time, however, making the acquaintance of libraries like that of Pembroke [18] and of congenial men like Thomas Wharton. He was already learning the conveniences of Cambridge as a residence and the possibilities of scholarship as a gentlemanly occupation. His stay in the university town after 1744 was therefore not so much the result of a decision as of the gradual evolution of his state of mind. The bookworm slowly turned scholar, preparing himself for future research long before he began in 1747 to dig deeply into Greek civilization. I wish now to show some of the steps in this transition and to describe Gray's chief interests from 1744 to 1747, especially those of a bibliographical nature, as illustrations of his methods of work.

II

Since Gray was widely read in many subjects before 1744, he had enough interests to keep him busy for a long time. He continued to enlarge the scope of his study with the help of such learned journals as the *Journal des Sçavans,* systematizing his work by keeping notebooks. From time to time his enthusiasm for some scheme of the moment took him deeply into a special field. Then a new interest would come to the front, causing him to abandon the old one. Inertia was the chief reason for these changes, encouraged by the scholar in him who could see in his study of the moment too vast a field ever to be fully mastered. His vivid imagination, with its restlessness and its desire for uni-

[18] The first books Gray borrowed from Pembroke (*c.* 1743) were charged to " Mr. Trollope " on the library register, but after 1745 nearly all to James Brown, later master of the college and coexecutor with Mason of Gray's estate.

versal knowledge, sent him to new subjects before the old was finished. His active mind made him a pioneer in learning, but he was content to let others get the credit.

Gray gathered his materials for research, at least in the well-documented fields of geography and the classics, chiefly from two sources: (1) from learned journals, such as the *Journal des Sçavans* or the *Mémoires de l'Académie des Sciences,* and (2) from formal bibliographies. He kept most of his findings in the omnium-gatherum that he called his Commonplace Book, which therefore presents typical specimens of his scholarly pursuits from beginning to end. At some point in his undergraduate years, probably about 1736, Gray began this Commonplace Book. His plan, based on "the Method of Mr. Lock," was to group quotations or notes under general subjects, leaving space for later additions. Only the first forty pages or so, nearly all in his early hand, follow this method. Before 1750 Gray was using his Commonplace Book as the chief repository of his learned discoveries.[19]

In the first part of the Commonplace Book, Gray again shows the broad interests of his youthful reading. In his first article, "Affectus," he quotes Aulus Gellius, Plutarch, and Cicero, among the ancients, and Locke and Pope, his youthful favorites, among the writers of his own day. Under the heading, "Comparatio," he traces several pictures from Homer or Vergil through Tasso to Milton, quoting copiously from the original languages. He is here most concerned with Italian Renaissance poets, for he was reading them with enthusiasm at Cambridge in 1737. Characteristically he remarks, after quoting three lines from Horace and seventeen from *Il pastor fido* of Guarini: "What a difference between Horace and Guarini! an Italian poet and one of the Augustan Age." He includes antiquities as well as literature. He copies out "tables of ancient monys taken from Arbuthnot," and compares the weights and measures of the ancients with those of his own country. He describes the situations of ancient cities bearing the same names, twelve Alexandrias, nine Seleucias, twenty-

[19] See Martin, *Chronologie,* pp. 134–147, for an analytical table of its chief articles.

one Augustas, and so on. He made additions to these articles, as the handwriting shows, but the principal entries belong to the period before 1744.[20]

In his Commonplace Book Gray has left the best indication of what he was studying, especially during the years 1748–1758, when he put into it the results of his most scholarly research, random articles on hundreds of miscellaneous subjects as well as extended series of studies in special fields. The sequence is roughly the one I have followed in the succeeding chapters of this book, though with constant overlapping. Classics and travel books, for example, seem to go hand in hand, for both of them begin in 1744 with the checking of Strabo's geography against the recent accounts of travelers like Shaw and Pococke, and both end about 1754 with Plato and India. Intensive study of Greek history, on the other hand, falls within the years 1746–1748, whereas the travel books yield their richest harvest in the articles on Oriental history, which may be dated in the early fifties. The study of poetics for a history of English poetry took most of his time from about 1754 to 1757, leading him in his search for the roots of early English poetry to a superficial knowledge of Anglo-Saxon and to an intimate acquaintance, through the medium of scholars who wrote in Latin, with what was available in his day of Celtic and Norse poetry. Early in 1758 he began a study of English cathedrals and their monuments, then of the science of heraldry needed to interpret his materials, all as a background for original research in the field of English history in the manuscript collections of the British Museum during the years 1759–1761. The Commonplace Book ends at this point, but not before Gray had inserted an article on Linnaeus and his new method of classifying natural history —

[20] An interesting article entitled "Lingua" (p. 33) shows an early interest in philology. In speaking of Greek, Latin, and Arabic, Gray makes this observation: "It is however to be remark'd, that, tho' the Stock of words in the two former of these languages did indeed grow greater in proportion to the extent of the Greek & Roman conquests, yet their purity was thereby as much diminish'd: Herodotus, Xenophon, & Thucidides, the authors whose style we chiefly admire, & look upon as fathers of the Ionic & Attick idiom, lived all before the Macedonian power arose; Demosthenes at the very time of the conquest of Persia, before it could have any influence on the tongue: the Latin too, after Augustus, grew corrupted, & infected with foreign terms & expressions, & as its copiousness increased, so its beauty & purity was impaired."

a prelude to the scientific research he carried on during the last ten years of his life. Thus the Commonplace Book really tells us what he was doing to stay busy and furnishes by connotation an ample reason for the slight output of poetry. More than a thousand folio pages in its three ponderous volumes, many of them closely written, contain the results of his researches. With the smaller notebooks and the marginalia in the books of his library, they furnish the materials for an account of Thomas Gray the scholar.

III

The casual observer may wonder how Gray became so learned. The poet gave his own answer when his youthful friend, Norton Nicholls, expressed astonishment at the extent of his reading: "Why should you be surprised, for I do nothing else," and added that "he knew from experience how much might be done by a person who did not fling away his time on middling or inferiour, authors, & read with method." [21] In a way, that is the secret of Gray's becoming a pioneer in several fields of scholarship. In the classics he chose the best available editions with their scholarly annotations. In the field of travel he supplemented early firsthand descriptions with the latest and most accurate accounts by his contemporaries. In the study of early English poetry he went to the works of Chaucer, Lydgate, and others, and then studied enough Anglo-Saxon to understand the seeming inconsistencies of Middle English verse. He went back of English poetry to its progenitors — the Provençal, the Welsh, and the Norse — and learned enough of the original language to understand the various meters, but saved time by relying on scholars who wrote from devoted study and who freely translated the foreign poetry into Latin. In the study of history Gray always went to original materials, relying upon manuscript documents and contemporary memoirs rather than upon second-rate historians.[22] In English history and in the scientific research of his later life, he used few

---

[21] Nicholls, "Reminiscences of Gray," in Tovey, II, 284, and Whibley, III, 1296.

[22] See his interesting comment on Boswell's *Account of Corsica* (Whibley, III, 1019): "The pamphlet proves what I have always maintained, that any fool may write a most valuable book by chance, if he will only tell us what he heard and saw with veracity."

books, preferring to make his own way, like a true scholar, through the new world of uncharted source material.

Gray saved time by going to the best authors for his reading and to the best scholars for his learning, but this was not by chance. The modern scholar, approaching a new field of study, prepares an elaborate bibliography. Gray did just that, too, even though his wide range of interests threatened at times to overwhelm him with a meaningless avalanche of titles. He kept a small notebook at first, in which the titles were arranged in a loose alphabetical order. When this system threatened to get unwieldy, he kept his lists on the flyleaves of the Commonplace Book or in random notes that have for the most part disappeared. A description of the small notebook will give an idea of the methods he used.[23]

This bibliographical notebook has always been described as an alphabetical catalogue of Gray's library, but it obviously is not that. Very few of the titles listed appear in Gray's library, as we know it from sales catalogues, and even then often with different editions or prices. For example, Hickes's *Thesaurus* is listed at four guineas, whereas we know that he bought his copy in 1760 for two pounds. Fourteen volumes of Fabricius's *Bibliotheca Graeca* are listed at £3 10s., but Gray picked up the first six volumes in 1760 for six shillings. Some very rare items are too expensive for Gray's modest income,[24] and the total sum represented by the prices given in the notebook would have been a hardship to him in his most affluent days. We know that he never spent much for books, for he bought them regardless of their condition, showing himself rather the scholar than the bibliophile.[25]

[23] Now in Pierpont Morgan Library. See Register II. 2.

[24] E.g., " Seb: Gryph: Commentarii L: Latinae. £12.12.0 rariss:" and London *Gazettes,* 1665–1720, at the same price.

[25] An interesting commentary on this trait appears in a description of Gray's books at the time of their first sale in 1845, in the *Athenaeum,* December 6, 1845, p. 1174: "We were somewhat disappointed . . . with the outside appearance of the poet's library. . . . Many of his books were very ordinary copies: ' Refuse of stalls, and gleanings of Duck Lane.' Many wanted their outside letterings — others were cropped to the quick, and there was not a book in the whole collection but would have horrified Dr. Dibdin, or would have stood the test of Mr. Miller's rule."

The manner in which the items are listed, moreover, shows clearly that Gray was collecting and putting into rough order miscellaneous information from many sources. Numerous items are listed in more than one edition or with several memoranda as to price or rarity.[26] Often he left space for information as to date, format, or price, which he usually filled in later, but sometimes left blank, particularly in the case of the author's first name. Gray also used the notebook for much bibliographical information, especially in the case of the last items under each letter. Compendious histories or collections he occasionally explained in long parenthetical notes, giving full information, for instance, as to the best edition ("uncastrated") of Mézeray's *Histoire de France* and of Ramusio's collection of voyages. He noted spurious works and the real authors of pseudonymous books.

Obviously interested in obtaining the best information in the quickest way, Gray went to the bibliographical sources — reference books and learned journals — and supplemented his information with prices from booksellers and sales catalogues.[27] It is not probable that he ever intended to read all the books, but he filed his notes away and tried to make a catalogue of them in alphabetical order. Under each letter he listed at the beginning various books on antiquities and editions of classical authors, for they represent his first serious interest in scholarship. From these he found it easy to send Thomas Wharton in 1746 a list of books to be recommended for purchase by the Pembroke library.[28] All he had to do was to copy the first items in his catalogue, omitting the prices and making a choice as to edition.

After the classics and antiquities Gray listed books relating to the modern history of Europe, a subject which he pursued all his life with interest and vigor. With the addition of a number of travel items he abandoned the idea, tiring of the labor required or

[26] E.g., Roger Ascham's *Discourse of the Affairs of Germany* (1552) is "scarce & commonly imperfect," and Gabriel Ackeleye's notes on Tacitus (1646) "rare & much esteem'd."

[27] These ephemeral catalogues were numerous but untrustworthy except for prices. See Adam Clarke's advertisement to his *Bibliographical Dictionary* (London, 1802), I, i–iv.

[28] Tovey, I, 140–143; Whibley, I, 242–245.

realizing the futility of his keeping an orderly bibliography. Whatever the cause, he discarded his alphabetical notebook in the early 1750's, after having listed some nine hundred titles.[29] This catalogue is evidence, nevertheless, of Gray's bibliographical method and of his interests during the first decade of his scholarly research.

IV

A glance at Gray's method of acquiring information shows that in scholarship as well as reading he went to the best authors. First he went through numerous volumes of the files of learned journals in Pembroke and elsewhere, thereby keeping up with the latest scholarship and at the same time gleaning a thousand curiosities for himself. Next he consulted the learned and elaborate bibliographical guides of his time, some of which he acknowledged as the sources of his preliminary lists on the flyleaves of the Commonplace Book.

The source most frequently cited by Gray is the Abbé Lenglet du Fresnoy's *Méthode pour étudier l'histoire,* the first two volumes of which are method, and the last two erudite bibliography, covering ancient and modern history, geography, and antiquities, and classified according to author and to subject. Fresnoy also included elaborate chronological tables of world history with a special table of Greece by Olympiads, the kind of thing that Gray was compiling for himself in 1747. Gray also drew on D. G. Morhof's *Polyhistor,* a compendious handbook which described the libraries of Europe and listed sources, printed and manuscript, for practically all branches of study from philology to poetics. J. Albertus Fabricius contributed a great deal to Gray's knowledge of the classics, not only through his compendiums of Greek and Latin literature, but even more through his *Bibliographia antiquaria,* with its convenient detailed catalogues of the contents of

[29] A number of new books, published in the 1740's, are listed, but none bearing a date later than 1748. Furthermore, we know that Gray was particularly interested in the classics from 1746 to 1748 and in travel books during the early 1750's. He abandoned both about 1755 for the study of poetry, for which he kept a bibliography on the flyleaves of the Commonplace Book without using his alphabetical notebook.

various other compendiums of classical learning, and through his *Bibliothecae Fabricianae historia,* with its elaborate discussion of editions and scholia of ancient authors. Draudius' *Bibliotheca classica,* another work used by Gray,[30] contains nearly seventeen hundred closely printed pages of bibliography classified by subject, besides an alphabetical index of authors at the end. For the study of antiquities or manuscripts — abbreviations, seals, monograms, paleography — Gray had such works as Mabillon's *De re diplomatica.* These ~nd many others were his immediate sources.[31] By their aid he found the easiest and best ways to learning, and from them he compiled for his convenience an alphabetical catalogue of the books which he might at some time consult on the subjects he was then pursuing — classical literature, antiquities, history, and travel.

Gray used the learned journals of his day, however, for more than bibliography. Such periodicals as the *Journal des Sçavans,* the *Mémoires de l'Académie des Sciences,* and the *Philosophical Transactions* of the Royal Society represented the last word in science and discovery. In their back numbers Gray could read the history of learning for the past two generations. Together with the *Acta eruditorum* and the *Mémoires de l'Académie des Inscriptions,* they furnished also the latest scholarship in the literature and remains of the ancients. With their reviews and their scientific accounts one might easily become a secondhand savant, acquainted at least by name with the learned world.[32] But Gray

[30] He borrowed a copy of Draudius from Pembroke library in 1744.

[31] B. G. Struvius, *Introductio in notitiam rei literariae et usum bibliothecarum* (Jena, 1710), contains useful information on libraries, bibliographies, and learned journals. Other noted works available in 1750 are J. Vogt, *Catalogus historico-criticus librorum rariorum*; J. H. Boecler, *Bibliographia critica*; and John Hartley, *Catalogus universalis librorum* (begun as a union catalogue of famous libraries). Gray knew William Oldys' *British Librarian,* which contains valuable summaries of books that he later used, such as Webbe's *Discourse of English Poetry,* Hakluyt's *Voyages,* Ashmole's *Order of the Garter,* Weever's *Funeral Monuments,* and H. Lhuyd's translation of the *History of Wales.*

[32] Gray translates (CPB. II, 687) a statement from an article in the *Mémoires de l'Académie des Inscriptions,* on the decay of belles-lettres, which sums up what he himself might have said: "by imitating them [the Middle Ages] voluntarily (in abandoning the knowledge of the learned Languages) we expose ourselves to the same Fate: our Dictionaries, Bibliotheques, Journals, & a thousand other

was seldom content with secondhand knowledge. He got what help was to be had from the best possible sources, then struck out alone into new country.

Although Gray used the learned journals of his day as sources of scholarly information, he chose from them, for preservation in his notes, items of the most curious sort. His interest in monstrosities and freaks of nature is never more apparent than in his first real venture of this kind, the quarto notebook dated January 1745, in which he begins with the *Journal des Sçavans* and continues with the *Histoire et mémoires de l'Académie des Sciences.*[33]

Gray sets out as if with the purpose of making a medical notebook, following up the early interest in " physick " that his uncle Robert Antrobus had tried to inspire in him. He collects a variety of odd scientific information — vital statistics from the great plague in England in 1665, dissection of a lion, unusual experiments, such as keeping a dog alive by blowing into his lungs or curing a madman by transfusion of calf's blood. He inserts a few historical or literary notes but seldom expands them beyond a line or so. Queer cases of medical treatment abound, and freaks of nature are on every page. Curiosities of one sort or another practically fill the notebook with specimens for a " believe-it-or-not " museum. Horns growing out of human bodies, a child living nine months without any brain, a human kidney nearly five feet in circumference, a child that stayed in its mother for twenty-six years, the secrets of Richardson the English fire-eater, a madman who fancied he was Christ and fasted forty days — such are the

---

Books of the same kind, wch are daily swarming among us, & that, while they facilitate to us the Means of appearing learned, keep us from making ourselves really so, seem to be the Forerunners of Barbarism & Ignorance."

[33] Now in Pierpont Morgan Library. Register II.4. For excerpts, see p. 164. The Castle Howard notebook (Register II.3) has two earlier but not extensive ventures along the same line: Mabillon's *Musaeum Italicum* (November 1744) and Ducatiana (December 1744). A few notes on *Acta eruditorum* and some antiquities from Fabricius's *Bibliotheca Graeca* and the *Mémoires de l'Académie des Inscriptions* appear in the same notebook. The registers of Pembroke library show that Gray borrowed several times a number of volumes of *Acta eruditorum* and the *Mémoires* in 1744-1745. He returned twelve volumes of the *Histoire de l'Académie des Sciences* on April 19, 1745. The last entries of such works for this period are in the autumn of 1746.

monstrosities Gray chose from these scientific journals, interspersing the description of them with occasional notes on the history of medicine or on methods of treatment of fairly ordinary diseases. The explanation of this queer assortment is easy: Gray was genuinely interested in science, even before he became an ardent disciple of Linnaeus; at the same time, he was a seeker of curiosities in the footpaths of learning. Did he not get pleasure in his reading from Athenaeus, Lydgate, and Crébillon, as well as from Plato, Chaucer, and Dante? Although he never lost sight of the truly great, he frankly showed his enjoyment of the unusual and the bizarre, even of freaks and monsters.

In the early 1750's Gray took notes on whole shelves of learned journals and compendiums, leaning in his interest more to literature and antiquities than to science and curiosities, but devoting enough space to nature's freaks to show that he had not lost his earlier interest.[34] These notes strengthen our picture of Gray's search for every available source of learning. Curiosities still find their place: spontaneous combustion of the human body, a buzzard with three testicles, a petrified walnut. On the whole, however, the notes after 1750 are of a more scholarly nature, both scientific and historical.[35] From all of the learned periodicals, the scholar in Gray, whether as scientist, classical student, antiquarian, or general historian, gathers material for study and in the process gleans his museum of curiosa.

Obviously, Gray knew how to study. With him to be busy was to be happy, but with anyone the employment must yield the

[34] The following list indicates the extent to which he continued, until about 1755, to consult the storehouses of recent scholarship:

[Le Clerc] Bibliothèque Choisie	V–XVII (1705–1709)	CPB, II, 512
Bibl. Italique	I–XVI (1728–1733)	CPB, II, 531 f.
Mémoires de l'académie des sciences	1742–1749	CPB, II, 533 f., 729–733
Acta Eruditorum	1738–1747	CPB, II, 595 f.
Commentarii Petropolitani	V–VIII (1730–1741)	CPB, II, 605 f.
Letters of Robert Boyle	(Works, vol. V, 1744)	CPB, II, 623
Mém. de l'acad. des Inscriptions	XVI (1741–1743)	CPB, II, 687 f., 691 f.
Lettres Edifiantes	I–XXIV	CPB, II, 753 f., 763 f., 793
Acta Philosophica Societatis Regiæ	XLVII–XLVIII (1751–1753)	CPB, II, 783, 789
[Lambecius] Commentarii de Bibliotheca Cesarea Vindobonensi	8 vols.	CPB, 785–787

[35] Gray's interest in travel appears very strongly, as in a long description of a trip into Peru (CPB, II, 533), or in the intimate accounts of foreign countries by the Jesuit missionaries in the Lettres édifiantes.

satisfaction that comes from progress. Although he was too economical of his energy not to utilize what aid he could find, he was at the same time too scholarly to use any but the best help. He availed himself of compendiums but deplored the taste of the age which depended upon them. In other words, he had the attitude of the sincere scholar who takes what he can find but tests it and verifies it at the source. We shall see in the succeeding chapters how this method works out in the various fields to which he devoted special study — namely, the classics, travel, poetics, history, and science.

CHAPTER III

THE HERITAGE OF GREECE AND ROME

I

GRAY was well acquainted with most of the classical authors before he undertook a formal study of Greek philosophy and history in the autumn of 1746. An intelligent student in the eighteenth century could scarcely avoid knowing classical literature. To knowledge, however, Gray added love and enthusiasm. He knew Latin well before he left Eton, and the classics were his chief love at Cambridge. By 1738 he had not only read most of Latin literature and dipped boldly into the Greek but had also shown his mastery of the Latin language by translating selections from Statius and Propertius into English verse and by composing original Latin poems, two of which were published at the time of writing. The importance of this thorough knowledge and love of the classics cannot be overemphasized. It not only furnished his mind with a plentiful stock of beautiful poetry which often crept unconsciously into his own writings, but gave him as well the knowledge necessary for sound criticism and the equanimity to rise above the difficult moments of life.

Gray was not one to leave his classical companions at the university. On the Continent in 1739 he read Livy as he rode down into Italy, and compared impressions of the Alps with him. On the same trip he read Silius Italicus for the first time,[1] and reviewed Tacitus and Seneca,[2] and perhaps many other classical authors as well. With new understanding he compared their accounts with the genuine remains of ancient Rome which lay before his eyes. Italy was at that time the Mecca of those who

[1] Tovey, I, 45; Whibley, I, 129.
[2] William Gilpin, in an unpublished letter to William Mason from Cheam, May 6, 1775, speaks of having seen a bundle of letters from Gray to Dr. Clerke, which had been found in a box almost forgotten: "In one from Italy he gives a very entertaining acc^t of some fr^{ds}, whose company he then enjoyed, Tacitus, & Seneca." I owe this information to Professor W. D. Templeman, who is preparing an edition of Gilpin's letters.

loved things classical, and Gray was the most ardent of pilgrims. He worshiped at the shrine for almost two years, and his knowledge of the ancient world increased tremendously.

He continued to compose Latin verses, more to amuse West than to show his own proficiency. His final farewell to Florence is typical. He was bored with his manner of life in that city before he and Walpole left it in April 1741 to go to the fair at Reggio. "Yet the place and the charming prospects demand a poetical farewell," he writes West, enclosing the composition in Latin verses full of Vergil and Silius Italicus.[3] He and West had exchanged verses from their days together at Eton. Latin, an easy medium for both, furnished them with a sort of intimate language not meant for the public eye. Gray continued the Sapphic ode he had written to West in 1738 with a stanza from Genoa in November 1739, bidding farewell to the frozen north. In 1740 he sent at least three: in January a few elegiacs on a visit to the site of the battle of Trebia, in May a song in Alcaics addressed directly to him under the name of Favonius, and in September some vivid hexameters on the desolation of the Gaurus by an earthquake in ancient times. In the same letter with the farewell to Florence he enclosed other Latin verses, spoils of the tedium of waiting for Walpole and longing for West, one of them a Latin imitation of an Italian sonnet, another the beginning of his most ambitious Latin poem, *De principiis cogitandi*.

In this didactic poem Gray himself recognized the contradiction which arose from mingling metaphysics and poetry. "It is Latin too to increase the absurdity," he added. He never finished it, although the fifty-three verses sent to West later grew to two hundred thirty-six, in which one naturally finds numerous echoes of Lucretius, as well as some of Vergil, Ovid, Horace, and Claudian. The subject itself is not a strange one for Gray, for the philosopher Locke, to whom it is addressed, was one of his first loves. But why should he begin writing it in Florence? To have something to do, for one thing, and also to enable him to send West a composition to match his epic poem in dignity.

[3] Tovey, I, 87; Toynbee, II, 6; Whibley, I, 182.

The poem itself contains some interesting ideas in its description of the development of reason in the human mind and of the part played in the process by the senses. Locke and Lucretius are not strange partners, but the driving force of the poem is West, the Favonius to whom it is addressed. When West died there was no incentive to finish the poem. What purports to be a fragment of a second book [4] is Gray's moving lament on the death of his friend, as if he were saying that he had planned a long poem which would reveal the secrets of Nature but that in the midst of the task the hope and reason of so much work (" spes tanti et causa laboris ") had been taken from him.

On his way to England from Italy in August 1741, Gray stopped for a second time at the Grande Chartreuse and in the album of the monastery wrote an Alcaic ode, one of his best poems in Latin. Here he expresses artistically what he had written on his first visit to the spot in a letter to West: " Not a precipice, not a torrent, not a cliff, but is pregnant with religion and poetry." By contrast he asks at this time, however, nothing but peaceful quiet for a weary youth and finally a restful old age far from the tumult of the crowd. The world had been too much with him. Walpole with his love of company and festivity had wearied him until he could stand it no longer. The quarrel at Reggio was long overdue, and Gray was merely demanding the quiet which he loved but which traveling with Walpole could not give him.

Gray was in London the following winter and, having no definite work in hand, indulged in an orgy of general reading, in which the classics naturally played a conspicuous part. He has great praise for Tacitus, whom West is translating.[5] He sends West a long fragment of a stilted poetical drama, *Agrippina*, taken mostly from Tacitus and modeled on Racine. He reads Thucydides and tries to translate him, but gives up in despair,

---

[4] The manuscript in CPB has " Liber Secundus," not " Liber Quartus," as in most editions. See *Works,* ed. Bradshaw, p. 165. Gray wrote Walpole that it was part "of the fourth Book, wch was intended to treat of the Passions" (Whibley, I, 267).

[5] Toynbee, II, 21, 29, 34; Tovey, I, 95, 100, 101. Nearly all the following description is taken from letters to West about the same time.

sending West instead his poetical version of an elegy of Propertius. He drinks and sings with Anacreon for a fortnight and quotes three verses of him for West. He browses in Theocritus, Pliny, and Martial. The last piece of his work that West ever saw was an Ovidian heroic epistle in Latin, *Sophonisba Massinissae,* which he acknowledged was "partly taken from Livy, and partly from Appian." [6]

West died June 1, 1742, and Gray's interest in Latin composition, except for his translations from the Greek Anthology and his uninspired technical verses on the orders of insects, ceased abruptly. His last attempt at original Latin poetry was the concluding fragment of *De principiis cogitandi,* written shortly after West's death. To my mind this is the only poem Gray ever wrote which portrays genuine personal emotion. Like Milton lamenting the untimely death of Charles Diodati in his *Epitaphium Damonis,* Gray chooses to conceal deep feeling in Latin phrases. " The harshness of the lingering disease seemed at last to have ceased, and unsuspecting, alas, I hoped, beloved Favonius, to spend long days alone with you as we used to do. . . . In vain, alas, are our sweet hopes and futile vows." The last three verses are full of the loss of his best friend:

> Respice et has lacrymas, memori quas ictus amore
> Fundo; quod possum, proptér lugere sepulchrum
> Dum juvat, et mutae vana haec jactare favillae.

Gray wrote no Latin poetry to equal Milton's, but Dr. Johnson thought he showed great promise in that field. John Mitford, in many ways the poet's best editor, considered Gray's Latin poetry " to be peculiarly forcible and correct." [7] Like many students in his day, Gray showed in his Latin verses not only a knowledge of the language but also a sufficient intimacy with such poets as Vergil, Lucretius, Ovid, and Horace, to enable him to borrow freely from them both meter and phrase; unlike most of them, he also displayed occasional feeling and originality. The classical

---

[6] Tovey, I, 105; Toynbee, II, 45; Whibley, I, 211. In the next letter Gray sent West his first English poem, *Ode to Spring,* not knowing that his friend was then dead.

[7] *Poems of Thomas Gray,* p. lxix.

poets, in fact, became a part of him until their thoughts, and to a certain extent their language, went even into his English poems.

In 1742 Gray went back to Cambridge, where he spent the next two years ostensibly in acquiring a degree in law, but at the same time he did not neglect his classical companions. The entries in the Commonplace Book from this period are full of Greek and Roman antiquities, with numerous references to Strabo's descriptions of the ancient world. The truth of the matter is that Gray seldom limited himself to a single line of study. He became a snapper-up of scholarly trifles, carrying out in more or less intensive study the varied tastes of his youthful browsing. In 1744 he became especially interested in bibliography as a background for future research. In 1746 he began an intensive study of Greek history, oratory, and philosophy, ostensibly for the preparation of a chronological table of Greek history, but really because he found in the Greeks the beginning of the story of human progress, which was to be for many years his study. Gray's own notes, most of them unpublished, fill out the meager picture of his classical studies that we see in his letters.

II

Gray showed that he was already in the mood for classical study by the list of books to be recommended to the Pembroke library, which he sent in a letter to Wharton from Stoke, September 11, 1746.[8] He compiled carefully his list of seventy-three " Ancients " and thirty-five "Antiquaries, Grammarians, &c:," choosing the best editions from his own bibliographical notebook,[9] where he was accustomed to set down alphabetically the various editions and prices of books that interested him. He had good reason for being interested in what books the Pembroke College library purchased.[10] For at least two years he had not only read in the library, but he had also borrowed books to take to his rooms, entering them in the register under the names of

[8] Tovey, I, 140 ff.; Whibley, I, 242 ff.
[9] Now in Morgan Library. See discussion above, pp. 42–44.
[10] According to the college records, however, the library did not buy the books listed by Gray.

one or another of the Pembroke fellows. The entries begin about 1744, from which time till the summer of 1746, when he sent the list of desiderata to Wharton, he borrowed numbers of books relating to the classics or to classical antiquities. The borrowings usually consist of formidable and expensive works of reference, such as the antiquities of Montfaucon and Gronovius, a three-volume lexicon of Suidas, and the classical bibliography of Draudius. The presence of several classical authors in the register easily explains the seemingly glaring omissions in the list sent to Wharton. Professor Northup looks upon the omission of Plato as accidental,[11] but Gray had already borrowed Plato twice from the library. He omits Plutarch for the same reason, and recommends Xenophon in two editions to add to the Stephanus edition he had borrowed. Gray probably knew more about the Pembroke library even at that time than some of the college fellows.

In the same letter Gray tells Wharton that he is reading Aristotle, "his Poeticks, Politicks, and Morals," and comments on the ancient author in so apt a fashion as to make one deplore feelingly that he did not write more criticism and fewer notes on natural history. After a brief interval of "dissipation" in town he is again in Cambridge, taking up a study of "Diogenes Laertius & his Philosophers, as a Proœmium to the Series of their Works."[12] He wrote Wharton on December 27 that he was in the midst of this study and was preparing an elaborate chronological table.[13] Thus the poet's general reading in the extant works of his classical companions led almost imperceptibly into his first serious effort in scholarship. Plato and Aristotle were interesting enough to warrant more knowledge of their less famous contemporaries. Diogenes Laertius contained precious information on the Greek philosophers up to the third century B. C. — biography, contemporary gossip, and, best of all, the teachings themselves of many whose writings had perished. Gray's notes show that he

[11] Introd. to *Essays and Criticism by Thomas Gray*, p. xl.
[12] Tovey, I, 152; Whibley, I, 259.
[13] Gray's notebook on Diogenes Laertius, now in the Morgan Library, is dated November 20, 1746. He used Meibomius' edition, Amsterdam, 1692. Register II.6.a.

used this valuable work not only as a background for a study of Greek philosophy but also for data to fill up the columns of his new table of Greek chronology. He gleaned the usual amount of curiosa and gossip, but the best part went into the tables.[14]

Gray was much interested in history. As a boy he read not only Tacitus, Livy, and other Romans, but also much in the memoirs and papers that made up a great part of modern European history. The reference books he used in his bibliographical research around 1744 were mainly historical, and many of them contained elaborate chronological tables. From Pembroke he borrowed, in 1744, Sir Isaac Newton's *Chronology of Ancient Kingdoms Amended,* and after that the works of the Frenchman Petavius, who had improved the chronology of Scaliger. When Gray came to make his own tables of Greek history in the fall of 1746, he allowed three columns for political events and six for writers; already he was showing his fondness for the social history that is to be found in literature, manners, education, and thought. He entered the birth of the philosophers in red ink on his tables and tried in other ways to indicate their importance. He continued for some time to fill in the columns with philosophers, orators, and poets, using as authorities the Greek writers he was studying, besides such modern antiquarians as Bentley, Dodwell, and Marsham.[15] The project led him, as I shall indicate, deep into Greek history and literature, culminating in the study of Plato. He thought it would be diverting " to compare the Times of all great Men, their Writeings & Transactions." His thoroughness in carrying out such diversion made him a competent classical scholar.

Gray continued to read greedily in many fields. Judging only from the nature of the books he borrowed from Pembroke, we

[14] See Toynbee, II, 62 f., for Gray's use of a thought of Pythagoras from Diogenes Laertius.

[15] These tables, often mentioned by Gray, have probably disappeared for the most part. The only fragment I have seen, which contains all nine columns, consists of two sheets (Olympiads LXXXVII.3 – CV.2) laid in Mrs. J. T. Fields's copy of Bentley's designs for Gray's poems (1753), now in the Harvard Library. Dr. A. S. W. Rosenbach recently had two loose leaves, which contained the first four columns of Olympiads LXXIII – LXXXVII.2. Register VI.7.a.

see that during the winter of 1746–1747 he was studying not only Greek literature and antiquities, but also voyages, early English history, scientific journals, and natural history. His chief work of the moment, however, was Greek chronology, and he continued to fill out his tables, varying the tedium of history with poetry. After Diogenes Laertius he took up Athenaeus, whose comment on food and drink is rich with countless references to writers whose work has otherwise disappeared. He began Athenaeus on January 4, 1747, although he had Pembroke copies of both Aeschylus and Pindar by him at the same time. As he put it in a letter to Wharton two months later:

My Works are not so considerable as you imagine. I have read Pausanias and Athenæus all thro', & Aeschylus again. I am now in Pindar & Lysias: for I take Verse and Prose together, like Bread & Cheese. The Chronology is growing daily.[16]

Everything is grist for his mill, but nothing seems to be ground out except the chronology and a lot of miscellaneous annotations. He cannot have lost his sense of humor, for the letter continues: "The most noble of my Performances latterly is a Pôme on the uncommon death of Mʳ W:ˢ Cat."

What did Gray find to interest him in Pausanias and Athenaeus? Pausanias, the second-century geographer, interlarded his description of Greece with numerous historical sketches in the manner of a modern Baedeker. Gray probably used this ancient guidebook both for chronology and geography. He was writing in the Commonplace Book about this time a number of descriptive articles, some of them quite long, on Delos, Leucadia, Lebodea, Cythera, Tenos, Chios, Delphi, Thebes, and Corinth, with an elaborate description of Athens. He took most of the descriptions from the modern travel accounts of Sir George Wheeler (1682), but the subjects are such as Pausanias might have suggested.

Gray found Athenaeus a great help in his chronology, for the *Deipnosophistai* is a veritable handbook of references to everything even remotely connected with food and drink in Greek literature from Homer to the Alexandrians of the third century.

---

[16] Tovey, I, 162; Whibley, I, 276.

But he got from Athenaeus more than data for his tables, as a few examples from his quarto notebook show: the neglect of Pindar soon after his death; famous collections of books, including those of Euripides and Aristotle; a bronze statue erected to " a Juggler, that played at Cups & Balls"; a burlesque on Aristotle's Problems " much like our Conundrums "; a " Poppet-Shew Man in the same Theatre that Euripides appear'd." Beginning with the description of wines near the end of Book I, the notes become much fuller, including names of wines, toasts, and poems in praise of wine, rich testimony to the interest in food and cookery that Gray maintained throughout his life despite the rigid diet often necessitated by the gout.[17]

Gray was interested in curiosities of any sort, and Athenaeus, aided by the comments of Isaac Casaubon, furnished him God's plenty. He probably got the idea at this time of making his own vast catalogue of allusions in classical literature to wines, foods, clothing, furniture, medicines, gems, marbles, servants, and other such curiosities. They fill some sixty-five consecutive pages (186–251) of the first volume of his Commonplace Book, showing that he probably worked continuously on the project. Coming almost immediately after the notes on Greek geography, this catalogue belongs certainly to the same period as the study of Athenaeus. Wines head the list, as they do in the *Deipnosophistai* — twenty-eight kinds with quotations and specific references to their occurrence in literature. Eatables (forty-two kinds) and clothing (thirty-eight kinds) together account for fifteen pages of references, but Gray shows that the antiquarian may easily turn to natural history when he devotes five pages to twenty-one kinds of birds, and four pages to twenty kinds of fish.[18]

Almost immediately after he finished his notes on Athenaeus, Gray started two new notebooks, both dated March 20, 1747. One of them is for orators, beginning with Lysias and continuing the next winter with Isocrates; the other for poetry, first Pindar and

[17] Register II.6.b.
[18] Mathias (II, 126–131) has printed a few specimens from these catalogues, in which one sees a number of entries from Athenaeus as well as many from Latin literature, especially Martial, Horace, and Propertius.

then Aristophanes.[19] As he wrote Wharton, he was taking " Verse & Prose together, like Bread & Cheese." The prose, however, is his main concern at the time, for "the chronology is growing daily " and more historical data can be gleaned from orators than from poets. Since his reading of Pindar and Aristophanes is obviously for relaxation, let us consider first his study at this time of the Greek orators and historians.

Gray comments very seldom on the orations of Lysias, although he very justly describes the funeral oration for the Corinthian allies as " a noble & picturesque Description of the State of Greece immediately before the Battle of Salamis." His notes are mostly of an antiquarian nature, the greater part relating to the details of Athenian law which naturally appear frequently in Lysias' court pleas. An interesting example of this sort of annotation is the law cited in the case involving the murder of Eratosthenes: "Areopagitic Law, that a Man who caught another with his Wife, might murther him, if he thought fit; & the same, tho' the Woman were but his Concubine. yet he, who ravish'd a married Woman, or forced a Free Man or Boy was liable only to a Mulct." [20]

After a few notes on Andocides and Antiphon, Gray takes up Isocrates, the contemporary and rival of Lysias. The notes are dated December 26, 1747, and fill fifteen closely written pages with observations showing careful study and often independent thought as well. Using the 1593 folio edition of Stephanus, which contains the notes and Latin translation of Wolf, Gray seems to have studied Isocrates more thoroughly than any other Greek author except Plato or perhaps Aristophanes. Isocrates dealt at length in his orations with the subject of contemporary affairs in Athens, so that Gray was able to garner from them numerous

[19] Register II.7 and II.8.

[20] The edition Gray used was that of Taylor (4to, London, 1739), whose notes furnished him much material, e.g., on the equivalents of Greek money in his own day, in the notes on Conon's will. He reads also how Mantitheus gives himself a good character by furnishing his two sisters with dowries of thirty minae each,

£ s
then jots in his notebook: " 30 Minæ (96–17–6) a handsome Fortune for a young Woman of Condition at Athens."

notes on history, law, government, and even customs. More interesting, however, is the criticism which from time to time almost
grudgingly creeps in, as for example when he comments on the
opening of the famous panegyric: " I do not at all see the Art of
this most magnificent Prœmium, wherein the Orator . . . dis-
claims all Pretence to Modesty, promises to make his Hearers
forget all, that others had ever said on the same Subject, & stakes
his whole Reputation on the Success of this Speech."

The excellent plea for a return to fundamental principles
which Isocrates makes in his oration " On the Peace " draws the
following note from Gray: " He finely shews, that Justice & Hon-
esty with the Reputation, that results from them, are as much y^e
Interest of every State, as of every private Man. This whole
Topick is admirably treated, & equal to any Thing of this, or any
other Author." Luxury often leads to corruption, tyranny usurps
democracy, and the result in Athens is the depravity shown by
the practice of bribery and the use of Asiatic mercenary troops.
Sobriety is recommended for individuals; why not for states as
well? Athens and Sparta both rose from obscure beginnings to
power and then fell into the danger of becoming enslaved. An
excellent example of what becomes of a luxury-loving people is
summed up as follows in Gray's note: " He gives Thessaly at this
Time, as an Example, of a strong & wealthy People reduced by
their own ill-management to a low & distress'd Condition: & sets
in Contraste with them Megara, a little State with rocky barren
Territory, no Mines & no Ports, yet by its Prudence preserving its
Independency in ye midst of three powerful States (Thebes,
Sparta, & Athens) & where particular Persons were as rich, as in
any Part of Greece." Gray was undoubtedly thinking of this
oration when he wrote *The Alliance of Education and Government,* the first part of which he sent in a letter to Wharton the
very next summer.[21] The general idea, the frequent use of rhe-
torical questions, and even some details of Gray's poem are to be
found in this oration of Isocrates. The nearest parallel is that of
the following verses of Gray to the passage about Megara:

[21] Tovey, I, 192; Whibley, I, 310.

An iron-race the mountain-cliffs maintain,
Foes to the gentler genius of the plain . . .
What wonder, if to patient valour trained
They guard with spirit what by strength they gained?
And while their rocky ramparts round they see,
The rough abode of want and liberty,
(As lawless force from confidence will grow)
Insult the plenty of the vales below?

The "Panathenaicus," which Isocrates wrote as a defense of himself in extreme old age (begun at ninety-four and finished at ninety-seven), seems to have interested Gray more than any other of the orator's works. His judgment of the oration is a very just one: "This prolix Vindication of himself against the Attacks of a few trifling & contemptible Men (& that in the Exordium of a Grand Oration in Praise of his Country) seems, tho' full of Good-Sense, to be improper, & not well-judged in a Person of his great Age & Character." He finds one particular passage (26–32) excellent, however, "where he [Isocrates] shews, that the greatest Proficiency in Sciences & Arts contributes little to the real Improvement of the Mind or Manners of such as learn, or teach them." Gray transcribes in Greek a long quotation describing the truly educated and begs us to "see the whole Passage, wch is admirable." The subject is one that interested him all his life to such an extent that we listen eagerly to his close paraphrase of Isocrates:

The first & lowest Rank is of those, who have attain'd to Common-Sense, i:e: that is, Prudence, & the Knowledge of Mankind. the 2d, to Good-Temper, Good-Manners, & the inferior social Qualifications. the 3d to Temperance, the Command of their Passions in Pleasure & in Pain. the 4th, to be above even Good-fortune & Prosperity with all the Insolence, all the Vanity, that attend them: to keep in spite of these the Rank of a reasonable Creature, & to place one's Pride in those Advantages, that are not in the Power of Chance.

One fine passage, however, does not make a good work, and Gray gives his frank judgment: "All this, that passed with Relation to this Work between his Friends & him [233 ff.], seems to me very prolix, uninteresting, & artless." Having come to the end, the reader is ready to agree with Gray's parting opinion of the Pan-athenaicus: "the old Man's Ostentation is remarkable (tho' his Praises are put into the Mouth of another Character) in this Oration."

The notes on Isocrates are the only ones to be dated at both ends. Gray has added in this instance "Finish'd, March 1st. 1747/8," showing that he had spent a little more than two months on the project. The very same day he began to take notes on Xenophon in the new edition of Hutchinson, which he had recommended for the Pembroke library. As early as April 19, 1745, Gray had borrowed from Pembroke the Stephanus 1561 edition of Xenophon's works,[22] and he began at that time the study, particularly of the *Anabasis,* which is found in another notebook in the Morgan Library. Let us turn to this earlier note-book before taking up the notes on Hutchinson's Xenophon. It begins with notes on Thucydides, which Gray almost immedi-ately abandoned, probably because he chose rather to insert mar-ginal annotations in his own copy. The next ten pages or so are filled with notes on the Stephanus Xenophon, consisting chiefly of statistics concerned with chronology or antiquities.[23] Then comes a break in the continuity that demands our special attention.

All references to this notebook describe it as "Notes to Thu-cydides and to Xenophon," but the greater part of it deals with Diodorus Siculus, beginning with Book V of the fragmentary *Library of History.*[24] Gray had probably taken notes on all the earlier books, for they contain the curious kind of travel lore that interested him in Strabo and in the voyages of the sixteenth and seventeenth centuries — tales of Egypt, Babylon, Ethiopia, Arabia, the mythical stories of ancient Greece, the fabulous accounts of

[22] Other borrowings of Xenophon recorded in the library register are May 1745 and March 14, 1747.

[23] Register II.5.c. Most of the notes are very dry, but occasional items of interest are to be found, as for example: "Xenophon sells his horse for 50 Darics (£80-14-7)" or "the whole of their March is reckon'd 34355 Stad.: (4356 ¾ Miles) wch they perform'd in 15 Months."

[24] These sheets seem to have been originally separate, for they are of a slightly different size, and the pagination is not consecutive. Xenophon ends on p. 11 and Diodorus begins with p. 10. Register II.5.c.

savage tribes in Africa and Gaul and Britain.[25] He had no high opinion of the authenticity of Diodorus, as we know from his letter to Wharton, June 5, 1748: " Your Opinion of Diodorus is doubtless right; but there are Things in him very curious, got out of better Authors now lost." [26] In his notes he points out numerous disagreements with the accounts of Thucydides, to him the most authentic of Greek historians. The account of the " great Battle in the Hellespont," for example, is " very different from Thucyd: (N:B: It seems, Diodorus never had seen the 8th Book of Thucydides)." Again and again Gray finds fault with Diodorus and checks him also with Xenophon and Dodwell, even with Strabo and Isocrates. His notes reëcho such derogatory phrases as " strange Blunder," " careless hasty Account," " trifling & false," or " most imperfect Account." Though Gray obviously did not trust Diodorus, especially when it came to Grecian history and dates for his chronological tables, he nevertheless read him with interest, as he did Athenaeus and Pausanias and Diogenes Laertius, for the many curious things he rescued from oblivion — as, for example: " Celtiberians bath, & wash their Teeth in Urine — the Spanish Banditti unconquer'd by the Romans — Plenty of Silver in the Pyrenees: the Phoenicians bought vast Quantities of the Natives for a Trifle." On the familiar ground of Grecian history Gray enjoys rebuking Diodorus; in the earlier books he revels in romantic curiosities.

In his notes on the Hutchinson edition of Xenophon,[27] Gray is less statistical and more critical than in the earlier notebook. He begins here with the *Cyropaedia,* from which he gathers much on Persian customs, a subject he had already been studying in travel books. He finds occasion for some interesting literary criticism. For example, he praises the conversation of Cyrus and his father about the duties of a ruler (I.vi): " under its Plainness & Simplicity [it] conceals the deepest & truest Good-Sense, w[ch] appears the stronger every time it is read." He notices the " manifest Allusion to the Death of Socrates " in the account of the execu-

---

[25] Seven pages of such notes, obviously the part missing in the Morgan notebook, have recently come to light. See Register VI.7.g.

[26] Tovey, I, 176; Whibley, I, 306.   [27] Register II.9.

tion of Tigranes' tutor (III.i.38) "wch it is strange nobody has observed."[28] He appreciates the naturalness and delicacy of Tigranes' wife when she shows her tenderness for her husband (III. i.41). He finds the speech of Cyrus to his troops (III.iii.35) very noble, " on the Vanity of supposing, that sudden Exhortations can raise the Spirits of Men to true Valour, who have been never accustom'd by Education & the Laws of their Country to the Practise of it." Finally, having taken Hutchinson to task on his contention that the Persians worshiped the Dioscuri, "w^ch, if any, were doubtless Gods proper to the Greeks," Gray concludes that the *Cyropaedia* is more Greek than Persian: " It is clear to me that the Persian Education, the Conversation of Cyrus, his military Precepts & Discipline, &c: are plain· Copies of the Spartans, the favourite People of Xenophon, & that is the Fault of this fine Work, that it has too much of the Greek Air."[29]

All this time Gray was studying verse and prose together. One of his quarto notebooks, now in the British Museum, dates the study of Pindar March 20, 1747, followed exactly three months later by that of Aristophanes.[30] The notes on Aristophanes have been printed by Mathias.[31] Except for the " Plan of the Aves," the annotations are similar to those in the Morgan notebooks, and of little value except for the portrayal of Gray's mental habits.

[28] Weiske makes the observation (1798).

[29] An interesting note on the authenticity of Persian customs in *Cyropaedia* is in Gray's Commonplace Book, vol. II, p. 613. Mathias (II, 377) has introduced it, with the usual number of changes, into Gray's notes on Plato's *Symposium*. Diogenes Laertius (III.34) says that Plato also declares the *Cyropaedia* to be a fiction, but Gray in his notes on the *Laws* (Book III) disagrees with this interpretation of Plato (Mathias, II, 477).

[30] This notebook (Add. MSS. 36817), devotes the first four and one-half pages to genealogies of the royal families of Greece. Since much of this material is legendary, e.g. the lines of Cadmus, Pelops, Sisyphus, Perseus, etc., it is probably intended as an aid in following the numerous allusions in the odes of Pindar. Register II.8.

[31] II, 132 ff. Mathias made his usual "improvements," but omitted nothing except a few lines on the first page, containing a quotation from Platonius followed by this note: " It was not any Oligarchy or Tyranny, that retrenched the Chorus in the Athenian Comedy (as is here said) or prohibited the representation of real characters." The edition used was that of L. Kusterus, Amsterdam, 1710. Gosse (*Works*, IV) reprinted Mathias complete, even to the mistake in date, "July, 1747."

The notes on Pindar [32] would be no exception, if Gray had not chosen the ancient poet as the model for his two later odes, *The Progress of Poesy* and *The Bard*. As it is, one wonders why Mathias chose to print instead the far less interesting notes on Aristophanes, for here is the real beginning of the 1757 *Odes*, both in technique and in ideas. Gray acknowledges his indebtedness to Pindar in his notes to the 1768 edition of his poems, but it is interesting to learn that he uses in his odes the thoughts which impressed him in 1747. From the second Olympian he quotes a long passage, containing the famous phrase, "Φωνᾶντα συνετοῖσιν," which was to make such a stir as the motto of the 1757 *Odes*, and the figure, used in *The Progress of Poesy*, of Pindar as an eagle soaring scornfully above the croaking ravens. From the first Pythian again he quotes some ten verses of the passage which he later acknowledges as the source of the first antistrophe of *The Progress of Poesy*, prefacing the quotation with this comment: " Describing the Power of Musick, as calming the Fierceness & lulling to Repose even the Eagle perched on the Sceptre of Jove; he has the following Lines, an Example of fine Expression & poetic Painting, equal to anything I have met with." From the fourth Pythian he quotes part of a description of the young Jason just come from the mountains, and comments: " the whole succeeding account of their Expedition to Colchi, is somewhat wild, but with great Magnificence of Expression, & in the Taste of Homer."

Gray was also interested in Pindar's technique, for he has thoroughly analyzed some of the odes, listing twenty-eight sorts of feet, with examples, from the " Pyrrhician " with two short syllables and " Iambic, a short & a long " to the " Dispondee, 4 long." He has named and described every conceivable combination, making in all " 4 Disyllabic, 8 Trisyllabic, 16 of 4 Syllables," and including such familiar names as trochee, dactyl, and anapaest, alongside many others never used in English verse unless as a tour de force. He then analyzes the meters of the first Olympian, and lists seventeen different kinds of lines. Whether original with

[32] The edition used is " Oxon: 1697. Fol:"

Gray or not, this shows an early interest in versification, one of his chief studies about ten years later. He wisely does not try to follow Pindar too closely in the meter of the 1757 *Odes,* but this analysis of the Greek forms has shown him the way to that variety of meter in a very strict mold which characterizes his own Pindaric odes, *The Progress of Poesy* and *The Bard.*

Two classical notebooks in the Morgan Library remain to be mentioned, one on Plutarch and one on Sophocles, neither of them very interesting. They have no date but probably belong to the same period as the undated Xenophon notes.[33] The annotations on Plutarch are full of the names of authors cited, as well as of the characters written about, for the ancient biographer probably furnished him with much the same kind of chronological data as he found in Diogenes Laertius. Occasionally the biographical matter reveals Gray's personal interest: "434. Aristotle observes that great geniuses incline to Melancholy, & instances Socrates, Plato, Lysander, &c: . . . . 443. Plato (then a young Man) comforts Antimachus, whom he admired." Chronology, history, customs, antiquities of all sorts fill the notes, leaving very little of a personal nature to add to our picture of Gray at this time.

The notes on Sophocles are meager, consisting mostly of a few remarks on the staging of *Ajax* and *Electra.*[34] The only item of particular interest is a critical note on the break in the unity of place in *Ajax,* "a rare & remarkable Instance of all the Characters, even the Chorus itself, leaving the Stage." He notes a difference of opinion among critics, but holds with the scholia that the scene changes to a desert place. In this event, he adds, " the Unity of Place is broke thro', wch however I take to be the Case here

---

[33] Register II.5. Gray borrowed "Plutarch V: 1 Fol: " from Pembroke library, December 2, 1744, and a little later, "Plutarch, Cruserii 2d V: "

[34] Reprinted by LaRue Van Hook, *American Journal of Philology,* LVII (1936), 5 f. The edition Gray used was the Stephanus quarto of 1603 with Latin translation and notes by Camerarius. Gray himself owned the Johnson edition which was popular in his day, and made in it numerous corrections and translations. Perhaps he abandoned the notes on Sophocles as well as those on Thucydides because he found it more convenient to annotate his own copies, a practice which he used more and more as he got older.

for the principal Reason, why the ancients observed that Unity seems to be, because the Chorus never left the Stage, & it would be absurd, for them to remain in the same Spot of Ground, & the Scene itself to remove to another Place."

III

Although none of his classical notebooks is dated later than March 1, 1748, Gray studied Plato, at least at intervals, until 1756. His elaborate notes on Plato, no matter what their intrinsic value may be, are a monument to the poet's love of philosophy and of Greek literature.[35] He has certainly made Plato the crowning point of his study of the classics. He is no longer searching for curiosities in the bypaths of ancient learning. The chronological tables have been finished or abandoned. All his former study seems indeed to lead toward Plato, the notes on whom are filled with references to Diogenes Laertius, Xenophon, Plutarch, Thucydides, Aristotle, Athenaeus, Aristophanes, Pindar, Pausanias, Aulus Gellius, and Isocrates. The notebooks which Gray kept on most of these authors seem to be merely feeders for this great work, and many of the earlier annotations have gone almost bodily to clarify an allusion in Plato. One would think that Gray was contemplating an edition of Plato, rather than of Strabo or of the Greek Anthology.

Strangely enough Gray does not seem to have owned a copy of Plato; he borrowed instead from Pembroke library the three folio volumes of the 1578 Stephanus edition with notes by Serranus. The Pembroke library registers record twelve different borrowings, beginning with the entry under Trollope's name about 1743 ("Plato, T: 2 dus, to Mr Grey of Pet:") and ending with Gray's own hand recording the return of the three volumes on December 4, 1756. The entries occur most frequently from 1748 to 1751, making those years a safe date for the bulk of the notes on Plato and therefore for the first part of the second volume of the Commonplace Book.

[35] Mathias, II, 299–547. The notes are scattered profusely through the second volume of the Commonplace Book between pp. 463 and 798.

Gray, it is true, added very little to the understanding of Plato. His most valuable conjectures are based on his study of Greek chronology from a comparison of various authors he had been reading. Interesting bits of criticism, however, are hidden away here and there. Occasionally his summary of a dialogue almost reaches the point of creative beauty, as in the *Phaedo,* the *Protagoras,* and parts of the *Republic* and the *Laws.* We sense the poet's love for the philosophy of Plato, an admiration that must have affected strongly his own personality.

Gray does not have equal praise for all the works of Plato. He admires the drama of the *Phaedo,* for example, portraying the death of Socrates with "the noble simplicity of nature," but the reasoning part, on death and immortality, "is far inferior, sometimes weak, sometimes false, too obscure, too abstracted, to convince us of anything; yet with a mixture of good sense and with many fine observations."[36] He considered the sixth book of the *Republic* to be the high point in Plato's work: "the thoughts are as just as they are new, and the elocution is as beautiful as it is expressive; it can never be read too often; but towards the end it is excessively obscure."[37]

Much of the poet's criticism of Plato is in the nature of apology. In the *Meno,* for example, he finds the doctrine of reminiscence "chimerical enough," but that which follows it "is worth attending to, where Socrates shews how useful it is to be sensible of our own ignorance."[38] In the *Euthydemus* he criticizes the philosopher for bothering with the arguments of punsters: "It is scarcely possible to see with patience Plato seriously confuting

---

[36] Mathias, II, 335.

[37] Mathias, II, 441. Gray in his Commonplace Book (I, 340, "Philosophia") quotes at length from this book and concludes: "This whole Book is indeed so excellent, that it cannot be sufficiently read." The rest of the article summarizes Plato's views on the influence of bad education on a good mind. Here is an alliance between education and government, a subject which interested Gray all his life. Plato has shown, he says, in the *Republic* that a very apt mind can easily be corrupted, for certain excellencies and endowments "lighting (as he expresses it) in an improper Soil, that is corrupted by a bad Education, & ill-regulated Government become the readier Instruments of Mischief to Mankind by so much more, as Nature meant them for their Good."

[38] Mathias, II, 355.

these childish subtleties, as low as any logical quibbles, used by our scholastic divines in the days of monkery and of deep ignorance." [39]

Gray gives us a great deal more of this sort of thing, but the real point of interest here lies not so much in his ephemeral criticism as in the influence of Plato's thought on his personality. Although we find little in the poet's writings which can be definitely traced to Plato, we can detect the philosopher's influence in Gray's lifelong search for truth in the bypaths of learning. Unconsciously he carried Plato with him in his conversations on education, history, literature, or philosophy. His remarks on the sixth book of the *Republic* seem to sum up his own calm life: "The love of truth is the natural consequence of a genius truly inclined to philosophy. Such a mind will be little inclined to sensual pleasures, and consequently will be temperate, and a stranger to avarice and to illiberality." [40] Plato's favorite point might easily become his own, "that philosophy alone is the parent of virtue, the discoverer of those fixed and unerring principles, on which the truly great and good man builds his whole scheme of life, and by which he directs all his actions," and that consequently the philosopher is greater than the artist or the statesman. [41] Such thoughts are more significant than parallel passages or borrowings. They indicate a depth of character which would have made Gray an important man, even if he had written no poetry.

Gray's study of the classics took him into the curious bypaths of Diodorus and Athenaeus as well as into the broad highway of Plato and Vergil. He probably added very little to the sum total of knowledge in the field of classical scholarship. [42] Most of the editions he used were already filled with the learned annotations of such early scholars as Stephanus and Casaubon, and practically every one contained a Latin translation in parallel columns with the Greek text. As usual Gray sought the very best work of the past and took from it whatever aid it might offer.

[39] Mathias, II, 383.   [40] Mathias, II, 441.
[41] Mathias, II, 367.
[42] J. E. Sandys, *A History of Classical Scholarship* (Cambridge, 1908), II, 417, devotes only a few lines to Gray.

Even though he was not so great a classical scholar as Bentley or Parr, Gray was nevertheless a thoroughgoing and industrious student. Wherever he turned, his mind seemed to lean toward history, but history to him meant more than rulers and wars. He filled out the columns of his chronological tables of Greece with poets and orators and philosophers as well as archons and tyrants. He gleaned as he went, poetry or philosophy or curiosities of all kinds. And when he was ready to stop he discovered Plato, into the study of whose philosophy he poured all of his former work on orators and historians. In all of his work he looked upon Greek literature as superior to Roman;[43] yet very few ancient authors, Greek or Latin, escaped him,[44] while many of them became his lifelong companions. After 1748 he studied no classical author intensively, except Plato, whom he lovingly followed for another eight years. His friends, his classical companions, however, never really deserted him, and their influence spread far beyond his notebooks.[45]

[43] He criticizes (Whibley, I, 268 f.) Spence's *Polymetis* for having willfully neglected the Greek writers, "who could have given him more Instruction on the very Heads he professes to treat, than all the others put together . . . but, to say the Truth, I suspect he was little conversant in those Books & that Language."

[44] In his Alphabetical Catalogue Gray listed some ninety classical authors with data on editions and prices.

[45] Just before his death he wrote to Norton Nicholls: "It would be strange if I should blame you for reading Isocrates. I did so myself 20 years ago, & in an edition at least as bad as yours. The *Panegyrick*, the *De Pace, Areopagitic,* & *Advice to Philip,* are by far the noblest remains we have of this Writer, & equal to most things extant in the Greek tongue: but it depends on your judgement to distinguish between his real & occasional opinion of things, as he directly contradicts in one place what he has advanced in another" (Tovey, III, 275; Whibley, III, 1121).

CHAPTER IV

THE ROAD TO CATHAY

TRAVEL books have been a source of inspiration to English poets since the stirring days of the Elizabethan voyagers. Spenser, Shakespeare, and Donne sang of the new-found-land, the America of untold wealth and fabulous possibilities. Milton spread his wings toward the gorgeous East, the splendor of Ormus and of Ind, the spicy odors of Araby the Blest. The romantic poets of the eighteenth century followed Milton's lead, as much to show the glory of England in her trade with India and America as to obey the romantic urge toward far-off places. James Thomson took his seasons from the English countryside and planted them in tropical forests and frozen wastelands. John Dyer started out to describe the technical history of fleece from the lamb to the wool jacket but ended with much of his poem describing trade routes to show that even then Britannia ruled the waves because of her wool. In the age of Elizabeth an intense patriotic fervor had inspired Hakluyt to publish the stories of Englishmen who explored savage countries and plundered Spanish gold. The eighteenth century built its patriotism around world trade and read travel books that emphasized the accurate description of foreign countries rather than the zest of adventure.[1]

Thomas Gray made considerable use of the varied material that was offered him in travel books. As a boy he read them for the pictures of distant lands, following the romantic trail " o'er Libya's deserts and through Zembla's snows " until it ended in his own poetry. As a young man he studied them carefully for the story of human progress in their descriptions of men and man-

---

[1] An idea of the chief travelers and their contribution to geography may be had in Edward Heawood, *A History of Geographical Discovery in the Seventeenth and Eighteenth Centuries* (Cambridge University Press, 1912). See also R. W. Frantz, *The English Traveller and the Movement of Ideas, 1660–1732* (Lincoln, 1934).

ners, arts and science. In later life he went back over them to add in the margins a part of his own knowledge, especially in the revision of the portions devoted to natural history.

Gray knew something of the literature of travel before he and Walpole went on the Grand Tour into France and Italy in 1739. He shows it in his letters and notebooks written on that memorable journey, for they constitute his own travel book in the manner of the time, expressing with youthful eagerness his impressions of the people, the manners, the civilization, and the natural scenery of a new and unexplored territory. His enthusiasm for Alpine scenery was different from that of Addison and other Englishmen who went into Italy and has therefore been heralded as a startling manifesto of a new romantic feeling.[2] Gray was, however, describing for his mother and his bosom friend West what he saw, much in the same way that travelers in the Orient had done in their books. One of the duties of a traveler is to give an idea of the topography of a region, even to the point of detailed description where an unusual sight presents itself. Add the enthusiasm of an imaginative youth like Gray, and the result is the beautiful description of the pass to the Grande Chartreuse near Grenoble, always an awe-inspiring scene.

So Gray wrote his own travel book, in which one finds many things besides scenery. Manners, history, art, antiquities — he sets everything down in great detail, the more trivial things in letters to amuse his mother, the serious side in his notebooks for his own edification. He would have been the first to admit that he had nothing new to give the world, for thousands of English youths had made the Grand Tour before him. The only ones besides himself who cared were a few at home, so he wrote his travels for them, using the same kind of material as that of the books of his day. In a playful mood he wrote in a letter to Thomas Wharton some proposals for printing " The Travels of T.G., Gent.," the particulars of which show the clever combina-

[2] See C. S. Northup, "Addison and Gray as Travelers," in *Studies . . . in Honor of J. M. Hart* (New York, 1910), pp. 390–439. C. D. Thorpe, in *Studies in Philology*, XXXII (1935), 463–482, cites John Dennis as a romantic traveler on his " grand tour " in 1688.

tion of a burlesque on travel books and a satire on foreign manners. The proposal itself is an indication of familiarity with the literature of travel, for travesty requires a thorough acquaintance with the object of ridicule.

After the enthusiasm of first impressions had worn off, Gray settled down in Italy to a thorough study of the culture of that country — its palaces, art collections, and music, as well as the relics it contained of the ancient splendor of Rome. All this background of antiquity and modern Italian art was the very meat of Gray's scholarly soul, much more to his liking than the courtly society which attracted Walpole. The books he bought in Italy were filled with the descriptions and engravings of antiquities and of such collections of art as those of the Barberini, Farnese, and Borghese palaces. In other words, Gray's first year abroad was that of the traveler with his vivid impressions of the land and the people, whereas the year and more which followed was a period of intense study of antiquity and the fine arts.

When we consider Gray's own travel and his interest in books of voyages, we are not surprised to find him turning more seriously to the subject at his first leisure. Even before he began, early in 1747, his intensive study of Greek history and literature, he turned to Greek geography as the beginning of serious study in travel. He discovered Strabo and clung to him, although he knew and used Ptolemy, Xenophon, Herodotus, Diodorus Siculus, Arrian, Polybius, and the minor geographers collected by John Hudson. Later in life he told his youthful friend Norton Nicholls that he placed Strabo " with reason at the head of all Geographers." [3] This mature judgment was also his opinion when he began the serious study of geography as early as 1744, if one may judge by the use he made of Strabo in his early research.

Gray advised Nicholls in reading Strabo "to miss the two first books & begin with the description of Spain." He seems to have done the same thing, extracting many things from Book III for one of his articles in the Commonplace Book.[4] He used Strabo's

[3] " Reminiscences of Gray," in Tovey, II, 284; Whibley, III, 1295.

[4] CPB, I, 135. From Book III Gray also added a note on the ancient Spanish language to an earlier article, " Lingua " (CPB, I, 33).

descriptions of Italy for several articles, including those on Latium, on the lake and grotto of Avernus, and on Vesuvius,[5] although he brought in Pliny's *Natural History* and other Latin works for support. For Greece itself he preferred, as we have seen, the more detailed descriptions of Pausanias. When he got to Strabo's accounts of Egypt, Persia, and India, however, he became intensely interested, and engaged himself in years of reading and research on the subject. Perhaps the lure of the Orient that was making itself felt in Europe in the early eighteenth century drew him on. Certainly vast quantities of material were available, not only in the form of fascinating accounts of travel but also in the critical work of ardent Orientalists in England and abroad. At any rate he began to compare Strabo's account of the ancient world toward the East with the descriptions of recent travelers like Thomas Shaw and Edward Pococke. Pursuing the subject more and more deeply, with his usual thoroughness, he arrived at a knowledge of Oriental history and geography that few Englishmen of his time achieved.

Gray's research into Oriental geography and history may be rather easily dated. Beginning with Strabo about 1743, he soon launched out into more serious study. We see him early in 1744 withdrawing from Pembroke library copies of Simon Ockley's *Introductio ad linguas orientales* (1706) and George Sale's translation of the *Koran* (1734) with a preliminary discourse of about two hundred pages on the history of the Mohammedans, the study of which resulted in an article on Arabs in the Commonplace Book.[6] The same year, probably in November, he borrowed Shaw's book of travels in northern Africa and took copious notes on the work in a small notebook, which he continued in April 1745 with Pococke's account of Syria. After that occur frequent articles in the Commonplace Book dealing with Oriental geography and history and covering hundreds of pages, often consecutively. The last of these articles is almost coincident with the last of the notes on Plato, which were probably written about

[5] CPB, I, 314–320.
[6] I, 280, 282. The article preceding this gives the ideas of Turks on hell, with quotations from Selden, whom Gray had quoted frequently in previous articles.

1756. Generally speaking, Gray pursued classical literature and Oriental travel as parallel interests from 1744 to 1756, grounding himself in the history, geography, and thought of two great civilizations.

Although Gray was at first primarily interested in the geography of the ancient world, his desire to check Strabo by more recent accounts of the same regions led him to vast collections of interesting material on a multitude of subjects. He came to rely on the compendious travel books of the seventeenth and eighteenth centuries, in which he might find firsthand accounts not only of the topography and the inhabitants but also of the climate, the flora and fauna, and the state of the arts and sciences in some particular part of the world. The earlier voyages of discovery naturally tended more toward the fanciful, perhaps because they were describing new worlds from the point of view of the man who is always on the move, whether he be soldier, missionary, or simply explorer. The more scientific nature of the later accounts probably derives from their having been written by men who for purposes of trade or religion or diplomacy lived in the foreign countries and who therefore concentrated more thoroughly on particular regions. Gray nevertheless read and used travel books of all periods, sifting and evaluating the material as a basis for his lifelong study of history, which to him included what one now calls social history — a knowledge of language, geography, antiquities, manners, and education as well as of chronology, laws, and government.[7] He took notes on all these phases of foreign countries, from their relics of antiquity as illustrations of ancient history to their fauna and flora as material for his later study of natural history.

This variety of material is well illustrated in the poet's first serious venture beyond Strabo into the literature of travel, namely his study, in the fall of 1744, of Dr. Shaw's travels, mostly in the kingdoms of Algiers and Tunis.[8] Northern Africa contained

[7] See Gray's sketch for his inaugural lecture as professor of modern history at Cambridge, p. 115 below.
[8] Quarto notebook at Castle Howard. See Register II.3. Notes on Pococke's travels, vol. II, are in the same notebook.

many ruins from Roman times, and Gray shows that this interest is uppermost in his mind by his frequent references to them and to the differences between the present account and the ancient ones, especially that of Ptolemy. He seems unusually interested in the site of ancient Carthage and accompanies his lengthy notes on that part of the book with a neatly-drawn chart, reproduced almost exactly from the original map, showing all points of interest and the difference between the coast lines in ancient and in modern times. After about nine pages of this sort of thing Gray adds three pages of interesting notes on Part II of the travels, describing the climate, plants, animals, arts and sciences, and government of Algiers and Tunis. The last three pages include miscellaneous observations on Syria and the Holy Land — a meager account of that interesting region, since Shaw in Part III of his travels, according to Gray, "remarks little, but what Maundrell has omitted or mistaken."

A few of the notes show Gray's interests at the time. For instance, he describes the locust plague, which he probably remembered from the Bible and from Milton's vivid use of it to illustrate the flight of Satan's cohorts in hell: " they appear'd the End of March from the S: & by April they darken'd the Sun, like a Succession of Clouds," devouring everything in their path " so that the whole Land appear'd a desolate Wilderness." Gray defines the new term "romantic" for us in his note on Shaw's description of a scene near Mount Lebanon which was designed to import mixed feelings of sadness and joy: " the Country about is peculiarly romantick, an uncommon Mixture of Woods, Waters, Grotto's, Rocks, Ruins, & the Sea." In such passages the writers of travel books gave Gray in his youth a feeling for the uncommon things in nature which comes into his letters from the Continent.

Gray was probably not satisfied with Shaw's description of the Holy Land, for in April 1745 he added in the same notebook four pages of material from Pococke's description of that region in the second volume of his travels, which had been published that very year. In both accounts of the Holy Land, however, Gray disregards such places as Jerusalem, Bethlehem, and Nazareth, which were full of sentimental association for most Christians. He notes the climate, the topography, and the modern customs, with particular emphasis on antiquities, whether Roman remains or Crusaders' castles or the pagan temples of Baalbek. Curiosities interest him always, such as the unusual tree which produces balsam, or the peculiar properties of the Dead Sea. He has the air of quoting from the text, but comparison with the original often shows some queer changes. For instance, he records the description of a meal: " They gave us Pillaw, fried Eggs, Honey, Coffee, Prunella's, Pistaches, & excellent White-wine," but he arrives at this combination by combining the accounts of three different meals.[9] The notes on Syria are hurried and the entire journey from Damascus to the Euphrates and back " is omitted for Want of Time." The description of Mount Lebanon, however, might almost be taken from Gray's letters about the Alps:

ascended 4 hours, pass'd by a romantic Vally, thro' wch the R: Abouali rushes, being hid with Trees. descend to Caunobius. the Monastery is chiefly Grotto's cut in the Rock on the Declivity. the R: of Tripoli runs in a deep Vale below with high Ridges covered with Pines on each Side . . . there are numberless fine Cascades . . . there is a fine Prospect of the inhabited Parts below, of the Lake Lamoun, of Cælesyria as far as Baalbeck, & the Sea beyond Tripoli.

Gray constantly compared such accounts as those of Shaw and Pococke with the descriptions of Strabo and Xenophon. He gradually continued this until he was familiar with the topography and history of northern Africa, the Near East, Persia, and India, in ancient, medieval, and modern times. He filled the last hundred pages of the first volume of the Commonplace Book almost consecutively with various accounts of travels in the Near East, as well as a descriptive history of the African kings, the Saracen caliphs, and other Oriental dynasties. This concentrated study of the Levant and its history, probably begun around 1748 and ex-

[9] Pococke, *Travels*, II, 95 f. A good example is Gray's note on the Druses in Syria: " they love Christians, & are descended from the Franks," whereas Pococke says (p. 94): " They themselves now say they are descended from the English," supplemented by a footnote: " Some say, they are descended from the Franks, whom Godfrey of Bulloign brought with him to the holy war."

tending as far as the winter of 1755–1756, is in itself considerable, even though it seems to have had little effect on Gray's thought or writing.

The first of this series of travel notes in the Commonplace Book takes up the journey of Rabbi Benjamin of Tudela during the latter part of the twelfth century from Spain as far as China and back, in which Gray limits himself to the descriptions of the Near East and Persia. Although he interested himself mainly in Jewish matters, Benjamin also described some of the remains of the Crusaders in Palestine and Syria,[10] which Gray followed with a few descriptions of the Holy Land by the Crusaders themselves. Of these he extracted descriptions of the expedition in 1095 by two eyewitnesses, Fulcher of Chartres ("Chaplain to Count Baldwin") and Robert of Rheims.[11]

After Syria Gray took up Egypt, giving it much more space since he compared the modern descriptions of Pococke with the ancient account of Strabo. The country, he finds, has obviously changed a great deal. Memphis was in Strabo's time still a great city, but Gray says he will pass over it "because no Footsteps of it are now left." He explains also why it is useless to attempt to describe the coast of Egypt: "I omit his [Pococke's] more nice Disquisitions about the ancient Branches of the Nile, as somewhat prolix and intricate. the face of the country seems now so changed, & the Accounts of Herodotus, Strabo, & Ptolemy are so different, that it is scarce possible to reconcile them all." [12]

Before going on to the geography of Persia and India, Gray dug deeply into the history of the Levant. He took a sketch of the kings of western Africa from Thuanus, and then turned to Lonicer's *Chronicon Turciae* for the Saracen caliphs, adding

[10] For a critical text of the travels of Benjamin of Tudela with translation and commentary, see M. N. Adler's edition, Oxford University Press, 1907. For concise accounts, see C. R. Beazley, *The Dawn of Modern Geography* (London, 1901), II, 218 ff. and *Jewish Travellers* (London, 1930), ed. by E. N. Adler, pp. 38–63.

[11] In the collection of the accounts of Crusaders, *Gesta dei per Francos,* Hanov. Wechel, 1611, I, 30–81 (Robertus Monachus, Historia Hierosolymitana), 381–440 (Fulcherius Carnotensis, Gesta peregrinantium Francorum).

[12] CPB, I, 355. The whole article is to be found, pp. 347–368.

numerous details from Pococke's translation of Abulfaraj's universal history (1663), and from Barthélemy d'Herbelot's *Bibliothèque orientale* (1697). He continued with the Ottoman sultans,
with the Buid, Seljuk, and Kharezmian dynasties, with Genghis
Khan and his successors, and finally with the Mongols, extracting
page after page of closely written notes from many sources.[13] The
vast amount of detail that Gray collected about Oriental mon-
archs, especially about the Saracen caliphs, serves to heighten one's
feeling that he was wasting precious hours. The works he consulted, however, were intrinsically interesting and helped him to
pass the time. Such were, for example, the Oriental studies of
George Sale; the seven-volume *Historia* of Thuanus (1553-1617),
whose library made Casaubon himself despair; Simon Ockley's
History of the Saracens; Sansovino's history of the Turkish empire;
the three-volume collection of voyages by Ramusio, the pred-
ecessor of Hakluyt; the later more scientific collection of De
Bry; Vaillant's histories of Eastern nations; and numerous accounts of travelers to the Levant, like those of Pietro della Valle,
of Jacob Spon and George Wheeler, and of Sir Thomas Roe.[14]

Although Gray's history of Oriental dynasties is his most
meticulous contribution to his study of the Levant, all of his
previous work in geography seems to lead towards the articles on
Persia and India which Mathias extracted from the Commonplace Book for publication. Tedious though they are, these
articles represent the climax of Gray's intensive study of geography
and show his method of work, which was to take the ancient
accounts, usually from Strabo and here from Arrian as well, and
by means of copious notes to compare them with the discoveries
of recent travelers. We have seen him doing the same thing

[13] CPB, I, 372-377, 384-385, 398-417, 424-427, 434, entirely devoted to
Oriental genealogies. For a typical excerpt, see Martin, *Chronologie*, pp. 158 f.

[14] Gray lists a number of other works on the subject, both in the Alphabetical
Catalogue and on the blank pages of the Commonplace Book. The following
reference is fuller than most but gives an idea of Gray's wide acquaintance with
the subject: "Della Legge, e Vita de' Turchi, di G: Antonio Menavino. Ven:
1548. 8vo. (the Author, a Genoese, was taken Prisoner at 12 years old, & brought
up in the Seraglio of Bajazet, till at his Death he went into the Troops of Selim,
A: D: 1512)." Much later Gray made a descriptive list of Venetian writers on
foreign history, most of whom deal with the Orient (CPB, III, 1037).

earlier with northern Africa, Egypt and Syria, but on a less extended scale.[15] His modern authorities in these articles on Persia and India are numerous and for the most part trustworthy — notably Pietro della Valle; J. B. Tavernier; the Thevenots, uncle and nephew; Adam Olearius; Johannes de Laet; Captain Alexander Hamilton; Jean Chardin; and numbers of others whose journeys are to be found in collections that range in time from Ramusio through Purchas and De Bry to the latest work on the subject in Jonas Hanway's *Historical Account of the British Trade over the Caspian Sea* (1753).[16]

If Gray projected an edition of Strabo, as Mason says he did, he was certainly prepared to write learned commentaries on the material covered by the Greek geographer. Obviously he did not read carefully all the travel books in his various bibliographies, but he was familiar with many of them before 1755 and continued to read others until his death. He did not scorn any account from whatever period in history, if it seemed to him sincere. He took the Jewish travels of Rabbi Benjamin in the twelfth century and added to them accounts of some Crusaders in Count Baldwin's expedition in 1095. He used Arabian accounts wherever they were accessible in translation: a Latin epitome of the famous geography of Al-Idrisi made for Roger of Sicily in 1153; " Account of India & China by two Mahometans in the 9th century, publish'd by Renaudot, 1733 "; John Greaves's translation of parts of the geography of Abulfeda; Bentinck's annotated translation of the genealogical history of the Mongols and Tatars by Abulghazi Bahadur; Jacob Golius' notes to the astronomy of Al-fragan; and others to be found in Hudson's *Geographi minores* or in d'Herbelot's *Bibliothèque orientale*.[17] He goes from such medieval

---

[15] An unpublished article, obviously meant as an introduction to his work on India and Persia, gives an account of the " Eastern Coast of Africa, of Arabia and Persia as far as the Indus, from Arrian " (CPB, II, 625–632). The note at the end, " continued above, p. 537," refers to the articles printed by Mathias, which occupy pp. 537–578 in vol. II.

[16] Numerous travel books are listed by Gray in his bibliographical notebook and on the blank leaves of the Commonplace Book. A formal but much less complete list in the CPB is printed by Mathias, II, 187–192.

[17] On early travels, see J. K. Wright, *Geographical Lore in the Time of the Crusades* (New York, 1925).

accounts to other early voyages in the extensive collections of Ramusio and Purchas. Between these two he perhaps thought he could dispense with Hakluyt, whom he seldom mentions among his sources.[18] On the whole he cared only for voyages having to do with the Orient from the Barbary Coast to China and Japan, in which field of exploration the English, with whom Hakluyt is chiefly concerned, took little part until the late seventeenth century.

Gray seems to have conducted most of this intensive investigation into Oriental geography and history in the five years or so after 1750. The last articles coincide with those on Plato in the Commonplace Book, and we can date both series by comparison with Gray's borrowings from the Pembroke library. From 1744 he had borrowed miscellaneous travel books from the library, notably individual volumes, one at a time, of a six-volume folio *Collection of Voyages and Travels* printed in London, 1704–1732. On June 1, 1752, however, he took out the voyages of Della Valle, Le Brun, and Tavernier, and eight days later the first volumes of the collections of Thevenot and Ramuzzio (*sic*). On December 7, 1755, he borrowed practically the same books again, replacing Le Brun with the new account of Persia by Hanway.[19] Although he was diverted to English poetry about 1755, Gray continued to be interested in travel. He evidently went on to study the history of Japan, China, and the Tatar khans, for in the Pembroke copy of Ramusio he added numerous marginal annotations to the accounts of Marco Polo and other travelers in the Far East. Later, America also caught his attention, for in 1760 he bought for his own library several books of voyages to the new world, among them the *Novus orbis,* Simon Grynaeus's version of the earliest

[18] Hakluyt translated much from Ramusio. Purchas took nearly half of his material from Hakluyt. See G. B. Parks, *Richard Hakluyt and the English Voyages* (New York, 1928), especially pp. 224 ff.

[19] This agrees with other evidence. The bibliography in Mathias, II, 188, says of Buffon's *Histoire naturelle*: "There are 5 vols. published, 1755." Gray's pocket book for 1755 has a list on the back flyleaf, presumably of the authorities he wanted to use on Oriental travel, including among the ancients Ptolemy, Strabo, Pliny, and Arrian, and among the moderns, in addition to many of those cited above, Kaempfer's *Amœnitates exoticæ* (mainly about Persia) and "Tamerlane & Genghiz-can's History."

records of Spanish exploration in America.[20] He also bought in 1760 Ligon's *History of Barbadoes,* Rochefort on the Antilles, the journal of La Salle's last voyage, and Diereville's trip to Acadia, not to mention a number of new works concerning the Orient which show that he had not forgotten his old love.

While he had long been interested in the descriptions of the natural history of foreign countries, Gray began to turn more particularly to them when about 1760 he took up the serious study of natural history under the guidance of Linnaeus. He continued to read travel books and reread numbers of them, this time with a critical eye for the descriptions of the fauna and flora of various parts of the world. He annotated his own books and some of those belonging to the Pembroke library, putting in marginal corrections to the natural history sections, usually in the form of identification of animals or plants by means of the new Linnaean nomenclature. He evidently continued this until the end of his life, for his copy of Edward Bancroft's *Natural History of Guiana,* published in 1769, has marginalia of this sort.[21]

The chronology of Gray's study of travel parallels that of the classics, reaching its high point about 1755 but forming both in earlier and later life a part of his general reading and diversion. Again his scholarly method has been thoroughly illustrated: he prepares his bibliography, covers the general field from many angles, and then centers his research on one particular line of interest. His vast erudition in the special field of Oriental history, however, is scarcely reflected beyond the articles in the Commonplace Book, those reminders of the man's industry and scholarly mind. Travel plays a very little part in his thoughts, and even there, as I have already shown, its romance works into his early poetry and into the letters from the Continent. Whatever reflection of travel books may be seen in Gray's writing, even as late as the savage youth of *The Progress of Poesy* who lives " in climes beyond the solar road," the spirit is that of the boy reading about the discovery of brave new worlds, not of the scholar following

[20] Gray filled the front flyleaf of his 1760 pocket book with a long note on the history and contents of this book.

[21] For more on this, see below, chap. VII.

the changes of Oriental dynasties. One exception remains, however, in Gray's accidental descriptions of his own tours late in life.

The irony of this situation is typical of much of Gray's whole life: he carefully kept the results of his lifelong study of travel literature to himself, seldom mentioning it even in his letters, and then unconsciously helped to start a vogue in travel descriptions of his own country that led directly to Wordsworth and romantic poetry on the one side, and on the other to such a deluge of " picturesque tours " as to call forth the pictorial burlesque of Thomas Rowlandson. Gray described the highlands of Scotland and the beauties of England's Lake District because he wanted his friend Wharton to enjoy them with him. As in the earlier letters from France and Italy, he unconsciously followed the informal technique of the more pretentious voyages he had read in abundance. William Mason published both of these descriptions in his life of Gray in 1775, and they became the forerunners of many other " journeys " of a more ambitious cast.

Even before his death, however, Gray had sowed the seed of nature description in the very fertile mind of the Reverend William Gilpin, whose tours later became the Bible of the " picturesque " cult. Gilpin proudly acknowledges it himself in his letter to Mason which serves as a preface to his first tour, *Observations on the River Wye . . . made in the Summer of the Year 1770,* dated 1782. Gray had made the same tour in the same year and, hearing of Gilpin's descriptions, wished to see them. He saw the little work, continues Gilpin, in London about the beginning of June 1771, and said some handsome things about it which made it seem creditable and therefore publishable. In June 1772 Gilpin made a tour of the Lake District and brought back with him a variety of remarks and sketches. He was very curious to see Gray's descriptions of the same country, which Mason had with him at that time. Mason continued to make plain in his letters to Gilpin, however, that he much preferred the minister's method of supplementing the descriptive sketches with drawings to Gray's power of words alone, a judgment which he repeated in 1775 in a footnote to Gray's journal. The world of taste began after 1775 to take

notice of Gilpin and continued until it catapulted him into fame
as the archpriest of the picturesque. Gilpin was nevertheless quite
free about acknowledging his indebtedness to Gray and to Mason
for their inspiration and encouragement, even though he actually
borrowed almost nothing from Gray's writings.[22]

[22] For this information I am indebted to the unpublished correspondence of
Mason and Gilpin kindly shown me by Professor W. D. Templeman. Some
excerpts from Gilpin's letters are interesting; e.g., from Cheam, July 18, 1772:
"I have a great curiosity to see M^r. Gray's acc^t. of the north;w^h. I suppose you
will print: if not, I hope you will contrive some way to let me see it. He did not,
I find, penetrate into some of the wildest parts of that rough scenery. I heard of
him through D^r. Brownrigg, an ingenious hospitable physician in those parts;
whom M^r. G., I believe, visited."

CHAPTER V

NOTES FOR THE FIRST HISTORY OF ENGLISH POETRY

GRAY seldom finished anything, and so it is not surprising that he gave up his projected history of English poetry, for he soon found himself faced with dark problems that his own exacting mind had stirred up. It is a pity, for the history would have dug from his reticence much valuable literary criticism. Gray came upon Pope's similar scheme through Mason, who in turn got it from William Warburton. That was in 1752, and Gray was at that time still interested in Plato and Oriental history, but he used Pope's idea of the influence of Italian poetry in England as the central theme of an ode he was then writing. Poetic genius, declares *The Progress of Poesy,* has gone with political liberty from ancient Greece to medieval Italy to modern England. The theme interested the poet, as it had in 1748, for its inevitable alliance of liberal education with liberal government. Gray finished his ode in 1754, and about the same time began to look seriously at English poetry and its origins.

Gray was familiar with the chief English poets long before 1754; he had as a boy absorbed Shakespeare, Milton, and Pope, and later had gone on to Spenser, Dryden, Chaucer,[1] and many others. As early as 1753 he was trying to get a deeper knowledge of the language and meter of Chaucer than the editions of his day afforded, for in that year he borrowed simultaneously from the Pembroke library the works of Chaucer and the learned *Thesaurus* of George Hickes, with its Anglo-Saxon grammar. By 1755, if we may judge from his pocket notebook for that year, he was well under way in his thorough study of poetics — Romance, Germanic, and Celtic — as a background for the historical origins of English prosody. By 1758 he had practically

[1] Urry's edition of Chaucer is Gray's first recorded borrowing from the Pembroke library, *c.* 1743.

abandoned the study of poetics for English antiquities, but meanwhile he had written articles in his Commonplace Book on early English poetry, on Welsh lore, and on things Norse that mark him as a genuine English pioneer in those fields. These three seemingly divergent interests unite in his study of the origins of English poetry. His study of Celtic and Norse poetry was so novel as to interest the new romantic generation and to gain a fame for him far beyond anything he wished or deserved. His more thorough study of English poetry, especially of Chaucer, has remained for the most part unacknowledged. I shall consider the three subjects in separate sections, taking them in the order of the articles in the Commonplace Book, English poetry first, then Welsh, and finally Norse.[2]

I

In his articles on poetics in the Commonplace Book,[3] Gray leaves the subject of meter and rhyme to the last, and, using as a preface the sketch made by Pope,[4] begins systematically with a "Catalogue of British Poets, that wrote before A:D: 1600, from B^p Tanner's *Bibliotheca Britannica.*" Spreading the names on the left-hand page, he added his own notes on the opposite page so copiously as to fill it completely with his own fine handwriting.[5] He supplemented this catalogue with a list of Elizabethan poets cited in Robert Allot's *England's Parnassus* (1600),[6] so that he had a working basis for the study of all English poetry before the seventeenth century.

The first of the full-length articles dealing with English

[2] Martin, *Essai,* pp. 220 ff., has a brilliant discussion of these subjects.

[3] CPB, II, 707 ff. They come almost consecutively in the next hundred pages, broken only by notes on learned journals. Roughly speaking, they lie between the notes on Plato and Oriental history (*c.* 1754) and the articles on antiquities of England (probably begun in 1758). All the articles, except a large part of "Cambri," were published, with the usual embellishments, in Mathias, II, 3–80, 104–110.

[4] "Given by Mr. Warburton to Mr. W. Mason in 1752." See Mathias, II, vi f.

[5] CPB, II, 707 f., 735–740.

[6] CPB, II, 462. This is the first numbered page in vol. II, probably left blank and filled in later. A note says: " (to be inscribed in the Catal: at P:707 infra)."

poetry is on Lydgate.[7] If one asks why Gray should have been attracted by "the drivelling monk of Bury," the question can be answered by a glance at the article. Gray was a seeker of curiosities, and Lydgate has plenty of them to offer. He was interested in manuscript material, and he had found an unpublished poem of Lydgate's in the university library at Cambridge. Most of all, he was at this time studying early English versification, in which field Lydgate presented even more difficult problems than Chaucer. Gray saw in the choppy quality of Lydgate's verse a symptom of the changes taking place in the English language. He believed, nevertheless, that the serious verse of the time had uniform meter, "not indeed to the eye, but to the ear, when rightly pronounced." This important observation leads directly to Gray's criticism of Chaucer's verse, especially in the article "Metrum,"[8] where he treats the whole subject more specifically than before and reveals a knowledge of Chaucer and his language far beyond that of the scholars of his day.

A genuine understanding of Chaucer was rare in 1755, for those who knew him at all usually read his works only in the modernizations of Dryden and Pope. Scholars like Richard Hurd and the Warton brothers repeated the criticisms of Dryden that Chaucer was a barbarous poet, with poetical fire but no understanding of metrical regularity. John Urry, in his edition of Chaucer published posthumously in 1721, had tried to regularize the Middle English by additions much in the manner of Percy's later improvements of the popular ballads. Chaucerian scholars have never forgiven Urry for his presumption and have therefore failed to give him credit for his attempt, more scholarly than is commonly believed, to show that we accuse Chaucer of irregularity through ignorance of the condition of English language and poetry in the fourteenth century. The fact remains, however, that the eighteenth century followed Dryden rather than Urry,

---

[7] CPB, II, 741–750, 755–756. Printed in Mathias, II, 55–80, but with many changes, notably the addition of artificial accent marks and the omission of many original passages quoted by Gray.

[8] CPB, II, 757–762, 765–770. Printed in Mathias, II, 3–30, "Observations on English Metre."

and continued to believe that Chaucer's verse was rough and barbarous.

In his articles on meter Gray shows that most critics, especially Puttenham and Dryden, had not understood Chaucer's principles of versification. He takes Urry's edition as a point of departure, criticizing his insertion of "words and syllables, unauthorized by the oldest manuscripts, to help out what seems lame and defective in the measure," yet agreeing with him "that many great inequalities in the metre are owing to the neglect of transcribers." At this point Gray shows the soundness of his method by trying to gain an understanding of the original language and the history of its changes. For this he fortunately uses what was probably the best work on the subject, the Anglo-Saxon grammar of George Hickes, supplemented with the Anglo-Saxon dictionary of William Somner. By the use of these works he is able to demonstrate just how some of the changes took place before Chaucer's time. The prefix ge- becomes y- and is often dropped. The inflectional final -n in infinitives, participles, and plural forms of the verb is usually dropped, and the resulting final -e may or may not be pronounced. This tendency, which applied to other forms as well, had become, he continues, well established in the fourteenth century, "but in verse, they took the liberty either to follow the old language in pronouncing the final syllable, or to sink the vowel and abridge it, as was usual, according to the necessity of their versification." In other words, it was not considered offensive to the ear to pronounce the final -e in verse, "though in time it was quite dropped in conversation." These conclusions are practically the same as those of modern Chaucerians, yet they date from about 1755, some twenty years before Tyrwhitt paved the way for a scholarly appreciation of Chaucer with his edition of the *Canterbury Tales*.

Gray shows an understanding of another principle of English verse which had been neglected in his own day, that is, the natural freedom of English verse based on Germanic rhythms as opposed to the strict regularity of the iambic line that was threatening to engulf all poetry in the early eighteenth century. He calls this *riding rhyme,* " which is confined to one measure, whatever that measure be, but not to one Rhythm; having sometimes more, sometimes fewer syllables." Gray himself used this freedom of rhythm in much of his own poetry, but ears attuned to the iambic regularity of Dryden and Pope could not appreciate it.

Gray also praises the freedom that comes in verse from the variation of the caesura, especially in the blank-verse line. Quoting Puttenham's strict rules for pauses within the line, he goes on to show how the best poetry disregards such uniformity. The twelve syllables of the Alexandrine require a uniform pause in the middle, which, he continues, " is just the reason, why we no longer use them but just to finish a lyric stanza," thinking perhaps of the way he himself used an Alexandrine to end each stanza of the two Pindaric odes he was then composing. He pays Milton the just compliment of being " the best example of an exquisite ear " for his variation of the pause in blank verse and even in the octosyllabic line. The decasyllabic " which is now become our only heroick metre for all poems of any length," no longer has a uniform caesura on the fourth syllable, he thinks, because Spenser and Milton shook off such fetters. He sums up his praise of the variety that is the glory of English poetry by showing how Milton used the pause to suit his purpose: " The more we attend to the composition of Milton's harmony, the more we shall be sensible, how he loved to vary his pauses, his measures, and his feet, which gives that enchanting air of freedom and wildness to his versification, unconfined by any rules, but those which his own feeling and the nature of his subject demanded."

Gray's table of the fifty-nine measures in use in English poetry, appended to his article on meter, is chiefly valuable in showing his wide range of intimate knowledge in that field. He wrote specific criticism of Chaucer, Lydgate, Daniel, and Milton, but he knew the works of many of their contemporaries. He placed Lydgate far above Gower and Occleve in choice of expression and smoothness of verse. He knew Gawin Douglas well, the interesting prologues to the various books of his translation of the *Aeneid* and the *Palace of Honour,* the latter so rare that Gray had a transcript of it made for his use. The unusual inventiveness of Spenser furnished the chief exhibits for the table of meters. Gray knew Dryden and Pope intimately, and wrote critically in his letters about the verse of his contemporaries, although he gave them little place in his metrical discussions, because, he says, they write mostly in octosyllabics and decasyllabics.[9]

Gray showed in writing these articles on meter a combination of critical approach and scholarly knowledge of the subject that would have made of his projected history an outstanding creative work. Instead of writing it, however, he went more deeply into the subject in search of the historical background of English poetry, following its roots into Latin and the Romance dialects — Italian, French, and Provençal — into the "Gothic" rhythms of Anglo-Saxon, Old High German, and Old Norse, and even into the multiple variety of Welsh prosody. A few examples from the memoranda on the flyleaf of his pocket diary for 1755 indicate how varied was his pursuit of the many elements that went together to make the glory of English poetry: Julius Scaliger's *Poetica* for a scholarly approach; Du Cange's glossary for such articles as "Sequentia," "Rhythmus," "Romancia," and "Antiphona" on medieval Latin verse; Aldhelm[10] and two German dictionaries for Germanic poetry; Jean de Nostredame and Claude Fauchet on Provençal; and Giraldus Cambrensis, supplemented by Henry Rowland's *Mona antiqua,* for Celtic matters.

Such an ambitious approach almost inevitably led Gray into new interests far removed from his original project. One problem that occupied his attention more than any other in poetics was the origin of rhyme. His first article on the subject, "Pseudo-Rhythmus," [11] begins with a consideration of the alliteration common to Old High German, Anglo-Saxon, and such Middle English verse as *Piers Plowman*. Coming to the question of rhyme,

[9] A convenient compilation of Gray's criticism may be found in Northup, *Essays and Criticism by Thomas Gray*, and in Whibley, III, Index I.

[10] A short article (CPB, II, 479) was written about 1754. In it Gray refers to *De metrorum generibus et schematibus* as one of the first books on meter. He got most of his knowledge of Aldhelm from William of Malmesbury's life of him in Wharton's *Anglia sacra*.

[11] CPB, II, 771–774, 791 f., 801 f. Printed in Mathias, II, 31–49.

he finds that it was used earliest in Latin, Welsh, and Arabic. He argues against Arabic as the source of rhyme in Europe, because Latin, being the mother of the various Romance dialects which chiefly used rhyme, was far more easily accessible.[12] In English poetry, he continues, rhyme appears for the first time in the twelfth century, presumably arriving from the Continent, since some of the Germanic tribes, notably the Norse, had rhyme before the Norman Conquest. He admits the possibility of the English having borrowed it from their neighbors, the Welsh bards, who wrote in rhyme in the sixth century. This possibility became more and more plausible to him as he began to learn more about Welsh poetry, until he was finally convinced in his own mind that the Celtic origin of rhyme was not only possible but almost certain. His study of Welsh poetry and history became the rallying-ground for a new branch of romantic poetry. He laid aside the history of English poetry in order to make new history.

II

Gray was more familiar with Welsh poetry and even with the Welsh language than is commonly supposed. He wrote an extended article in the Commonplace Book, dealing with the Welsh — their prosody, their bards, their history, and even their language — and expounding his most mature reflections on the question of the origin of rhyme. He makes himself quite plain: since Welsh and English prosodies have many kinds of feet in common, his native measures " not improbably might have been borrow'd from the Britons, as I am apt to believe, the rise of Rhyme itself was. Once I was (I own) of Monsig' Crescimbeni's opinion, that it was derived from the use of the Roman Church in its Hymns, and from thence pass'd to the People of Provence." He was aware of his radical departure from the traditional beliefs, and for that reason developed very thoroughly his arguments concerning the relation between English and Welsh poetry. The whole article, which Gray entitled " Cambri," is much more extensive and

---

[12] He follows the theories of G. M. Crescimbeni, *Commentarii intorno alla volgar poesia storia*, 5 vols. (Rome, 1702-1711).

scholarly than the greatly mutilated excerpts of Mathias would indicate.[13] The whole question of Gray's relation to the Celtic revival of the late eighteenth century should therefore be reviewed in the light of this manuscript evidence, apparently overlooked by Professor Edward D. Snyder in his otherwise very creditable study of the subject.[14]

Gray begins his article with a general description of Welsh poetry, taken from the material furnished by the Welsh antiquary, Lewis Morris, in Thomas Carte's *History of England* (1747-1754). From Morris he got a reference to David ap Rhys's more particular studies of prosody in his book on the Welsh language.[15] This he consulted at length for its extensive analyses of intricate Welsh forms, and found in it numerous examples of verse forms, not only catalogued but scanned, with diagrams to show the complex rhyme schemes. He discovered that instead of barbarism Welsh poetry was full of sophistication and of a richness that, as he expressed it, " appears both for variety and accuracy to equal the invention of the most polish'd Nations." He copied out a number of these illustrative poems letter for letter in his notes, marking each foot carefully to indicate the original meter. He obviously was not satisfied with a description of the old poetry and demanded to know what its actual sounds were, for he confesses his frank enjoyment of the original even while as yet knowing little of the language:

he [Rhys] produces a great number of passages from ancient Writers as examples to the several rules; from w[ch] (tho' entirely unacquainted with the Language) one may perceive something of the Measure, Alliteration, and Order of Rhymes, of w[ch] their Verse consists. the Rhyme seems to be entirely monosyllabic, as it is (for the most part) in our own tongue; and is sometimes in couplets, sometimes triple, or quadruple, or continued for

---

[13] CPB, II, 799–800, 803–806, 809–816. The article consists of seven folio pages of text in Gray's finest hand, with copious footnotes on opposite pages. Mathias (II, 50–54) printed garbled versions of some two pages of the text and a part of one note. The whole has been recently printed from the manuscript: Martin, *Chronologie*, pp. 170–199.

[14] *The Celtic Revival in English Literature, 1760–1800* (Harvard University Press, 1923).

[15] John David Rhys, *Cambrobrytannicae Cymraecaeve linguae institutiones* (London, 1592).

a great number of lines together, & often alternate. the Composition is generally in Stanza's regularly answering one another.[16]

Gray seems to be especially interested in the use of alliteration by the Welsh poets: "there is a conceal'd harmony, arising from the regular return of similar letters or syllables in the beginning or middle of a Verse, doubtless very pleasing to ears accustom'd to the Cadence of their Poetry & Language: . . ." In this instance, as in many others, Gray's footnote is more revealing than the main passage itself: "they had not reduced it to rule, but practised it wildly & without art, as we do at present. the Poetry of our Forefathers, the Saxons & Danes consisted of nothing else, than this Alliteration, & Measure, without any Rhyme."

Gray's own poetry reveals the same distinction in the use of alliteration. He himself had before 1755 practiced it "wildly and without art," that is, as an adornment for tone color. This kind of alliteration is prevalent, for instance, in the *Elegy,* along with the recurrence of similar vowel sounds for tonal effects. No rule is apparent in such phrases as "the pomp of power," "a youth to fortune and to fame unknown," and "craz'd with care, or cross'd in hopeless love." Seldom has alliteration, aided by a felicitous use of word order, been more effective, however, for purposes of tone color than in "The ploughman homeward plods his weary way" or "The moping owl does to the moon complain."

The alliteration employed in *The Bard,* on the other hand, has a more definitely studied cast, resembling what Gray had seen in Welsh poetry. He cites in his notes an extreme example "call'd peculiarly *Gorchest Beirdh,* or the Excellent of the Bards; I suppose from its peculiar difficulty." We can like Gray detect the complex structure without knowing any more Welsh than he:

> I rhwydh 'air hîr,
> I'w chwydh och wîr,
> I'w swydh a'i sîr,
>   Y sydh saeth:

---

[16] CPB, II, 799. This and the following two excerpts, omitted by Mathias, come in the text immediately after Gray's reference to Rhys.

I glai a' glyn,
I rhai o'r hyn,
I dhai y dhyn,
I Dhuw dhaeth.[17]

Alliteration appears, moreover, to be a definite part even of the less complicated Welsh stanzas transcribed by Gray in his notes. From this research Gray derived a very genuine feeling for the rhythm and devices of Welsh poetry, which he uses to great advantage in *The Bard,* particularly in the passages containing the speeches of the bard himself or of the ghostly chorus of his slain brothers. The opening line sets the tone, " Ruin seize thee, ruthless King!" and the rest of the bard's speeches reëcho it, increasing the air of wildness that appealed to the rómantic poets in such phrases as "highborn Hoel's harp" and "cold is Cadwallo's tongue."

Since the epode demands a change from the identical structure of strophe and antistrophe, near the end of each epode in *The Bard* Gray introduces the effect of the Welsh short line by the use of two verses with internal rhyme. Opposite the first occurrence of this device, " No more I weep. They do not sleep," he wrote in his own copy of the *Odes* the following note, which he neglected to insert in the 1768 edition: " The double cadence is introduced here not only to give a wild spirit and variety to the Epode; but because it bears some affinity to a peculiar measure in the Welch Prosody, called Gorchest-Beirdh, i:e: the *Excellent of the Bards.*" [18] Thus *The Bard* became one of the most successful examples of romantic metamorphosis, whereby the most formal metrical schemes of ancient Greek and medieval Welsh prosodies are combined to impart an air of wildness to an English poem. *The Progress of Poesy* was truly " An Ode in the Greek Manner," as Gray originally entitled it; *The Bard* is Pindaric as well, but a new sublimity has been added to it as the result of Gray's study of Welsh meter.[19]

[17] CPB, II, 804, "as invented, & practised by none but consummate Masters." Gray took the illustration from Rhys, *op. cit.,* p. 220.

[18] Gray's copy of his 1757 *Odes* is now in the Morgan Library.

[19] Gray tells us that he took the image of the bards weaving the web of

Apparently, therefore, Gray was not only diligently studying Welsh poetry but was also using his knowledge for metrical experimentation in *The Bard* as early as 1755.[20] Pursuing the scholarly aspect of his study in the article " Cambri," Gray concludes that such variety in metrical form must have developed over a long period of time, making it not only possible but very likely that rhyme originated among the Welsh. He has drawn largely on Carte's history and Rhys's Welsh grammar for the first part of the article. On the subject of rhyme he seems to be on unexplored ground. His argument is, briefly, that in the sixth century when rhyme first appeared in Church Latin it was already an integral part of a highly artistic prosody among the Welsh, which the bards received by oral tradition from long development at the hands of the Druids. The reasoning is sound, as may be seen from its scientific use by modern students of folklore.

Gray shows the feasibility of his scheme by summarizing the historical relations between the Celtic and the Germanic peoples in Britain. " I mark these Periods," he says after describing many instances of intimate connections, " to shew at what time the Britons might be so connected with the Saxons, as to give them possibly some knowledge of their tongue, and some tincture of their manners." Even then too many baffling difficulties present themselves to him. His many questions show that he is not satisfied with the results. His critical insight leads him instinctively, however, to the powerful influence of popular tradition on the use of rhyme: " Who can account for the Caprice of Time; & shew why one Monument has, & another has not escaped the Wreck of Ages? perhaps Rhyme might begin among the common People, & be applied only to the meaner Species of Poetry,

---

Edward's fate from the Norse poem which he adapted as *The Fatal Sisters*. As his unpublished note in his own copy of his *Odes* expresses it: " The image is taken from an ancient Scaldic Ode, written in the old-Norwegian tongue about A:D: 1029." This poem also uses alliteration with some rhyme, but not in so pronounced a manner as the Welsh poems. At any rate Gray found much in Welsh poetry to imitate, and we have his own word that he was using it on one occasion. If he borrowed anything from Norse meter at this time, it was the use of the parenthetical refrain, e.g., "(Weave we the woof. The thread is spun)."

[20] Snyder (*Celtic Revival*, p. 39, n. 2) conjectured this influence without proof.

Adages, Songs, & vulgar histories, passing by tradition from one to another." [21] The question of the origin of rhyme is even at the present day probably not completely settled, for the beginnings of most forms of art have a baffling way of being hidden in the mists of oral popular tradition. Gray was on safer ground when he conjectured that the Welsh bards borrowed their elaborate use of alliteration from Anglo-Saxon poetry.[22] In the matter of rhyme, moreover, he correctly concludes that, no matter what its origin may have been, the prevalence of rhyme in English verse was due to the coming of the Normans and the subsequent close political relations between England and the Continent.

Having disposed of the question of rhyme, Gray continues his article with many things of interest to students of the Celtic revival in the eighteenth century. He cites Giraldus Cambrensis as the best authority on Welsh civilization in the Middle Ages, and transcribes from the *Descriptio Cambriae* several passages on the Welsh language, poetry, and music.[23] He then uses Rhys's grammar again as the authority for a thorough classification of the types of Welsh poetry. After this he comes to a detailed treatment of a subject which had long interested him, the Welsh bards, their traditions, and their relations with the English rulers.

In his discussion of the bards Gray first describes, on the authority of an article in Bishop Thomas Tanner's posthumous *Bibliotheca Britannica* (1748), the custom of periodic contests among the bards for the silver harp, the token of poetical supremacy. This contest, as appears from a commission of Queen Elizabeth, was to discourage the vagabond minstrels. The winner of the metrical battle was to be accorded great privileges and was given precedence even over the very powerful court bard, who was himself eighth in rank among the king's own attendants.[24]

[21] CPB, II, 805.

[22] Gray's footnote on the *Cymeriad*, or use of alliteration in Welsh poetry (CPB, II, 806), summarizes his views perfectly: " as this art was not practised by the most ancient Bards, whose works are yet extant; it is highly probable, that the Welch borrow'd it from the Anglo-Saxons & Danes, who in their turn caught the art of Rhyme, & some of their measures from the Welch."

[23] Gray used David Powel's edition, 8vo, London, 1585.

[24] Gray describes the privileges and duties of both kinds of bards, using as his authority William Wotton's edition of the *Leges Wallicae* (London, 1730, folio), which he cites on every point.

Gray goes on to discuss at length what seems to have bothered his commentators considerably, the persecution of the bards by Edward I. It has long been known that Gray got the idea for his poem from a hint in Carte's history,[25] but not that he was himself aware of its lack of authenticity. He noted Carte's manuscript source for the tradition and in the hope of later seeing it entered " J. Wynne's Account of the Gwedir Family " as a memorandum on the flyleaf of his pocket diary for 1755. In his historical review of the relations between England and Wales, Gray showed that he was skeptical about the tradition: " he [Edward I in 1284] is said to have hanged up all their Bards, because they encouraged the Nation to rebellion, but their works (we see,) still remain, the Language (tho' decaying) still lives, & the art of their versification is known, and practised to this day among them." [26] Farther along in the article he brought out the true situation by quoting records and documents from the reigns of Edward I and Henry IV, extracted from William Wotton's appendix to the *Leges Wallicae*, and by prefacing them with this statement: " Whatever severity Edward the first might exercise at the time, when he reduced that Country, on some of the Welch Bards; yet it appears, he proceeded no farther against them in general, than to order that they should not travel (as usual) about Wales, nor ask any rewards from the Inhabitants." In this instance, as in many others, Gray showed plainly that he was both historian and poet. The poet in him, however, was wise enough to realize that the tradition was far more dramatic than the historical documents.

The next point Gray took up was the ancient history of Wales, filled with the romantic tradition of King Arthur, which had interested the English people for centuries, as a curious mingling

[25] *History of England* (1750), II, 196. See Snyder, *Celtic Revival*, pp. 42 ff., especially the correspondence of Bishop Percy and the Reverend Evan Evans. A previous note in Carte had listed this account as from a Mostyn manuscript, but Gray probably thought he would be able to see it later. That he did not appears from Percy's letter to Evans, October 15, 1761, for which see Snyder, p. 42, n. The manuscript (Sir John Wynn's history of his family) was published in 1770 by Daines Barrington as *The History of the Gwedir Family*, of which Gray owned a copy.

[26] CPB, II, 803. The entire sketch was omitted by Mathias without indication.

of romance and history in the Middle Ages and as food for patriotic antiquarianism under the Tudors.[27] Gray was aware of the
controversies that had raged over the authenticity of the Arthurian
stories. He read about them in Carte's preface to his history and
in William Wynne's justification of Geoffrey of Monmouth in
the preface to his edition of David Powel's *History of Wales*.
From these and other sources Gray drew the conclusion that
Geoffrey's history, "wch abounds with childish fables," is nevertheless with a few exceptions " really a Version from the Welch." [28]
He plainly shows that he includes the Arthurian tradition among
the fables when he complains of the attitude of Giraldus Cambrensis: " tho' he declares Geffrey a Lyar, yet he follows many of
the most improbable opinions advanced in that Writers work, as
the coming of Brutus the Trojan, the fabulous exploits of K:
Arthur, &c: so that they appear to be very ancient traditions, &
firmly believed by all the Welch Nation long before Geffrey or
the Author, whose work he copied."

The last subject in the article " Cambri " is the Welsh language,
for Gray was by way of being an amateur philologist, deeply
interested in several languages without mastering them. The
Welsh nation, he says, "gradually received the Customs and
Manners of their powerful Neighbours, the Saxons," and extended
their borrowings to the language, of which he lists nearly seventy
words with their Anglo-Saxon or Norman cognates. No matter
which nation borrowed from the other, he continues, " either case
alike suffices to shew the intercourse between them, wch is the
intention of producing them here." Numerous Welsh borrowings from the Latin are easily explained in the light of the Roman
occupation of Britain. Gray laughs at the assertion of Giraldus
and others that the Welsh is a dialect of the Greek, and concludes,

[27] C. B. Millican, *Spenser and the Table Round* (Harvard University Press,
1932), gives an interesting and very learned account of this latter phase. See also
Roberta Brinkley, *Arthurian Legend in the Seventeenth Century* (Johns Hopkins
University Press, 1932).

[28] *"Brut-y-Brenhined*, i:e: the History of the Kings of Britain, ascribed (tho'
falsely) to Tyssillio." Gray cites as authority two manuscripts, one at Jesus College, Oxford, the other belonging to "Mr Davies of Llanerk in Denbighshire."

sanely enough in the light of the knowledge of his day, that the Celtic is itself an independent family:

this is sure, that tho' this Language has been for so many Centuries impoverish'd by being confined to a few narrow Provinces, & corrupted by the unavoidable mixture introduced by foreign nations, yet the foundation of it, its Grammar, & by far the greater part of its Words yet in use, have no similitude to any other in Europe, & bear the marks of a surprising antiquity.[29]

Just how much Welsh Gray knew is difficult to ascertain. He was obviously interested in its sounds as they were reflected in the intricate structures of Welsh poetry, but, as he himself affirms, one could detect the meter without knowing much of the original language. Rhys very carefully analyzed the structure of Welsh poetry, but failed to explain in his meager Latin text many of the Welsh phrases he used. In his notes Gray usually supplemented Rhys with a literal translation of the original, which served immensely to clarify the technical terms. For example, he uses Rhys's table of the types of Welsh poetry, the first of the three chief divisions being " the *Clerwriaeth,* or Stimulatorium, of wch there are two Species, one call'd *Sennu* (from *Sen,* a Reprimand.) this is wholly satyrical, & was often perform'd Extempore. the other *Canu serthed,* i:e: lascivious Song, running on obscene subjects." [30] For this kind of work and later for the numerous Welsh names of plants and animals that he added to the margins of his Linnaeus, Gray used John Davies' *Antiquae linguae Britannicae dictionarium* (1632), although he was usually willing to accept the Latin translations of his sources if he judged them adequate.[31]

Gray's study of the Welsh was well under way by the summer of 1755, when the blind harper Parry set the learned body at Cambridge a-dancing and inspired Gray to finish *The Bard*. He used his knowledge of Celtic lore the next winter correcting blunders in Mason's poetical drama *Caractacus* and in pointing

[29] CPB, II, 815.

[30] Rhys, p. 146. CPB, II, 809.

[31] Gray definitely refers to "Dr Davies," as the source for his information on Welsh borrowings from the Latin. Gray's note (CPB, II, 816) is from Davies' preface "Ad lectorem," sig ** v^o.

out the errors of such supposed authorities as Keysler, Pelloutier, and even Mallet.[32] Early in 1760 his interest in old poetry was revived by the Erse poems (part of Macpherson's *Ossian* in manuscript) shown him by Walpole. About the same time the Reverend Evan Evans sent him by Daines Barrington the manuscript of his *Dissertatio de bardis* " with specimens of their writings." Evans seemed to be anxious to get Gray's criticism, for he wrote Richard Morris, April 28, 1760: " He [Mr. Justice Barrington of Carnarvon] says he will show the Dissertation to Mr. Gray, to have his judgment of it, and to correct it where necessary." [33] Probably soon after this, Gray used Evans' translations for his own imitations from the Welsh, which consist of four fragments from two poems, Aneurin's *Gododin* and Gwalchmai's *Ode to Owen Gwynned*. He undoubtedly intended to do other specimens for his history. A flyleaf at the front of the second volume of his Commonplace Book contains three lists of poems: (1) " Gothic," the Old Norse and Anglo-Saxon poems discussed below; (2) " Erse," five pieces from *Ossian,* " very ancient if genuine"; and (3) " Welch." [34] The Welsh poems he lists but fails to use are: " Some Stanzas (chosen) of Taliessin, about A:D: 570," with " Battle of Argoed Llyfain " added on the side; " Gwalchmai's Delights (the beginning) about 1260"; and " Gruffudd's Lamentation for Prince Llewellyn, about 1284."

Gray was early recognized as an authority on Celtic matters, especially on the history of the Welsh bards. He turned to Celtic study very little after 1756 and even then only when stimulated by the desire of Mason or Evans for criticism or by the sensation of the Ossianic poems. In 1770, just a year before he died, he made a trip into Wales with Norton Nicholls, but he has left us no souvenir of it except in the encouragement to William Gilpin that resulted in the first of the numerous " picturesque tours." He had started a flame long before, however, when he wrote *The Bard,* and the fire swept into the Romantic movement itself.

[32] See the correspondence of this period, esp. Tovey, II, 12 f., 22, 26; Whibley, II, 550, 557, 567.

[33] Snyder, *Celtic Revival*, p. 27. See Tovey, II, 146; Whibley, II, 680.

[34] Printed in Martin, *Chronologie,* pp. 167 f.

III

Gray included in his scheme for a history of English poetry an account of its ancestry, with some illustrative specimens from the poetry of the Germanic peoples who settled in England, namely the Anglo-Saxons and the Danes. He grouped all the early Germanic poetry together under the name of "Gothic," in which the Scandinavian element was most prominent, probably because the Norse poems were more easily available, both in text and in translation, more picturesque in their wildness, and, according to general belief, more ancient. Gray's study of Old Norse and his place in the Scandinavian revival have been so thoroughly treated that I should be merely bringing coals to Newcastle if I attempted here to do more than present new evidence, including in my summary the findings of Professors Kittredge and Farley.[35]

Gray knew considerable Norse history before he took up Norse poetry.[36] Before 1755 he had read Torfaeus's history of Norway and the Orkneys, for he tells us that he found there the Norse poem on which he based his *Fatal Sisters* and from which he took the idea of the web of fate in his *Bard*. By January 1758 he was already well versed in Norse religion and history when he wrote Mason that he had seen the Gothic Elysium in "Mallet's Introduction to the History of Denmark . . . , and many other places."[37] Presumably Gray was studying Norse history and culture along with his research in English poetry. He wrote a general article on comparative Germanic philology, chiefly with reference to Norse and Anglo-Saxon, which in the Commonplace Book

[35] G. L. Kittredge, "Gray's Knowledge of Old Norse," in W. L. Phelps, *Selections from . . . Thomas Gray* (Boston, 1894), pp. xli–l, and F. E. Farley, *Scandinavian Influences in the English Romantic Movement* (Boston, 1903).

[36] The first indication of Gray's serious interest in Scandinavia comes in his notes (CPB, II, 605) on the *Commentarii Petropolitani*, vol. V (1730–1731), which can be dated about 1751–1752. As in many other fields, the historical interest seems to come first: "Character of the old Northern Historians, good sense of Snorro Sturlæus, far superior to Saxo Grammaticus. Thormodus Torfæus' Prolegomena in Historiam Norvegicam & Orcadensem. Arngrimus Jonas' Crymogæa and Specimen Islandicum. . . ."

[37] Tovey, II, 12 ff.

precedes his article on the Welsh.[38] He found it easy and interesting to turn from one Germanic language to another in the
remarkable *Thesaurus* of George Hickes, which he frequently
consulted, not only for Anglo-Saxon, but also for " Franco-Theotische " (Old High German), Icelandic, and Gothic. In the
Thesaurus and similar works he could find frequent examples
of poetry to illustrate the grammar or syntax of the various Germanic languages. He read many of these poetical excerpts and
transcribed some of them in his notes, doubtless pausing to observe
their sounds or to make a comparison with an English cognate
but learning their meaning from the Latin translations which
almost invariably accompanied the originals.

Some time later, probably about 1761, Gray wrote a second
article, also called " Gothi," which consisted chiefly of critical
apparatus for *The Fatal Sisters* and *The Descent of Odin*.[39] In it
he copied out the Norse versions of the two poems and their Latin
translations in parallel columns, and accompanied the poems
with copious notes. If we may judge from this article, Gray was
very much interested in the original language of these Icelandic
poems but at the same time depended almost altogether on the
Latin for his knowledge of their meaning, as Professor Kittredge
demonstrated without the help of the Commonplace Book.[40] In
almost every note of importance Gray gives a specific reference
to book, chapter, and page in *"Bartholin, de contemptu mortis,"* [41]
his chief source. He transcribes in full the Latin, the " literal
translation " as he calls it, but omits much of the Norse. Obviously
he would not have gone to such pains if he had not read the
poems in the original Norse, cherishing the foreign sounds and
taking the meaning from the conveniently placed Latin trans-

[38] CPB, II, 775–782, printed in Mathias, II, 104–110, with the omission of a
lengthy note on Middle English manuscripts, which Gray derived chiefly from
Wanley's catalogue in Hickes's *Thesaurus*.

[39] CPB, III, 1041–1048, 1067–1070, over two hundred pages after " Cambri "
and just before the English versions of the Norse poems (1761). Intervening
notes are on English antiquities (1758–1760).

[40] See also Martin, *Essai*, p. 238, n. 283.

[41] Thomas Bartholin, *Antiquitatum Danicarum de causis contemptae mortis*
(Copenhagen, 1689). See Kittredge, *loc. cit.*

lation. He felt the wildness of the trochaic rhythm beating a quickening pace through the older poems, and he was not slow to use it in his own Norse imitations, as he had already done in *The Bard*. The Norse refrain, " Vindum vindum/Vef Darradar," for example, reëchoes in *The Bard* as " Weave the warp and weave the woof," and in *The Fatal Sisters* as the repeated motif " (Weave the crimson web of war)."

From his Norse material in the Commonplace Book Gray chose " certain little Notes " to enlarge the " two ounces of stuff " he put in the 1768 edition of his poems, lest his works " should be mistaken for the works of a flea, or a pismire." Mason added a few more notes from Gray's manuscript in the 1775 memoirs, omitting some that would have been helpful in showing the artistic metamorphosis in the Norse poems. For example, the " griesly band," weaving with bloody hands the fate of Edward in *The Bard,* becomes more ominous when we see the gruesome picture that Gray took from Torfaeus: " the threads, that formed the texture, were the entrails of Men, the shuttles were so many swords, the weights were human heads, the warp was all of bloody spears. as they wove, they sung the following magic song: Vitt er orpit. . . ." [42] Another example shows a more specific knowledge of the Valkyries than does the 1768 edition:

> They are often described as spinning, or flying thro' the air, dress'd in the skin of a swan; some of them were married to mortal Men, (as Svanhvitr, Aulrunr, and Alvitrar) with whom they cohabited for a few years. They also are call'd Disir. (see Bar. 3.1 and 2.11) There were a great number more of these Valkyriar, as Hrist, Mist . . . &c: whose office it was to serve the departed Heroes with horns of Mead & Ale.

In an additional note to *The Descent of Odin,*[43] Gray shows his interest in the Norse prophecy concerning the end of the world:

---

[42] The note on " Darradar," translated from Bartholin, continues with examples from Egil Skallagrimson and Eyvind. Gray quotes a couplet from Egil, with Latin translation, and gives as his authority for the whole note Bartholin, p. 624, and Olaus Verelius.

[43] Gray introduces it as " The Vegtams Kvitha (from Bar. 3.2 p. 632)." The Norse and Latin versions are given as before. With the exception noted, Mason has reproduced Gray's notes fairly accurately. I cannot help noting Gray's " blew " for blue and " lent " for leaned.

Ragnarockr, the *Twilight of the Gods,* is the End of the World, when not only all the human Race are to perish, the Sun & the Stars to disappear, the Earth to sink in the Sea, & Fire to consume the Skies, but Odin himself & the Gods (a few excepted) must come to an end. after wch a new heaven & a new earth will appear, the Ruler of all things (a nameless God) will come to Judgement, & *Gimle,* the Abode of the Good, & *Nastrond,* that of the Wicked, will subsist for evermore. (see the Voluspa).

Gray ends his article " Gothi " with a fragment of the *Biarkamal* in Norse and Latin, also taken from Bartholin,[44] which he probably thought of translating along with other Norse poems into English verse. He had long been interested in the older poetry, and in 1760 the Welsh poems from Evans and the Erse from Macpherson awakened in him a tremendous enthusiasm, which led to his Welsh imitations and to his lists of Welsh and Erse poems on the flyleaf of his third Commonplace Volume. At that time or earlier he prefaced these two lists with a much longer one entitled " Gothic," in which he included poems from both Old Norse and Anglo-Saxon. He checked off the two Norse poems which he actually translated,[45] as we have already seen he did with the Welsh, so that we may look on the other titles in the list as poems that he at least contemplated translating at one time or another.

Gray describes each poem in the list, giving the author (where known), the date of composition, and the immediate source of information. The Norse poems in his list are, with one exception, identical with the poems which went into Bishop Percy's *Five Runic Pieces,* published in 1765 but contemplated, as the preface tells us, as early as 1761. It was in 1761 that Percy, visiting the libraries of Cambridge, first met Gray and spent an evening with him in his chambers at Pembroke. Can it be that Gray, with his customary inertia and aversion to publicity, suggested to Percy that he give the Northern poems to the English public?[46] The

[44] " Apud Snorron: in Chronico & Bartholin: 1.10," beginning " Dagr er upkominn."

[45] " Incantation of Woden (call'd Vegtams Kvitha) in Bartholin. p. 632. very ancient," and " The Song of the Weird Sisters, or Valkyries — In Tormodus Torfæus, after 1029. (Orcades and Bartholin)."

[46] Whibley (App. N) and Martin (*Essai,* pp. 240 f.) summarize the relations of Gray and Percy.

only one of Percy's five runic pieces not found here is the *Ransom of Egil,* which Gray himself transliterated from the runic characters of Wormius and quoted in one of his treatises on rhyme.[47] Gray included in his list what would have made Percy's book far more valuable, two poems from that treasure of ancient Norse poetry, the Poetic Edda: the *Voluspa* (which he had seen cited so often in Hickes's Anglo-Saxon Grammar) and the *Havamal.*[48] These, with the *Vegtams kvitha* (the source of his *Descent of Odin*) make up the only part of the Poetic Edda that was printed before his death.[49]

Besides the Norse poems the "Gothic" list contains four Anglo-Saxon pieces, all taken from Hickes: (1) "Part of the Dano-Saxon Paraphrase of Genesis," which Hickes never tired of citing and part of which he judged equal to if not better than Milton's treatment of the same subject in *Paradise Lost;*[50] (2) "Gospel of Nicodemus," which Hickes said had been published on account of its elegance and suavity of style by a very good friend of his;[51] (3) "Triumph of Aethelstan, A:D:938 (Hickes, V:1.p. 181, and Gibson's Chron:Saxon:)"; and (4) "Death of Eadgar, A:D:975."[52]

The sequence of the whole list — Old Norse, Anglo-Saxon, Welsh, and Erse — is plain in the light of Gray's note in the 1768 Poems: "In the Introduction to it [the History of English Poetry] he meant to have produced some specimens of the Style that reigned in ancient times among the neighbouring nations, or those who had subdued the greater part of this Island, and were our

[47] "Pseudo-Rhythmus" in Mathias, II, 32, n.

[48] The entire note serves as an example of his manner of reference: "Some Parts of the Voluspa (cited so often in the Edda) or Oracles of Vola; & the Havamaal, or Sublime Discourse of Woden, preserved by Sæmund Sigfusson (in the first Edda) who was born in 1057. In Mallet & Resenius."

[49] Kittredge, in Phelps's *Gray,* p. xlii.

[50] *Thesaurus,* I, 116: "Miltonoque nostro, optimo poetæ sed pessimo civi, qui in carmine vere rhythmico, quod inscripsit *Paradise Lost,* tartarum and cacodæmonum mores depinxit, æquandus, me judice, si non anteferendus."

[51] *Thesaurus,* I, 71: "quod ob orationis nitorem, & suavitatem, vir mihi amicissimus publici juris fecit." Hickes gives the friend's name as Edward Thwaites (I, 45).

[52] Hickes, I, 185 f. Hickes gives the Anglo-Saxon originals of the last two pieces without translation.

Progenitors." From the "very ancient" *Vegtams kvitha* to the Dano-Saxon historical poems of the tenth century Gray has carefully chosen from the available material pieces which may still be considered representative of the poetic style leading up to the beginnings of modern English poetry in the fourteenth century. He did not include any of the heroic poetry of the Anglo-Saxon epic, for he perhaps knew no more Old English than Old Norse. The unique manuscript of *Beowulf* was available in the Cotton collection, but Wanley's dry description of it in his *Catalogus* would never lead anyone to investigate its contents. Gray must have noticed the magnificent Finnsburgh fragment, discovered and printed by Hickes, for it immediately preceded in the *Thesaurus* Hickes's famous translation of the *Waking of Angantyr*,[53] but in this instance the author left no translation or description to guide him. Obviously Gray was more familiar with older Germanic poetry than most of his contemporaries, even though his two imitations from the Norse, printed in 1768, constituted the only proof that the English public had of his knowledge. *The Fatal Sisters* and *The Descent of Odin,* however, aided by Macpherson and Percy, kindled a romantic enthusiasm for things Scandinavian that went far into the nineteenth century.

IV

The search of Gray for poetic origins leading to a history of English poetry took him, as we have seen, into many strange places. Again the fertility of his ever-curious mind prevented him from writing what would for its time have been a masterful work. The thoroughness of his research, however, made him an unacknowledged pioneer in Chaucerian scholarship, the original instigator of the Celtic and Scandinavian interests which became important in the Romantic movement, and a student of early English poetry far ahead of his time. In spite of such achievement Gray was never the genuine scholar in the field of poetry that he later became in English history or in natural science. He knew the manuscript

---

[53] Hickes, I, 192 ff. Gray in his list cites Hickes as the source of his knowledge of *Angantyr*.

sources of his material, but only in a very few instances did he consult them. Although he depended upon translations for a complete knowledge of Welsh and Norse poems, he nevertheless was familiar with them in the original language, enough at least to follow their rhythms and their structure and after that to grasp the meaning of words and phrases as well. He had a feeling for the kinship of languages and could recognize cognates and loanwords as invincible proof of the historical relationship between peoples. The evidence I have presented demonstrates, however, that he never even approached a mastery of Welsh or Old Norse or Anglo-Saxon, the three medieval languages he knew best.

Gray became a recognized authority in so many branches of literary antiquarianism mainly because he consulted the best available authorities. The *Thesaurus* of George Hickes furnished him with everything he needed for his researches into Germanic philology or the beginnings of English poetry. The *Grammatica Anglo-Saxonica et Moeso-gothica* of Hickes gave him an understanding of the older languages that set him right in his interpretation of the meter and pronunciation of Chaucer's poetry. By means of its constant comparison of Anglo-Saxon, Old Norse, and Gothic, and its numerous details on the influence of Scandinavian on English it also gave him an insight into the kinship of the Germanic languages. This and the " Franco-Theotische " (Old High German) grammar in the same collection supplied him with some knowledge of the older Germanic languages and poetry.[54] Similarly he came to the study of things Celtic by reading the *History of England* of Thomas Carte, who, it must be remembered, got his knowledge of Welsh history from Lewis Morris, probably the best contemporary authority on the subject.[55] Gray went to Carte's sources, particularly to Rhys's study of the language, Giraldus Cambrensis' account of medieval Wales, and William Wotton's

---

[54] Gray would not have needed to consult Runolphus Jonas' Icelandic grammar, which was also in the *Thesaurus,* although he probably studied there the names and equivalents of the runic characters. He borrowed Hickes's *Thesaurus* from Pembroke library in 1753, but the three folio volumes proudly head his list of "books bought in London, 1760," the (for him) extravagant price of £2 being paid for them.

[55] Snyder, *Celtic Revival,* pp. 17-25.

edition of the old Welsh laws. After that he learned from Welsh-men — from Parry, Evans, and perhaps Lewis Morris. He was distinctly interested in the language, especially in its relation to English and in its adaptability to the complicated meters of Welsh poetry. He consulted John Davies' Welsh dictionary for the trans-lation of words and phrases that interested him, whether in the field of poetry or of natural history, so that before he died he prob-ably had a fair knowledge of the language, certainly beyond the meager acquaintance hitherto attributed to him.

Gray carried on these studies of poetics between 1754 and 1758, and found so much material that he could never bring himself to write the history of English poetry he projected. In its place he wrote several interesting articles and two poems, *The Progress of Poesy* and *The Bard*. He had an excellent opportunity to con-tinue the study of English poetry in the British Museum, but most of his research during the two years (1759-1761) that he spent there was in the field of English history. In 1760 the simultaneous appearance of the Ossianic poems and Evans' Welsh specimens excited him to the point of composing the Norse and Welsh imita-tions and accompanying them in the Commonplace Book with scholarly annotations. In 1768 he sent these poems to the publishers in order to fill out the slim volume of his works, and in 1770 sent Thomas Warton a belated sketch of the arrangement he had once prepared for his history of English poetry — a beautiful gesture, for he had really abandoned the project when he took up English architecture and antiquities in the spring of 1758 [56] as a prelude to an intensive study of English history for the next three or four years.[57]

[56] Gray's note in his article on the "Pseudo-Rhythmus" (Mathias, II, 39), which acknowledges his indebtedness to Percy in 1761, proves little as to the date of the article, as Kittredge suggests (Phelps's *Gray,* p. xlvi, n. 3). The handwriting in the Commonplace Book shows that Gray was habitually adding to and correct-ing his articles.

[57] See Register VI.13, for description of Gray's random notes on English poetry.

CHAPTER VI

PROFESSOR OF MODERN HISTORY

ON JULY 29, 1768, Gray with mingled shyness and pride kissed the king's hand and received the professorship of modern history and letters at Cambridge. For about twenty years he had considered it desirable. He had openly sought it six years before, when Shallett Turner died after holding the position for twenty-seven years, but it was given instead to Lawrence Brockett. When Brockett broke his neck by falling from his horse ("drunk, I believe, as some say "), the Duke of Grafton only three days later wrote Gray a handsome letter offering him the place. Vice-Chancellor Marriot went posthaste to London to ask for the office but arrived just in time to carry the news of Gray's appointment back to Cambridge. The reason for the prompt offer lay unquestionably in the fact that Richard Stonhewer was the Duke's secretary and was ready to propose the name of his very good friend, knowing his desire to obtain the professorship and his ability to do the office credit.

This position was a crown appointment and might easily have gone to any one of the five other applicants if Stonhewer had not been so forward with his candidate. Gray was well-known as a poet but scarcely any more so than he had been in 1762, when he personally asked for the same place. At either time he was a thorough scholar in the field of modern history, a fact which Stonhewer probably knew but which the public and those who made the appointments had no way of knowing. As early as 1748 Gray considered himself eligible for the professorship: "I certainly might ask it with as much, or more Propriety, than any one in this Place [Cambridge]." [1] He was in mature life more historian than poet, whether in the ancient or modern, Oriental or English fields. Perhaps he sought the professorship for the income it afforded,

[1] Whibley, I, 313. See note explaining the date of this letter to Chute, hitherto dated 1762. Gray had temporarily abandoned the idea by 1759, when he wrote to James Brown (Whibley, II, 623): "Old Turner is very declining, & I was sounded by D^r G: of Lincoln about my designs (or so I understood it). I assured him, I should not *ask* for it, not chusing to be refused."

but he was a credit to it and sought to increase its prestige and usefulness. His love of history and the accessibility of materials for original research made him a scholar in the field.

Gray's first serious study of history began, as did almost everything else he undertook, with the Greeks. His first piece of research, as we have already seen, was to prepare his elaborate chronological tables of Greek history, the columns of which he filled not only with rulers and political events but also with poets, philosophers, and orators. History led him, one might say, to Athenaeus and Isocrates and Plato, for Gray looked upon history as the study of man's progress in thought and emotion even more than in politics and war. At any rate he filled his Olympiads of Greek chronology not only from Thucydides, Herodotus, Xenophon, and occasionally Diodorus Siculus, but also from Athenaeus, Pausanias, Lysias, Isocrates, Aristophanes, and Plato.

Even before he came to the study of Greek history, Gray was familiar with the glory of Rome from his youthful reading of Tacitus, Livy, Caesar, and Silius Italicus, as well as from hundreds of evidences of past grandeur he had himself seen still standing in Italy. Something of the history of northern Africa, Egypt, Palestine, Syria, and Persia, he knew from Strabo, Xenophon, Herodotus, and other ancient writers. This knowledge he naturally increased by consulting travel books by such modern authorities as Pococke, Shaw, and Wheeler. The history of the Levant led to that of the Far East, again chiefly through the lure of travel books. Gray might have more easily been taken for an authority on the Tatar khans or the Ottoman sultans than on the Welsh bards, but few seemed to care about more than a hazy knowledge of Oriental history. This part of Gray's study, however, is so closely linked with his interest in travel books that I have described it in that connection.

Plainly Gray was at heart an historian as well as a poet. Throughout his life he seemed to have an instinctive desire to ferret out the monuments of various civilizations and where possible to bring them into coördination. This historical frame of mind at times became linked with some other field of study, ancient history

with the classics, Oriental history with travel books, Welsh and
Scandinavian history with the beginnings of English poetry. In
a miscellaneous way he was meanwhile reading widely in modern
history as well, especially English, French, and Italian. About
1758, however, when his enthusiasm for the history of English
poetry was waning, he came to a study of English architecture and
heraldry that was to make him an original investigator in the field
of English history. How did he accomplish this?

I

Early in 1758, to counteract his low spirits, Gray began compiling a catalogue of antiquities. As he explained it to Wharton in
his letter of February 21, " the drift of my present studies is to
know, wherever I am, what lies within reach, that may be worth
seeing. whether it be Building, ruin, park, garden, prospect, picture, or monument." [2] Such a design sounds more like the preparation of a guidebook than a study of history, but as a matter of fact
the work was much more serious than Gray's chatter to Wharton
would indicate. At any rate he abandoned his research in English
poetry for the time and took to history. On January 2, 1758, Gray
borrowed from Pembroke library a number of books relating to
English history and antiquities: three volumes of Strype's rework-
ing of Stow's *London,* the first two volumes of Rymer's *Foedera,*
containing state documents of English kings, and Dugdale's *St.
Paul's* and *Warwickshire.* These works, together with the nine
volumes of Leland's *Itinerary of England* which he borrowed on
February 14, became the basis of a thorough study of English
history that lasted for at least three years.

Gray had been interested in the subject for a long time. One of
the earliest articles in the Commonplace Book (*c.* 1742) is the beginning of an outline of English history by periods from the reign
of William and Mary, showing a detailed chronological table of
ministries, magistracies, Parliamentary and civil affairs, military
actions by land, naval affairs, and events in neighboring countries. [3]

[2] Tovey, II, 23; Whibley, II, 564.
[3] " Anglia," CPB, I, 56 f., continued to 1701 on pp. 106–112.

A little later he wrote a formal summary of Saxon history, obviously taken from books he had been reading but without any references.[4] He was not in this instance concerned with original scholarship, yet his survey covers the subject thoroughly.

Much of the emphasis in this article, as in short articles on Parliament[5] and on the Normans[6] which follow almost immediately, is on laws and institutions, a subject Gray was studying in 1743. He speaks with praise of Alfred's collecting the Saxon laws and enacting others, and leaves a blank space for reference to another article on the subject which he never wrote. The article on the Normans has to do almost altogether with the institutions arising under William the Conqueror which led to the Magna Charta. The Magna Charta itself — its history, regulations, and procedure — is explained in still another article,[7] and the two intervening pages are given over to an elaborate genealogical chart of the kings of England.[8] These notes on English history are all of an elementary nature when compared with Gray's later work in the field, but they show an early interest in the subject, stimulated probably by the study of law in 1742–1743. That he continued to be interested in English history is shown by his borrowings from Pembroke library,[9] by his study of Carte's history of England in connection with the Welsh bards, and even more by the constant mention of contemporary events in his letters.

From such general reading in English history Gray came in 1758 to a thorough study of the antiquities throughout England, Scotland, and Wales, which led immediately to his catalogue of notable sights, and showed its more learned aspects in a succession of articles in the Commonplace Book on the cathedrals and abbeys of England. His method of study was to begin with the pedantic treasure house of John Leland's *Itinerary* and *Collectanea,* supple-

---

[4] "Saxones," CPB, I, 124–127, 130–132. The article comes just before those on Greek geography, probably about 1744.

[5] CPB, I, 137, 148 f., 172 f.

[6] CPB, I, 150 f.

[7] CPB, I, 154 f., 160.

[8] CPB, I, 152 f., 204.

[9] 1746, White Kennet's *History of England,* vol. II, and Bohun's *Character of Queen Elizabeth;* 1749, "State Tryals, Vol. 1"; June 1753, "Cambden, 2 Vol."; Jan. 3, 1754, Strype's *Annals* and Wood's *Institutes;* and Feb. 15, 1754, Rymer's *Foedera.*

mented with the works of such antiquaries as William Camden
and John Stow. From these he made his lists as exactly as possible
and then verified details concerning architecture, dates, or monuments from personal observation or from the most reliable modern
source he could find.

The cathedrals at York and Durham he had seen while on
a visit to Wharton in the summer of 1753. The following summer
he visited a number of country estates, where he found not the
pure Gothic of religious architecture but a deplorable mixed style,
" wch now goes by the name of the *Battey Langley* Manner." [10]
Gray's refined taste led him correctly to find at least a comparative purity of Gothicism in Walpole's Strawberry Hill but allowed
him to take none of the domestic Gothic very seriously. After beginning his study of architecture in 1758, he himself visited still
more cathedrals and abbeys, checking up on his old information
and adding new details. In this search he was aided by his friends,
especially William Palgrave,[11] whose information helped him to
fill accurately the blank spaces as his articles grew over the years.[12]

Gray was obviously studying the architecture of England as
an aid to the understanding of English history. He indicates his
method when he prefaces the articles on cathedrals with systematic
and detailed catalogues of "monuments of the royal family of
England, that remain at this day undestroy'd." He tabulates the
monuments with a great deal of descriptive detail on the left-hand
pages, devoting the opposite pages to copious notes of an antiquarian nature, usually on genealogy and heraldry. He follows
this with a second catalogue, arranging the same monuments
according to the time when they were erected, and a third

[10] Tovey, I, 248; Whibley, I, 404.

[11] Many details in the CPB are attributed to " W:P: " When describing Lichfield
Cathedral, pp. 903 f., he writes " I wait for more particular information, concerning
the superb West Front and other parts of the building." A long description follows, marked " W:P: in 1760," showing that this part of the Commonplace Book
is definitely earlier than 1760.

[12] An example of his method is CPB, II, 859, a note on Framlingham Castle:
" Thomas, the third Duke, died at Kenyinghall in Norfolk, but where he was
buried, I do not find: perhaps it might be here. N:B: I have since found that he
lies under a stately Monument of freestone, adorn'd with columns, niches, &
statues of Prophets, &c: in Framlingham-Chancel."

which describes "the monuments and places of residence belonging to the present nobility of England." In this way he
brought his material up to date and showed again that he was
interested in the light that the past was continually throwing on
the present.[13]

Gray then describes every important cathedral in England and
Wales in his Commonplace Book, some of them naturally with
far more detail than others. He was, for example, greatly interested in the various periods of Gothic to be found in the cathedral
at Ely, not far from Cambridge, and consequently lavished so
much study on it that he had enough material to spare some for
criticism when James Bentham sent him his *History of Ely* in
manuscript. Gray's remarks show his obvious predilection for
Gothic. York is "the noblest & most magnificent Gothic Building
on the inside now in England: the outside, tho' richly ornamented,
has moulder'd away, & been much injured by the weather,"
whereas Durham, the best specimen in England of Norman architecture, is merely "a great & very ancient structure." Gloucester is
"a noble structure, & extremely well-preserv'd," Salisbury "a most
stately Edifice,"[14] and Winchester, "a great & ancient Fabrick."
In spite of his love for Gothic, Gray was interested less in aesthetic
criticism than in the wealth of historical material to be found in
the cathedrals, not only from the sepulchral monuments they contained but also from the stories of their checkered careers as buildings. Whether he had seen them or not, he got together what he
could learn about the great cathedrals, treating in succession, besides those mentioned, Lincoln, Oxford, Peterborough, Chester,
Lichfield, Hereford ("one of the most ancient buildings of its kind
in England"), Worcester, Bristol, Bath, Wells, Exeter, Chichester,
Norwich, Rochester, Canterbury ("great and stately Pile"), St.

[13] The three lists are in CPB, II, 843–890. The cathedrals extend from p. 891
into the next volume, p. 952.

[14] In October 1764 Gray made a trip to Salisbury and wrote a long detailed
description of it in the small notebook he took with him on such expeditions.
Then as now the view of the cathedral from the bishop's garden was the finest
sight in the town: "the Close (wch has been surrounded with a stone wall em-
battled still standing for the most part with 4 or 5 old Gateways) is the most
pleasant airy part of ye city."

David's, Llandaff, Bangor, St. Asaph's, and St. Paul's, followed by Westminster and other abbeys.

Most of these antiquarian articles were from secondhand information, checked in many cases by later observation. In June 1758, however, Gray was inspired by his studies to take an antiquarian tour to the cathedrals at Ely and Peterborough and to the near-by abbeys of Crowland, Thorney, and Fotheringay. He obviously enjoyed the expedition, wrote Mason that he was " grown a great Fen-Antiquary," [15] and started the third volume of his Commonplace Book with long articles on the three abbeys and a supplement to his earlier account of that " noble old Fabrick," Peterborough Cathedral.

This expedition, although it did not take Gray far from Cambridge, inspired him to begin an article on Gothic architecture which unfortunately ended with what should have been merely an introduction, namely a criticism of the Norman architecture that preceded the Gothic in England. Gray's tastes were plainly for Gothic, but he understood the main characteristic of the Norman and used as examples specimens he himself had seen in the massive lines of Durham and in the older parts of Ely and Peterborough. He was interested in Norman architecture for historical reasons, placing its chief development in the twelfth century when strength was more necessary than beauty. He could, however, appreciate its ponderous simplicity, for, " though far surpassed in beauty " by Gothic buildings, " these huge structures . . . have really a rude kind of majesty resulting from the loftiness of their naves, the gloom of their aisles, and the hugeness of their massive members." [16] Gray did not continue with his remarks on Gothic architecture except in the individual articles on cathedrals, but the aid he gave Bentham and Walpole was in itself enough to gain him a reputation as a critic of the subject well in advance of his time.[17]

[15] Tovey, II, 33; Whibley, II, 573.   [16] Mathias, II, 103.

[17] Kenneth Clark, *The Gothic Revival* (London, 1928), p. 37: " Compared with this [Batty Langley's ideas on Gothic architecture] Gray's theories were scholarly and profound, and his method of research scientific." I think Clark is wrong (p. 35) in suspecting " that Gray's interest in the architecture of the Goths grew out of his study of their literature."

The cathedrals of England were of genuine antiquity, and their varied architecture was tangible evidence of changing English history. They contained, moreover, not only artistic evidence but also actual monuments of royalty and nobility who had helped to make history, " the boast of heraldry, the pomp of power." Great people were buried not in country churchyards but in the aisles and chapels of the cathedrals and churches themselves. The inscriptions on their tombs contained eulogies which did not hide the historical truth underneath. Dates, family relationship, and even the list of achievements furnished the antiquarian with elusive facts that went to make history. Even the crest that marked the man of rank was important evidence, so that the historian had to turn to the study of genealogy and heraldry.

Gray had very definite ideas on the preparation needed for the study of history. The following sketch of his proposed inaugural lecture at Cambridge, found by Mitford among the poet's papers, gives a better idea of the breadth of his conception of history than any summary:

Preparations and accompanyments.

1 Knowledge of antient History.
3 Geography } Mem. Technica
4 Chronology }
2 Languages
8 Moneys
9 Antiquities
5 Laws. Government
7 Manners
6 Education

Dates to commence from (Mod: Hist:) different in diff^t nations. arbitrary, yet distinguished by some favorable & convenient point of Time.

Sources of Hist:

Original & Contemporary
Public Papers, Treaties, Letters of Princes & Ministers, &c.
Relations of Embass:^rs
Private Correspondence, Memoirs
Chronicles, Monkish Histories.
Character & Condition & opportunity of the Writers Interests, prejudices

& parties, understanding, age, & profession.

Proper distance from the times we live in.

History itself.[18]

From this sketch one understands much of Gray's interest in travel books, with their accounts not only of geography but of government, manners, and education. His own study in law and in ancient history, in languages and in antiquities, fits symmetrically into his scheme for preparation. The sources of history are those he had been studying, whether in printed form or in manuscript.

An additional preparation necessary for research in English history is a knowledge of heraldry, a subject which Gray took up seriously when he was studying cathedrals and their monuments. His articles on heraldry in the Commonplace Book fill some sixty pages immediately following the notes on the architectural trip into the Fen Country in June 1758. He begins with the leading noblemen in 1300 by giving the " Names & Arms of those Barons who subscribed the letter to Pope Boniface asserting the Liberty of the Crown of Scotland with respect to the pretensions, & its dependence on the Kingdom of England," a hundred and four names in all, with copious historical and genealogical notes and a supplement showing when " these Peerages were extinct or devolved to other families." [19] Following this are fifty pages of alphabetical notes on noble families of England as if for a peerage book. Space was left after each letter, and all the notes show constant revision.

Gray was already prepared to do original investigation in heraldry by the time he went to study at the British Museum. Among the books he bought at London in 1760 were three authorities he had already used: Milles's *Catalogue of Honour,* Dugdale's *Baronage of England*, and Guillim's *Display of Heraldrie.* He bought only the first volume of Dugdale,[20] and put in it frequent

---

[18] Mitford MS. III[2], 99 f.

[19] CPB, III, 953–958. Gray describes arms in the heraldic manner but does not draw them in his notes.

[20] Gray's copy is now in the British Museum. According to the sales catalogues, Gray's copies of Milles and Guillim contained "numerous notes." I have not been able to locate either book.

annotations on the nobility after the Norman Conquest, in addition to a long note on the first flyleaf giving " Names & Bearings of several great Persons (many of them Barons by Tenure) omitted by Dugdale." [21] The sources are of three kinds, indicative of the way Gray assembled his materials: (1) printed books, particularly Milles, Camden, Leland, and the *Parliamentary History*; (2) personal observation; [22] and (3) manuscripts in the British Museum. Gray refers specifically to several manuscripts, but the ones he used most often were Matthew Paris's history of England, [23] and the " Banieres d'Angleterre " [24] from the collection of Sir Robert Cotton, and from the Harleian library Robert Glover's collection on heraldry, a beautiful manuscript with numerous seals and arms, some of them in color. [25] From these various sources Gray checked Dugdale and then in his usual manner made his additions in the margins of his personal copy.

In the years 1758–1761 Gray was eagerly studying architecture, heraldry, antiquities, documents, and manuscript papers of all kinds. In short, he went to the firsthand materials for English history and almost turned antiquarian in the process. From the cathedrals with their documents in stone he turned to written records, manuscript memoirs, state papers, and unpublished historical data of all sorts. For these he went, as we have already seen him doing in the study of heraldry, to the best possible source, the manuscript collections in the newly-opened British Museum.

[21] Of thirty-eight nobles (from the reigns of Henry III and Edward I) in the list, thirteen are marked with an asterisk as being "undoubtedly Barons." The volume contains 424 notes in all.

[22] A long note on p. 313 describes in detail the sixteen quarterings in the arms of Dorothy Neville, wife of Thomas Cecil, Earl of Exeter, which Gray had seen, "in a window of the Hall at Stoke-Pogeys-House in Buckinghamshire." On Katherine Swinford's burial in the Cathedral Church of Lincoln (p. 298) he adds, "where her monument still remains." A similar note (p. 174) on a monument in Northamptonshire is dated 1761.

[23] There were two such manuscripts: (1) Chronicon abbreviatum, Cotton Claudius. D. vi, beautifully illuminated, and (2) Historia Anglorum, Cotton Vitellius D. ii.

[24] Cotton Caligula A. xviii.I. Cf. W. H. St. John Hope, *A Grammar of English Heraldry* (New York, 1913), p. 68.

[25] Harl. 827 is in Glover's own hand, but Gray's reference is to the fuller Harl. 245, a transcript (from original manuscripts now in the College of Arms) made by W. Smith in 1600.

II

When Gray began in July 1759 to study in the Museum " with all its manuscripts and rarities by the cart-load," he went at it eagerly, for he had done very little the past year. He spent most of the summer of 1758 waiting for his aunt, Mrs. Jonathan Rogers, to die, making the time pass by reading " French plays & novels, Willis's mitred Abbies, & the History of Norfolk in 3 volumes Folio." [26] Mrs. Rogers died near the end of September, and from then until Christmas he was busy settling her estate and moving his portion of her household goods to London. For three months he suffered severely from the gout, but became more active as warm weather approached. By April 1759 he was reading several works on early English history just off the press and looking at the new Museum, which was then crowded with curious sightseers. [27]

On July 23, 1759, Gray wrote Mason that he had that very day gone into the reading room of the Museum, where there were only four students, the antiquary Stukeley, three professional writers, " and I, who only read to know, if there were anything worth writing." [28] He was greatly attracted by the manuscript treasures which were being shown to the public for the first time. He had the spirit of a pioneer in learning, and it was constantly driving him back to the Museum for the next two years. Except for the summer of 1760, he stayed most of the time in London until June 1761, taking lodgings in Southampton Row in order to be near the Museum. His chief amusement and work for nearly two years was to study in the manuscript collections of the Museum.

Gray's main interest at this time was English history, and his particular line of study at the Museum was in the manuscripts of the famous collections of Sir Robert Cotton and of Robert Harley, first Earl of Oxford. The Cottonian Library had been catalogued in 1734 by its keeper, David Casley.[29] One of the first

[26] Tovey, II, 48; Whibley, II, 585.
[27] Tovey, II, 83 f.; Whibley, II, 620. The books were William Murdin's collection of Elizabethan documents, Hume's history of the Tudors, and Robertson's history of Mary Stuart and her son.
[28] Tovey, II, 91; Whibley, II, 630.
[29] Gray refers to this catalogue in his letters to Walpole. See Toynbee, II, 188, 195, 279.

projects of the Museum was to publish a catalogue of the Harleian collection. Gray says they printed a thousand copies and in July 1759 had sold only fourscore. He himself bought a copy for £2 10ˢ, a fabulous sum in comparison with the prices he usually paid for secondhand books. He began enthusiastically copying out historical documents or using the new material to annotate books, as he did in the case of Dugdale's *Baronage*. On September 18 he wrote Wharton that he was living in the Museum and writing " volumes of antiquity," which included the trial of Sir Thomas Wyatt, later printed by Walpole from this very transcript, some documents having to do with Richard III, " and several more odd things unknown to our Historians." The four hours he spends at the Museum are not enough: " when I come home, I have a great heap of the Conway Papers (which is a secret) to read, and make out. In short I am up to the ears." [30]

His interest in history is evident from his letter to Mason a fortnight later: " My only employment & amusement in Town . . . has been the Musæum: but I have been rather historically than poetically given. With a little of your encouragement perhaps I may return to my old Lydgate & Occleve, whose works are there in abundance." [31] Whether Mason encouraged him or not, no evidence of his study of poetry at this time is to be found in his letters or notes. Ossian the next year inspired him to a poetic enthusiasm, but the history of English poetry, " my old Lydgate " and the others, had already proved top-heavy for Gray's meticulous methods. He carried poetics along with other abandoned projects into the later years of life. Among the books he bought in London, 1759–1760, Hickes's *Thesaurus* (in three folio volumes that included Wanley's Catalogue) proudly heads the list at two pounds; he also bought Samuel Daniel's poetical works and several black-letter books, including Speght's Chaucer and Stephen Hawes's *Pastime of Pleasure*. But the history items outnumber the poetry by more than ten to one. Whatever study of early English poetry Gray did after 1757 was in the way of temporary diversion.

[30] Tovey, II, 102; Whibley, II, 642.
[31] Tovey, II, 109; Whibley, II, 646.

He was naturally curious about poetical manuscripts in the Museum, but historical papers were the chief game.

In January 1760 he writes Wharton again: "The Musæum goes on as usual: I have got the Earl of Huntingdon & Sr Geo: Bowes's letters to Cecil about the Rebellion in the North." [32] He does not often bother to mention his work in his letters except where the correspondent might be particularly interested, as Wharton would be in the rebellion centering in his own region. Only his concern over the possible loss of the valuable Conway Papers gives us an inkling of the fact that he had studied them for nearly a year and in returning them to Walpole had divided them into two packets, one " Papers of Queen Elizabeth, or earlier," the other a larger bundle, " Papers of King James and Charles the First." [33]

An interesting confirmation of Gray's study of English history at this particular time comes from the gossiping pen of his antiquary-friend, the Reverend William Cole, which was easily set in motion, as the numerous volumes of his papers in the British Museum testify. Transcribing two epitaphs of Gray's relatives is excuse enough for a long comment on " my ingenious and learned Friend, Mr Thomas Gray." After a long note on Gray's life, Cole continues:

After what I have said of Mr. Gray in respect to the beauty and judicious elegance of his poetical compositions, it will hardly be believed that he has condescended to look into the studies of antiquities: yet dining with him at his chambers in Pembroke Hall, the last time I was at Cambridge, viz. one day the beginning of this very month of Dec. 1761, he told me that he was deeply versed in Dugdale, Hearne, Spelman, and others of that class; and that he took as much delight in that study as ever he did in any other: indeed I myself saw many Specimens of his industry in his collections from various MSS. in the British Museum, near which he took lodgings for the 2 last years, merely on Account of being within reach of consulting them: his Collections related chiefly to English history, little known, or falsified by our Historians, and some Pedigrees.[34]

[32] Tovey, II, 126; Whibley, II, 661.
[33] Tovey, II, 149 f.; Whibley, II, 683.
[34] Cole MSS., XXXII (Brit. Mus. Add. 5833), 12. First published in part by Mitford, *Poems* (1814), p. ci.

Gray took his study of history seriously, and he delved into the Harleian and Cottonian manuscripts with the same enthusiasm that he prepared the elaborate chronological tables of Greek history or the long articles on Oriental history in his Commonplace Book. Nearly everything he undertook turned eventually toward history, for he had a broad conception of the subject that embraced the greater part of human activity. He spent his four hours a day with manuscripts, but his mind was ranging even then into many fields. The list he kept of the books bought in London the first year he was there gives a good impression of his casual reading. Besides the works on poetry and heraldry already mentioned, most of the books he bought were along some line of history: biography, memoirs, antiquities, travel, early histories of England, pamphlets, and historical works on European countries, particularly France.[35] History dominates; but early poetry hangs on, and natural history appears. At this time Gray bought the tenth edition of Linnaeus' *Systema Naturae* (1758-1759) for fifteen shillings — a significant portent, for Linnaeus and the world of nature soon became and remained his chief study.

Gray studied diligently in London for nearly two years and widened his knowledge of English history considerably. With some patience and more hard work he could have written a new history of his own country that would have been scholarly, if inertia had not again prevented him. In his enthusiasm he made transcripts of many documents which he filed away or gave to more ambitious friends. Walpole wisely used the results of Gray's researches in his own historical works,[36] although he usually preferred the fervor of his own rapid composing to the cold exactness of Gray's critical information. Perhaps the two would have made a good combination at historical writing, but Walpole, though he

[35] See the complete list with prices paid, p. 157. In French history he advises (Tovey, III, 299 f.) the reading in order of Villehardouin, Joinville, Froissart, Monstrelet, and Philip de Comines, excellent firsthand accounts from the late twelfth to the sixteenth century.

[36] Walpole later printed one of Gray's transcripts, that on the trial of Sir Thomas Wyatt, in *Miscellaneous Antiquities* (Strawberry Hill Press, 1772), pp. 21-54. Cf. Toynbee, II, 195.

incorporated Gray's notes into the *Anecdotes on Painting* (1762–1764) [37] and in at least one instance in the *Historic Doubts on Richard the Third* (1768),[38] felt that critical additions to his work really cramped his style considerably.[39] Gray was nevertheless interested in his friend's historical works and did his best to see that they were accurate. His critical letters to Walpole, both before and after publication, show the exact knowledge of English history which enables him to question all previous work on the subject.

Gray presumably wrote very few articles in his Commonplace Book after 1759, so that little is left by which to judge his ability as an historian, except in letters and in marginal annotations. Most of his notes on English history and later on natural history are to be found in the books he owned. We have seen an excellent example of his method in the field of heraldry. The same scholarly method is evident in the marginal corrections to his copies of Gilbert Burnet's *History of His Own Time* and the Earl of Clarendon's *History of the Rebellion,* both now in the Bodleian Library. In dealing with so recent a period, however, Gray is dependent mainly on printed sources. He goes nevertheless to the records themselves, citing exact references in almost every instance from the volumes of the *Parliamentary History.* He annotated the *State Papers* of Roger Boyle, Earl of Orrery, from the same period, frequently identifying the persons mentioned and giving full genealogical notices of them. His knowledge of the period of the Tudors, which must have been profound, is shown only in his letters.

Another chapter in Gray's life ends with the same sad commentary. He was interested in history throughout his life. Nearly

[37] See Gray's letter to Walpole, September 2, 1760, in Toynbee, II, 186–206; Whibley, II, 696–703.

[38] Gray to Walpole, December 24, 1767, in Toynbee, II, 262 f.; Whibley, III, 985.

[39] Walpole to Gray, February 18, 1768: "and you may perceive that the worst part of Richard, in point of ease and style, is what relates to the papers you gave me on Jane Shore, because it was tacked on so long afterwards, and when my impetus was chilled" (Toynbee, II, 271).

everything he studied took an historical turn. The philosopher in him saw history as the progress of human thought and endeavor, embracing the arts and manners as well as the government of a people. The scholar in him sought the minutiae that go together to make the true picture that is history. He was learned in many branches of the subject: in geography, in the customs and governments of widely separated civilizations — ancient Greek and medieval Tatar and modern European — and in the architecture, heraldry, and chronicles of his own people. The manuscript treasures made available in the British Museum tempted him to two years of almost continuous study in early English history. His enthusiasm added rich stores of untouched source-material to his own preparation in the study of English chronology and antiquities. As usual, however, his enthusiasm waned with the achievement, and the rich stores remained in his mind, to be tapped occasionally in his marginalia or in his criticisms of Walpole's work. He continued to collect material on architecture and heraldry as he went on his summer excursions through the countryside, but the dominant interest in these expeditions was natural history.[40] He became in 1768 professor of modern history at Cambridge and for three years until he died graced the position with dignity, although his rapidly failing health did not allow him to carry out his ambitious projects to reform the professorship. One of his proposals, now in the British Museum, provides among other things for the professor to reside at least half of every term in the university, to give at least one public lecture, as well as regular private lectures, in modern history, and to direct students in their reading.[41] The spirit was willing but the flesh was too weak. He

[40] The Murray notebooks show only the following antiquarian notes of any consequence: July 1761, Wingfield church and castle in Suffolk; October 1764, Salisbury (elaborate five-page description of the cathedral) and Stonehenge; 1765, churches near Durham and Arbroath Abbey in Scotland (very few notes); and June 1766, Barston and Hythe churches in Kent.

[41] P. Toynbee, in *Times Literary Supplement*, March 4, 1926, p. 163. Whibley, App. S, sums up Gray's entire relations with the professorship, and shows that Gray's proposal came as the result of a memorandum to the king from the Oxford heads of houses. On the history of the professorship, see D. A. Winstanley, *Unreformed Cambridge* (Cambridge University Press, 1935), pp. 154–162.

left us the outline of his proposed inaugural lecture as a reminder of his desire to serve and of his ability to do his task well. He finally decided that he would have to resign the professorship because he was too sick to give lectures, but death relieved him of that necessity.

CHAPTER VII

THE DISCIPLE OF LINNAEUS

I

GRAY devoted the later years of his life largely to natural history, but his interest in the subject began early. When he went to Eton he found in his uncle, Robert Antrobus, an enthusiastic student of science who taught him the rudiments of natural history and tried to steer him into the medical profession. At any rate, when he died before Gray left Eton, Antrobus instructed his brother to give his nephew from his library all the books " relating to the practice of physick " if he should follow that profession. The boy probably chose instead the items concerning natural history, for among the books he kept in his library was the edition of Albin's *Natural History of English Insects,* with its colored plates of butterflies in their various states of metamorphosis, a rare and expensive book to which Robert Antrobus was one of the original subscribers.

The study of natural history made phenomenal progress in the eighteenth century. The philosophy of Shaftesbury, expressed in poetic terms by Thomson's *Seasons,* sought in nature an answer to the riddle of the universe and a panacea for the evils of civilization. This romantic search led to a more or less scientific study of the riches of nature on the part of many Englishmen. The serious aspect of enthusiasm for nature turned more and more toward research into natural history, especially from 1735, when the Swedish scientist Karl von Linné, better known as Linnaeus, first proposed his classification of the natural world in the *Systema naturae.* Gray followed these changes, along with his other interests, for many years. He studied the latest scientific treatises on the one hand, and on the other observed nature, keeping calendars in which he noted the weather, the crops, the flight of birds, and the flowering of trees.

Although he later became a virtuoso in the field, Gray came to the study of natural history because of his aesthetic and philosophical interests. He loved the grandeur of Alpine scenery and found in it a revelation of the greatness of God. He knew also the simpler beauty of trees and flowers. Having no garden of his own except the hyacinths and jonquils in his window, he went to the " physick gardens " at Chelsea and Cambridge or took in the beauty of plants in meadow and moor. He kept track of the birds as they first began to sing around Cambridge, learning their melodies as well as their measurements. When he wanted a pictorial record of their characteristics, he copied, with the meticulous accuracy of a quill pen, the heads of several birds from the plates of Brisson's *Ornithologie*. He found a beauty in the smaller creatures, in butterflies, moths, and dragonflies, even in beetles and gnats. When he wrote the *Ode on the Spring* for West in 1742, he filled three of the five stanzas with moralizing on the " insect youth," whether floating on the wing, skimming on the current, or showing " their gaily-gilded trim Quick-glancing to the sun." He loved nature and knew the solace of its quiet beauty as well as the enthusiasm of its grandeur. He gave Wordsworth a text, when he depicted the joy of the convalescent in his *Vicissitude* ode:

> The meanest floweret of the vale,
> The simplest note that swells the gale,
> The common Sun, the air, the skies,
> To him are opening Paradise.

From his aesthetic interest in nature Gray went gradually deeper into scientific study. He found in Thomas Wharton, his physician-friend of Old Park near Durham, an interested amateur of natural history. In his letters to Wharton he describes his progress in the field and occasionally exchanges observations on nature. In the summer of 1750 he writes Wharton that he has already read the first three volumes of Buffon's natural history.[1] The first of his " Georgicks in prose " occurs in a letter to Wharton, describing the face of the country as he journeys in September 1753 from Durham to Stoke. South of York he found " the Country extremely beautiful, broke into fine hills cover'd with noble

[1] Tovey, I, 206 f.; Whibley, I, 328.

woods," in which the colors of autumn were scarcely beginning to show. A flock of geese in full song, the fields in Yorkshire "plough'd up, or cover'd with Turneps," the meadows in Northamptonshire brown from drought, the marvelous grapes at Cambridge, the lime trees in London which put out fresh green shoots after the old leaves were ruined by smoke, the progress of harvest at Stoke — all this and much more he described for Wharton, having nothing better, he adds, to send him.[2]

Not until 1759, however, did the prose georgics really get under way. Wharton had gone to live permanently in the north country, leaving behind him a thermometer which Gray was to observe at specified intervals for comparison with temperatures at Old Park. Gray sent his first report in July, although the broiling weather and a gouty foot kept him indoors. He described from hearsay the progress of crops and flowers, but he could see from his windows the wheelbarrows of cherry hucksters and the jessamine on a near-by garden wall, while his nosegays from the market in Covent Garden consisted of "nothing but Scarlet Martagons, Everlasting-Peas, Double-Stocks, Pinks, and flowering Marjoram." Obviously he had no firsthand calendar, so he sent instead his account of a cold, rainy July in 1754 when he had kept detailed memoranda of wind, weather, and the growth of plants from March to September.[3]

The calendars of nature became from that time a regular part of Gray's letters to Wharton. Where he cannot observe, he inquires, until his pocket diaries are filled with notes on weather and plant life. In January 1761 the casual observations take on a serious cast when Gray sends Wharton a Swedish and English calendar for 1755, bidding him to observe "how the Spring advances in the North, & whether Old-Park most resembles Upsal, or Stratton."[4] The Swedish calendar was by a student of Linnaeus, the English by Benjamin Stillingfleet, the botanist-philosopher,

[2] Whibley, I, 385 ff.

[3] Tovey, II, 85 ff.; Whibley, II, 624 ff. The manuscript journal for 1754, fifteen and a half pages small quarto, was sold at Hodgson's, December 15, 1916. Besides nature observations it contains remarks on health.

[4] Tovey, II, 199 ff.; Whibley, II, 725 ff.

who had been directing the movements of Gray's thermometer for some nine months past.[5] To these Gray added a third calendar from his own observations in 1755, incomplete but extending far enough to show that on December 2 the scarlet geranium and several kinds of wallflower were still in blossom.

Gray kept up his observations of nature the rest of his life, whether at Cambridge in winter or on some visit or excursion in summer. He wrote them in his pocket diaries and from 1767 in the "Naturalist's Journal," a special book for the purpose prepared by Benjamin White. From 1765 his expeditions presented such a wealth of scientific booty that he carried with him small notebooks in which he hurriedly jotted down on the spot descriptions of his specimens. At Cambridge he was always on the alert for something new in nature, whether out of doors or in the microscopic life from his own cultures. Much of Gray's activity during the last ten years of his life might be written from his notes on natural history, nearly all of which found their way into the orderly annotations in his copy of Linnaeus' *Systema naturae,* at first on the margins in his usual manner, later on blank leaves bound in for the purpose.

II

The tenth edition of Linnaeus was published in 1758–1759, and Gray bought his copy new soon after he came to London in 1759.[6] Almost immediately he began to annotate its margins with the English names of animals and plants, adding to them the equivalents in several foreign languages, particularly French, Italian, Swedish, German, Latin, and Greek. Other marginalia, nearly all in English, describe the size or appearance of some particular species, whether from observation or reading it is difficult to say. Gray's interest in food is shown in numerous marginalia

---

[5] Tovey, II, 139; Whibley, II, 672. Gray to Wharton, April 22, 1760: "mind, from this day the Therm:r goes to its old place below in the yard, & so pray let its Sister do. Mr Stillingfleet (with whom I am grown acquainted) has convinced me, it ought to do so."

[6] It appears in Gray's list (1760) at fifteen shillings. The note on the "Inkfish" in Gray's letter to Wharton, September 18, 1759 (Tovey, II, 105), is almost identical with the marginal notes on *Sepia loligo* in Gray's Linnaeus, p. 659.

concerning the edibility of certain animals, the quality and appearance of their flesh, and the usual methods of cooking them. Such annotations are not profound. They show not the scientist but the person of many interests who is often an enthusiastic observer of nature. They take their place beside Gray's calendars of wind and weather, of birds and flowers, only a step beyond the account of his window garden of hyacinths and jonquils. They furnish amusing diversion from early English poetry and Tudor manuscripts, but are not themselves the stuff of scholarship.

In 1761 Gray went back to Cambridge after two years among the manuscripts in the British Museum. Having gone as far as he cared into the secrets of English history, he turned to something new, as was his custom. What had been his diversion gradually became a serious study, so he interleaved his copy of Linnaeus' *Systema* throughout in order to have room for notes that were crowded off the printed page. Linnaeus himself was constantly revising his own ideas and classifications, notably in *Fauna Suecica* (1761), *Species plantarum* (1762–1763), and the twelfth edition of *Systema naturae* (1766–1768). Gray kept up with these and other changes, altering his tenth edition accordingly. As he did so he added a great deal from the writings of other scientists, as well as gradually more and more of his own material.

Gray was unquestionably stimulated by the interest Englishmen of his own day were showing in natural history, especially in the study of botany. In fact, England had already contributed much to this branch of science. Since the sixteenth century ardent botanists had been at work in England, observing plant life and classifying their numerous specimens in their own ways. Before the founding of the Royal Society men like John Goodyer had made considerable progress in the knowledge of botany.[7] During the last half of the seventeenth century John Ray advanced the knowledge of all branches of natural history to such an extent that he made a permanent contribution to pre-Linnaean classification.[8]

---

[7] R. T. Gunther, *Early British Botanists and Their Gardens* (Oxford, 1922).

[8] See Erik Nordenskiöld, *The History of Biology* (New York, 1928), trans. by L. B. Eyre, pp. 199–202, and L. C. Miall, *The Early Naturalists* (London, 1912), pp. 99–130.

He and his wealthy patron, Francis Willughby, had brought the study of birds and fishes to a high point; while Martin Lister had contributed notably in the field of shells and insects. Sir Hans Sloane's herbarium is best known as the collection which caused the founding of the British Museum, but it also increased the knowledge of botany in England. Sloane was the chief factor as well in the development of the Physick Garden in Chelsea, where during most of Gray's lifetime Philip Miller was in charge, adding to his knowledge of plants the vast amount of material that was to go into the successive editions of his *Gardening Dictionary*. Linnaeus visited him there in 1736 and borrowed from him a number of specimens. Gray knew and constantly read the dictionary, which Linnaeus praised as a lexicon not for gardeners but for botanists.

In London Gray was thrown with naturalists. Benjamin Stillingfleet, more famous for blue stockings than for botany,[9] became his guide in the new field. William Hudson, who in 1757–1758 studied in Sloane's herbarium while sub-librarian at the British Museum, was preparing the famous *Flora Anglica* with the encouragement and advice of Stillingfleet. Very likely, therefore, Gray knew Hudson, for according to Mason the *Flora Anglica*, published in 1762, was one of the most fully annotated of the books in Gray's library. Many of the specimens in Gray's collection of insects were caught around London, some of them in Chelsea, where he may have met the famous Miller.

Natural history had for some time past been a thriving subject at Cambridge, the scene of most of Gray's research in that field. John Ray was a Cambridge man, and his first scientific work was a catalogue of the plants around Cambridge (1660). About 1755 Israel Lyons, son of the Cambridge Jew who was both silversmith and teacher of Hebrew, decided that he could learn more by himself than in the university and started collecting materials for a " Flora Cantabrigiensis." In 1763 he published his work, bringing Ray's catalogue up to date and acquiring such a reputation as a

[9] His most notable contribution to science was his fervent plea for the recognition of Linnaeus in England, in *Miscellaneous Tracts Relating to Natural History* (London, 1759).

botanist that in 1764 he was invited by Joseph Banks to give lectures on the subject at Oxford. Meanwhile a botanic garden was established at Cambridge on the site of the old Austin Friary, very near Gray's rooms at Pembroke. In 1762 Charles Miller, second son of the Chelsea gardener, was made its first curator; he supervised the garden and taught botany until 1770, when he went to Sumatra. In 1762 Thomas Martyn became professor of botany, and the next year gave the university its first course of lectures on the Linnaean system. Gray knew all these young men and probably went with them often on expeditions around Cambridge. Perhaps he gave them the botanical specimens he collected on his tours, in return for insects to add to his own collection. At any rate many of his specimens came from them,[10] whereas numerous others were caught, probably by Gray himself, in the Cambridge garden.

Michael Tyson, fellow of Benet's from 1767 and often a companion of Gray during the last years of his life, was an accomplished naturalist as well as antiquarian. He was a good friend of Sir John Cullum, whom he considered the best botanist in England, and was acquainted through his friend Richard Gough with the early work of Thomas Pennant.[11] He was much interested in all the manuscripts Gray left, but he wanted most of all to see the interleaved Linnaeus "which has been the employment of his latter years." Mason let him see it, and he spent every leisure moment making extracts from its "truly valuable" notes.[12]

George Ashby, fellow and later master of St. John's, was before his death an excellent naturalist but seemed at first to depend somewhat on Gray. His Linnaean notebook, erroneously attributed by Mitford to Gray, mentions specimens seen at Gray's chambers in Pembroke. Numerous entries, all in red ink, are identical with certain marginalia in Gray's Linnaeus before it was interleaved,

[10] Gray's Linnaeus, p. 364, has this note on *Coccinella 2-punctata*: "N⁰ 8 (*C. 7-punctata*) dimidio minor: cum illâ tamen in coitu junctam vidit D: Lyons, & cum C: 6-pustulata D: Miller." Other references to specimens of Miller, pp. 459, 462, 472, et al.

[11] See the correspondence of Tyson and Gough in John Nichols, *Literary Anecdotes of the Eighteenth Century* (London, 1814), VIII, 567 ff.

[12] Nichols, VIII, 597, 604. According to Cole (*ibid.*, p. 209), Tyson wrote the account of Gray's natural history in Mason's life.

which seems to show that Ashby borrowed Gray's notes and copied out many of them for his own use, at the same time scrupulously acknowledging the adopted items by writing them in red ink.[13]

After 1760 Gray's annotations in his copy of Linnaeus grew rapidly, until the margins of the more popular sections were filled and flowed into the blank leaves. This book, bound now in three thick volumes, became the repository of nearly all Gray's discoveries in the field of natural history. His best friends knew of the treasure and said he had it by him constantly in his later years. In it he put whatever he found in the works of other scientists that would help him in his study or would bring the whole subject up to date. Linnaeus had brought together most of the knowledge available and had whipped it roughly into his new system of classification. The *Systema naturae* is a general catalogue of all animal and plant life, backed with references in each instance to the sources of information. Linnaeus himself recognized, however, that his work was only the beginning, for each new book or edition from his pen contained numerous revisions. When Gray became seriously interested in natural history, he took the latest edition of Linnaeus' *Systema* as the basis of his study and added to that his own discoveries, whether from books or from life.

III

The story of Gray's interest in natural history has already been told from the point of view of the finished product in his interleaved Linnaeus.[14] The study and experiments which made him

[13] This notebook, now in the Harvard Library, has hitherto been designated as Gray's rough notes for the interleaved Linnaeus. The handwriting is not Gray's and is in the earlier entries the same as that in a few notes which are signed " G.A." The manuscript is dated " 28 July 1759." Another date on the flyleaf, " 21 Jany 1762. Pembroke," has led many to ascribe it to Gray, but the entry is in red ink, probably to indicate that on that day Ashby saw and used Gray's notes at Pembroke. At any rate, the notebook is not Gray's and is probably all Ashby's, except for a few notes added by Mitford. The description of a hornet (p. 605) pursuing the author for two or three miles, though he galloped, is enough to assure me that it is not Gray's. The description (p. 610) of a white ant, seen " 2 March 1770 at Mr. Gray's," moreover, is signed " G.A."

[14] C. E. Norton, *The Poet Gray as a Naturalist* (Boston, 1903).

an excellent naturalist and an authority on insects may best be seen, however, in his rough notes. The story of evenings of work with a microscope by candlelight in his chambers, of specimens caught in the fields around Cambridge, of long walks along the Kentish coast, of watching marine life on the sands at Hartlepool, of attempts to classify roughly the creatures at Old Park — all this and more may be read between the lines of random notes. Most of the notes that finally went into the Linnaeus are scientific, purged of the crudities that picture the man.

Since Gray spent every winter, spring, and autumn after 1761 in Cambridge, he must have done much of his work there, not only in refining the rough notes from his summer expeditions but also in reading and in carrying on original research. Obviously he did most of his reading in the winter. He owned a number of books on natural history but depended on libraries for the more expensive items with their elaborate engravings. He read all the chief authorities and referred to them constantly in his notes — Buffon on the larger animals, Brisson on birds, Baker, Réaumur, Geoffroi, and Scopoli on insects, to mention only a few. For his own convenience he often copied in his notes meticulous drawings from some of the books he studied, adding to them from time to time cruder sketches of his own specimens. He acknowledged the source of his drawing of insects (mostly from Réaumur and Linnaeus' *Amoenitates academicae*) and shells (from Rumphius and Lister). He made elaborate drawings of the heads of birds, practically all from Brisson but without reference to the source. Most of them were not meant to illustrate species but, as in the original work, merely to show the characteristics of the different genera of birds.[15]

Gray studied natural history as much as possible in books, especially where collecting specimens would be cumbersome, as with most of the vertebrates, or impossible, as with the fauna and

[15] The dove, pheasant, owl, falcon, starling, bullfinch, gull, nuthatch, hoopoe, and roller, most of them birds well known to Gray, were taken from three plates (5, 6, 7) in M. J. Brisson, *Ornithologie* (1760), vol I. See facsimiles of Gray's drawings in Norton, where one may note that the drawings were done before the lists of birds were inserted.

flora of foreign countries. Exotic specimens were familiar to him in his much-loved travel books, in many of which he proceeded to identify animals and plants with their Linnaean classification. He knew birds in actual life, yet he preferred to note their habits rather than the minute details of their physical differences. He knew the times of their first singing, but his observation was in the spirit with which he noted the flowering of the hyacinths and narcissus in his window. The same condition might have applied to his study of fishes, if vacations spent near the sea had not stirred his curiosity to find out more about English marine life. Insects were small enough to be kept in his rooms, however, and plentiful enough to occupy his time, in winter or summer, indoors or out. Whatever the reasons, Gray's notes and reputation make it plain that his forte lay in the knowledge of insects.

A few of Gray's notes on his indoor experiments have survived, and from them one may get a picture of his attempts to follow the life cycles of some of the smaller creatures.[16] The first descriptions are of twelve insects in their larval form, which he kept alive in a cup of water until they changed into gnats or flies and flew away. He compares one specimen with another and tries to identify them, watching them as they swim with wriggling motion slowly on the bottom of the vessel. He can barely see what Linnaeus calls *Monoculus pulex*[17] (perhaps the common Daphnia) with the naked eye, but under a magnifying glass the reddish speck " appears greenish, & very transparent." One of the " animals " commonly lay still on the surface of the water, until " out of it came a hair-colour'd 2-winged Tipula, less than a gnat." The three stages of a mosquito which he identified in Linnaeus as *Culex pipiens* interested him very much. The second stage he described as " a large Nymph of a pale green colour," through whose integument " are plainly seen the body, legs, & large reticulated eyes of the future fly." It would lie on the top of the water until dis-

[16] MS. now in Harvard Museum of Comparative Zoölogy. Register V.3.

[17] All the classifications I have used are Gray's own terms, taken usually from the tenth edition of Linnaeus. Scientists who are interested in the history of classification will, of course, be aware of the numerous changes from 1758 to the present day. I am indebted to my colleague, Dr. James C. Gray, for aid in identifying the specimens described in this section.

turbed, when it wriggled away with great swiftness. Gray must have watched his larvae closely, for he tells how two specimens of a species changed into gnats " about 8 o'clock in the morning, & again about midnight." He was enjoying himself, watching wriggling larvae turn to gnats, describing the future antennae in the transparent shell as resembling " the forelegs of Sea-Horses, as the Painters represent them," or comparing the fine white fila-ments of *Tipula plumosa* to " the hair of a shock-dog." The results of these experiments go nevertheless into the finished notes, where his drawings of his own specimens serve as illustrations of Lin-naeus.[18] Metamorphosis interested Gray very much, as the numer-ous notes on pupae and larvae in many parts of his Linnaeus will testify.

Gray also used a microscope and with it studied by candlelight some of the small animals " in a little drop of slimy water, wch had had flowers in it for a fortnight." This new world of beings fascinated him, although he admitted he could not tell much about them. The " Mill-Animal, as described by Baker," probably one of the *Roterifera,* was too small: " I could never distinguish the rotation of its mills with the 2^d magnifier." He watched the " snap-per," perhaps one of the *Copepoda,* swimming madly around in every direction after its prey, sometimes moving " by short inter-vals like the moment-hand of a clock." In the drop are also many " beetles," the prey of the rest, of which he thinks " there may be many species, for some appear even in the Microscope not much larger than Mites to the naked eye."

Clearly, he was interested in this new world, but presumably he got no farther in its discovery than had van Leeuwenhoek a half-century before. He used the lens, or ordinary magnifying glass, often and with good effect. He studied aquatic life and the details of land insects with his lens and often made drawings of the enlarged head, leg, or wing.

By means of such gradual accumulation of details Gray learned what was necessary to fill out the knowledge of English insects. The story of his collecting specimens is too long to tell here. In

[18] See Gray's Linnaeus, pp. 585, 602.

his own windows, in the botanic garden, in the Hogmagog hills or on Feversham Moor near Cambridge, at Newmarket or Gamlingay, and in the neighboring counties of Suffolk and Bedford, he found insects. Having classified them roughly on the spot, he took them home and wrote his descriptions, modeling his style on the terse Latin of Linnaeus. The surroundings of London added specimens to his collection — Hyde Park, Chelsea, and even the rotting wood of Covent Garden Theater. His summer visits with friends all over the island — with Lord Strathmore in Scotland in 1765, with Billy Robinson in Kent in 1766, and with the Wharton family at Old Park at fairly frequent intervals — brought him new species as well as scenery.

He was seldom interested unless his specimen differed from the usual descriptions. He had a special mark ⊕ to designate the ones he described most fully, presumably therefore the ones he kept in his own collection. In each instance he gave the place and time the specimen was caught. To take a few of his beetles as examples, he caught two kinds in Kent as they flew in the June twilights; others he dug out of dung at Chelsea. He noted that the largest of English beetles (*Scarabeus cervus*) makes a great noise as it flies in the evening, like the droning flight of the beetle in the *Elegy*. He found the eggs of *Silpha vespillo* (a scavenger beetle) in the cadaver of a *Talpa* (the European mole) at Cambridge and noted that they produced larvae after fourteen days. Ugly and beautiful alike interested him: the leaf-beetle *Chrysomela graminis,* a most beautiful creature gleaming with gold, and the foul-smelling ground beetle *Carabus violaceus,* caught running in a garden path one August evening.

He describes the *Cicada sanguinolenta,* caught near London, as one of the most beautiful of all his specimens, with its reddish wings, shining head, black scutellum, and white antennae. With butterflies and moths he is more interested in metamorphosis, but finds the specimens beautiful. The changeable color in the dragonfly called " Peacock's Neck " (*Libellula virgo*) strikes him as being very lovely, but *Cimex bicolor,* which he found among the nettles in April, stinks terribly. The habits of insects interest him, the copulation of dragonflies in mid-air and of bees or flying ants near the ground, the shedding of the water scorpion's (*Nepa cinerea*) coat, the queer antics of great numbers of small sand hoppers (*Cancer cicada*). Hundreds of other personal notes may be found in the descriptions of thousands of specimens, but the industry and thoroughness with which he went about the study of natural history may be seen from these examples.[19]

Gray collected specimens wherever he went, especially when he visited Thomas Wharton at Old Park in 1762, 1765, 1767, and 1769. He and Wharton had been exchanging calendars of nature since 1761. The Wharton family caught insects for him, not only around the house but in the field and by the sea. Hartlepool was not far away, and Gray often went there during his visits at Old Park.[20] From Old Park he went also in 1765 to Scotland, in 1767 and 1769 to the Lake District in Cumberland, and he often stopped off at Aston in Yorkshire to see William Mason. In addition to these trips to the north Gray went to Southampton in 1764, and to Billy Robinson's at Denton in Kent in 1766 and 1768.

Each of these summer expeditions gave him renewed health and the pleasures of companionship that he found only in the society of intimate friends, and they also invariably produced rich spoils in natural history. England is a small country, yet each region has its own fauna and flora. The fact that names for the same species often varied with each new dialect made it necessary to study a specimen very carefully to determine its classification. The complete history of English insects or birds or fishes had not been written in 1760, and only through the gradual accumulation of such minute data as Gray collected was it possible for such a history to be compiled. Gray made lists of animals found in Great Britain, followed by comparison with the fauna of Sweden as shown in the works of Linnaeus. The idea of knowing thoroughly what part of the world of living things could be found in his own

---

[19] One should by all means consult Norton's facsimiles and selections, realizing, of course, that even he could only give a small part of the entire manuscript material.

[20] Gray's rough notes on these expeditions are now in the possession of Sir John Murray. See description, p. 176.

country interested him. He knew Cambridge animals and plants well, and was fairly well acquainted with those in the vicinity of London. By his contact with Wharton he compared the south with the north, and added, on his visit to Glamis Castle, what was distinctive of the Scottish highlands. The short stay at Southampton in 1764 showed him the possibilities of comparison, which he began to realize on his visits in Kent in 1766 and 1768.

The extensive tour in the summer of 1765 was the first to add much to Gray's natural-history collection. On June 13, just a week after he had written Wharton from Aston that he was beginning to walk a little after an attack of gout, he was collecting plants in the lane at Old Park, and he kept this up until he had more than a hundred species from moors, hedges, meadows, " the wood by the were," ditches, and rills. He followed these with numerous insects from the same places. On this trip, and again in 1767 and 1769, Old Park furnished many specimens. The dried plants collected earlier in the year by the Wharton family have music in their names: harebell, pilewort, fleabane, dog's mercury, barren strawberry, sea pimpernel, and many others. The family and he collected plants and insects not only around Old Park but at Durham, in neighboring villages, and even as far away as Gibside, the seat of Lord Strathmore near Newcastle.

A week after his first botanical expedition at Old Park he was at Hartlepool, and again on July 15, each time observing the kinds of fish caught around there, as well as the numerous insects in the water, in the fissures of the rocks, or on the sands. He talks to the fishermen, examines the catch, and notes the price in the market. He watches the great hordes of sand hoppers in the evenings, leaping like fleas and dancing on the sand, at midday hiding in holes or swimming in the water. He sees *Hydra carduus* give birth to young which immediately spreads its tentacles like its mother, and watches a hermit crab (*Cancer Diogenes*) of its own accord emerge from its shell with numerous eggs on the back of its tail. He even asks about the birds that come there in autumn or winter, and writes their picturesque names in his notebook with a short description of the less familiar species.[21]

In August 1765 Gray was in Scotland at Glamis Castle, where he observed many new plants, as well as some birds and insects. Lord Strathmore's trees interested him very much, especially the large ones around the house: a beech sixteen feet around, a pine twelve, an oak and an ash more than nine, and a maple six. Best of all on this trip were the species not common farther south, such as heather, moorfowl, or the young pelican brought alive from Dundee.

The visits to Kent in 1766 and 1768 were equally productive of specimens peculiar to the southern coast. His first notations at Denton, plants on one page and "animals" (mostly insects) on the opposite, are dated May 20, 1766. On June 5 he was at Margate, whence he went along the coast at Ramsgate, Sandwich, Deal, Dover, Folkestone, and Hythe, meeting on his way with "creeping things innumerable" and stopping for a look at Hythe Church, with "a huge pile of human skulls & bones very clean" in its vault. He was at most of these places again in June 1768, just before he went to London to receive his professorship from the king. On this second trip he went also, on June 19, to Canterbury, to Shooter's Hill and Gillingham. The specimens of plants, fishes, and land and water insects collected on these two pleasant journeys to Kent enriched immensely the notes in his Linnaeus.

From such expeditions the fauna and flora of England became gradually like an open book to Gray, but he never stopped his search while life lasted. During the winters at Cambridge he not only worked indoors with his books, experiments, and notes, but also went into the market and looked at the game and fish displayed for sale. These creatures he classified and then served as food, describing like an epicure the peculiar taste of each one. Wild geese caught at Cambridge in the winter months went into

---

[21] E.g., "A very small Bird (of variegated plumage, & little beak) arrives with the Woodcock, & said to come on it's back," or "Glead (a blew-gray Hawk, size of a Crow)."

his notes, described even to measurements and taste, the last of them recorded on February 3, 1771, a few months before his death.

Gray collected and recorded the English species, yet in some ways exotic life, especially that of the fertile tropics, interested him more. He bought books of travel and borrowed many from the libraries at Cambridge, enriching all of them alike with marginalia which identified specimens with their Linnaean classifications. Occasionally he saw some of the animals alive in collections or traveling exhibitions. He records two such collections that he saw, one near Charing Cross on July 4, 1766, the other, a smaller one, "at the corner of Pickadilly next the Haymarket, Nov: 1767." Many creatures never seen in Europe were exhibited, and Gray noted them: gaily-colored parrots and other tropical birds, two huge vultures, an eagle, several monkeys, a mongoose, a grunting porcupine, a very beautiful leopard, a beaver, several species of wild cat, a baboon (" penis nudus propendens "), two crocodiles (one so sluggish in front of a fire that he would not open his eyes though the children jumped around, the other agile and trying to bite), besides other live specimens and an accompanying museum of stuffed animals and birds. Occasionally such animals were also to be seen at Cambridge. George Ashby records in his Linnaean notebook having seen a camel there in November 1759 and a Spanish raccoon at Pembroke Hall in January 1762.[22] Gray's humor leaves us in doubt as to what young Foljambe's " Flying Hobgoblin from the E: Indies, & a power of rarities," consisted of, but the " jewel of a pismire " and queen of the white ants he gave Gray [23] is vouched for by Ashby, who saw it in Gray's chambers and called it the Indian wood louse or white ant (*Termes fatale*).[24]

Gray was plainly interested in all sorts of specimens and remained so until his death. This last line of study might well have

[22] Ashby notebook in Harvard Library, pp. 48, 65.

[23] Tovey, III, 294.

[24] Ashby notebook, p. 610: " Vidi 2 March 1770 at Mr. Gray's . . . the earth she lived in seem'd as if baked clay, & of a ferrugineous color." Gray had notes on this species in his Linnaeus, but no mention of his own specimen. Had he abandoned the tenth edition by this time and started using the twelfth edition? A sale catalogue of Ashby's books, laid in his Linnaean notebook, lists an interleaved twelfth edition of Linnaeus (1766-68) which formerly belonged to Gray.

continued to a point at which he would practically have been compelled to give some of his knowledge to the world. Death intervened on July 31, 1771, and Gray's unpublished notebooks went to Mason, along with the interleaved Linnaeus at which he had so zealously worked. Those who knew Gray's work as a naturalist spoke of him with praise, although the history of science has not recorded his years of assiduous research. He was nevertheless helping gradually to increase the knowledge of natural history in England. Since he was perhaps the oldest among the energetic Cambridge naturalists of the 1760's, his influence was widely felt. Around him gathered such young men as Ashby and Tyson, whose work is linked with that of Pennant and other eminent naturalists of the late eighteenth century. Associated with Gray were excellent botanists like Charles Miller and Israel Lyons at Cambridge, and probably William Hudson at London, not to mention his first master in the field, Benjamin Stillingfleet. By no means least were the friends who were probably led to natural history by his example and perhaps even by his teaching — men like Norton Nicholls and Victor de Bonstetten, to say nothing of the whole family of Dr. Thomas Wharton.

As with almost every other study he took up, Gray became a master of his subject. Through reticence and inertia he failed to publish his findings and has therefore remained unrecognized. He was a genuine pioneer in making Linnaeus known in England and in widening the field of British entomology. His chief influence, however, lay in his personal contact with others, especially with the younger men who carried on his work after him.

CHAPTER VIII

SCHOLAR AND POET

THE story of Thomas Gray is drab on the surface but exciting within. It is ever so with reflective natures — with Doctor Johnson, for example, who fortunately had a Boswell to preserve the drama of his many-sided mind. Gray had more learning than Johnson, his poetry was admittedly better, and he had a gift for sharp criticism that often equaled the best quips that Boswell reported. Both men were cursed with disease and inertia. But Johnson had two decided advantages: poverty that commanded him to write for a livelihood, and a personality that made him tower above his fellows. No greater contrast may be found than in these pictures: Johnson in his garret pouring his scholarship into the Dictionary and his criticism into the magazines, and Gray at Cambridge neatly writing erudite articles in his Commonplace Book; or, Johnson the " great bear," huge and slovenly, roaring at the Literary Club, and Gray, small of stature and fastidious in appearance, talking in a high voice to a few close friends.

And Gray had no Boswell. He revealed himself best in his letters: his first biographer wisely quoted many of them, and even now the recent edition of his correspondence is better than any life of him that can be written. Norton Nicholls waited until 1805 to write his reminiscences of Gray; consequently, the little he remembered has not the freshness of Boswell. Walpole was so desirous of preserving his friend's good reputation that he left little of a personal nature concerning him. From Gray's own letters and notebooks, however, we can piece together the picture of an interesting man who had a great mind.

We must not forget that, first and last, Gray was essentially a poet. Under the warming influence of his love for West he composed plentifully, and then on the death of his friend in 1742 he lost the urge. But even with his retirement to scholarly pursuits, his fondness for poetry and beauty never became entirely submerged in erudition. His love of Vergil and other great classical poets led him to the study of Greek civilization and history. His love of travel and the romance of distant lands ended naturally in a thorough knowledge of Oriental history. His interest in poetry, especially in the work of Chaucer, Spenser, Shakespeare, and Milton, found rich pasture in the study of early English poetry and of its roots reaching back into the French, Italian, Welsh, and Scandinavian prosodies. His love of Gothic architecture was a part of the background of his research in English history. His lifelong interest in the beauties of nature led him to a passionate and scientific study of natural history. The poet in him was always alive, even when dimmed by the varied tastes of the eighteenth-century gentleman. Guided by the appeal of beauty, he was willing to dig deeply into a subject until his knowledge assumed scholarly proportions. The very pursuit thus instigated by his poetic nature left him, however, little time or energy for creative work.

More closely linked with scholarship was Gray's literary criticism. He had excellent taste: he went, as he advised Nicholls to do, directly to the best writers, to Vergil and Plato, to Shakespeare, Dante, and Milton. He had the gift of concise and penetrating criticism. Years before Percy's *Reliques* came out, he hit exactly upon the nature of the popular ballad: " it begins in the fifth Act of the Play; you may read it two-thirds through without guessing, what it is about; & yet when you come to the end, it is impossible not to understand the whole story." [1] He praised the realistic characters of Fielding's *Joseph Andrews* when that novel first appeared. He sensed that the difficulty of Aristotle's *Poetics* lay in the dry conciseness (" it tasts for all the World like chop'd Hay ") that was the result of " Transcribblers."

In spite of his omissions Nicholls gives the best picture of Gray the critic: " He placed Shakespear high above all poets of all countries & all ages." " What he admired in Plato was not his mystic doctrines which he did not pretend to understand, nor his sophistry but his excellent sense, sublime morality, elegant style, & the perfect dramatic propriety of his dialogues." " He was

[1] Whibley, II, 505.

a great admirer of Tacitus . . . thought the narrative of Thucydides the model of history." "He had a perfect knowledge . . . of the Poets of Italy of the first class, to whom he certainly looked up as his great progenitors; & to Dante as the father of all." Nicholls thus dips into his memory and retrieves only a few samples from the deep well, yet he gives enough to show that Gray was potentially a first-rate critic. Prodded by necessity he might have given the world a body of criticism that would have equaled Johnson's. As it was, he gave it to his friends, and no Boswell was there to record it.

I have shown in this book that Gray was, at least in accomplished work, more scholar than poet or critic. And yet, in reality, all three are inextricably intertwined. Gray went easily from classical poetry into Greek history and Greek philosophy, but although he became an accomplished classical scholar, the only original contribution in the field was his criticism of Plato. Again, when he projected the history of English poetry, the only results evident to his contemporaries were some translations that added new ideas to the repertory of romantic poetry, whereas his scholarly discoveries and his criticism of Chaucer, Milton, Daniel, and other English poets, had to wait for later recognition. Yet even with genuine native ability at criticism, his judgment was rendered far more valid because of his learning.

He had also a natural gift for poetry, yet the universal appeal of his few poems owes much to his wide reading and his ability to borrow ideas without remembering the original words. He was himself free to acknowledge his borrowings, as he showed when he appended a number of unnecessary notes to his poems in the 1768 edition. Later editors, like Wakefield and Mitford, have added countless other parallel passages, faintly reminiscent phrases from hundreds of sources. "He congratulated himself," says Nicholls, "on not having a good verbal memory; for, without it he said he had imitated too much; & if he had possessed such a memory all that he wrote would have been imitation, from his having read so much." [2] To imitate and not plagiarize, and thereby

[2] Whibley, III, 1296.

to sum up what many had thought but none had so well and so universally expressed — that was the poetical gift of Gray, a gift that received abundant food from his love of books. He plundered the best of the ancients and the moderns, and was thankful: " do not wonder therefore," he warned Edward Bedingfield in 1756 after quoting several of his sources for *The Bard,* " if some Magazine or Review call me Plagiary: I could shew them a hundred more instances, wch they never will discover themselves." [3]

Thus his poetry borrowed from his learning, even as his love of poetry had led him in the beginning towards learning. He might have more evenly mingled scholarship and creative work but for his inertia, born of ill-health, and his contempt for professional writing, born of his desire to be a gentleman. Milton before him had done it, guided by a fixed purpose; Johnson in his own day was driven to it by necessity; and Goethe in the generation after him was able to become both scholar and poet through his abundant energy. Gray had the mind for it, but he failed, and the failure has interested thousands who have felt his power in the *Elegy.*

He failed to live up to his native abilities as a creative artist, whether in poetry or criticism. He failed even to seek acknowledgment for his achievements in scholarship. He might have made a name for himself in several fields. He deplored the neglect of Plato at Cambridge and could have written some excellent, probably original, criticism on the subject. A readable account of his findings in Oriental history would have been welcome to an age interested in every thing that came from the East. His projected history of English poetry, as I have shown, would have advanced our knowledge of Chaucer and early English poetry by at least twenty years, to say nothing of its being the first book on the subject. He did much original research in English history, but although he criticized Hume's history, he did not even plan to write one of his own. He forwarded the knowledge of natural history in England and became an authority on English entomology, but, as far as I know, not even a single species of plant or animal life has been named for him. Even the professorship of modern history owed

[3] Whibley, II, 477.

more to Stonhewer than to any amount of research in the manuscripts of the British Museum.

Why he failed I have tried to show. The reasons are many and are mixed up with his own rather complex personality. His introspective nature led him to books, and his varied interests guided his reading. His insatiable curiosity often led him into strange by-paths, but his taste and his desire to avoid " middling and inferiour authors " always brought him back to the highway. He would have no profession, even though trained to the law, and so he took to scholarship in order to fill his time in a manner congenial to his tastes and his code of a gentleman. This he did somewhat casually at first, but as his health grew steadily poorer, it became habitual. He despised the taste of the general reading public to such an extent that he would publish nothing of his own accord. When the public acclaimed the *Elegy,* he bore their approval with indifference; when they criticized his Pindaric odes, he withdrew into his recluse's shell. Sensitive to an extreme, he hated to offer his poems to the world. As a result of all these circumstances, he played the gentleman by reading and studying at Cambridge in winter and visiting his friends at their homes and estates in summer.

Gray then was a gentleman of letters. His tastes fit the tradition of the more literary landed gentry of his time: he loved the classics, read widely in travel books, dipped into antiquarianism of all sorts, and reveled in gardening and the study of nature. He would have been pleased with the quiet dignity of an estate, and he would gladly have filled his time — for his philosophy demanded that it be filled — with his garden and his small park, and his neat shelves of books, and the antiquities of the surrounding region. But he had no estate, nor ever should have, even with the steady accretion of small sums from the bequests of childless relatives, and so he became a gentleman of letters, with chambers in Cambridge as his manor and the whole intellectual world as his estate. He was proficient in poetry and composed occasionally for his own friends, but disdained the profession of writing. He studied with the varying taste of a dilettante, and yet his active mind carried him so deeply into literature and history and science that he became, paradoxically, an intellectual frontiersman.

The complexity of Gray's life merges into a sort of unity. The complete picture of the man shows, without speculation on the coldness of the age, why he wrote so little poetry. He overcame melancholy by practicing moderation and making the adjustments necessary to happiness. He achieved a personal victory over handicaps, both physical and psychological, even though it meant gradually abandoning the creative for the reflective life. Posterity lost when it was forced to exchange the unwritten poems for volumes of learned notes, but Gray himself won a degree of happiness and in doing so imparted a richness to the lives of his friends. And as to posterity, Gray asked Wharton in 1758, "What has it ever done to oblige me?"

Thus ends the story of Thomas Gray, scholar and sometime poet. His *Elegy* has endeared his name to so many millions of readers that the man has been almost entirely obscured. The tremendous sweep of his mind was nevertheless acknowledged by his contemporaries, for many of them had personally felt its genial warmth. He was versatile and extremely gifted — too much so, in fact, for he quickly reached a point of achievement in several fields of thought where to rest was impossible and to go on would take more energy than he was willing to give. If he had not been quite so versatile in scholarship or if there had been others like Richard West to challenge him to more creative work, he might have become one of the foremost figures in English letters, in criticism if not in poetry. After West's death in 1742, however, Gray turned restlessly from one study to another, until he had touched upon almost all of human thought. His love of beauty usually determined the subject of his research, and his philosophy of history gave it meaning. But the poet was almost lost in the scholar, and meanwhile the " gentleman " had turned " virtuoso."

ADDENDA

ADDENDA

TEXT OF GRAY NOTEBOOKS IN PIERPONT MORGAN LIBRARY

I. GRAY'S EARLY CATALOGUE OF HIS LIBRARY

Libri Classici

T: Livii Historia, cum supplem: Freinshemii, & Notis Creverii; 4 Vol: 4to. Parisiis, 1735.

Thucididis historia, cum not: integris H: Stephani, Hudsoni, Wassii, & Dukeri, cum Annal: Dodwelli, &c: Fol: 1731 — apud Wetsten: Amstelæd:

Callimachi opera, cur:^te Grævio, cum Icon: 2 Vol:
. . . . Ultrajecti. 1697
Taciti Opera, cur: Gronovio, 2 Vol: . . . . ap: D: Elzev. 1673
Catulli, Tibulli & Propertii Opera, cur: Grævio . . . Ultraj: 1680
Claudiani Opera, cur: N: Heinsio. . . . . ap: D: Elzev: 1665
Sallustii Opera . . . . ap: Hackios, 1677
Phædri Fabulæ, cur: Burmanno . . . . . ap: Wetsten, 1698
Lucani Pharsalia, cur: Schrevelio . . . . ap: Hackium, 1669
Cornelii Nepotis Vitæ . . . . ap: Wetsten: 1707
Statii Opera, cur: Veenhysen: — 10^s . . . . ap: Hackios: 1671 ⎫ 8vo cum Notis
Petronii Opera, cur: Hadrianidis . . . . . . ap: Blavium: 1669 ⎬ Variorum.
Ovidii Opera, cur: Schrevelio, 3 vol: . . . . Lugduni Bat: 1661
Q: Curtii Historia — cur: Schrevelio . . : ap: D: Elzevir: 1673
Flori Historia — cur: Blancardo . . . . . . Lugduni B: 1648
Martialis Epigrammata, cur: Schrevelio . . . ap: Hackium: 1656
Suetonii Vitæ, cur: Schildio . . . . ap: Hackium: 1662
Val: Maximus, cur: Thysio . . . . ap: Hackium: 1660
Senecæ Tragœdiæ, cur: Thysio — 6^s . . . . . Lugduni B: 1651
Luciani Opera — cur: Grævio, 2 vol: . . . . ap: Blavium, 1687
Ciceronis Officia, &c: cur: Grævio . . . . . . ap: Blavium, 1688 ⎭
Sallustii Opera . . . . 1634 ⎫
Terentii Comœdiæ, recen: Heinsii, ... 1635 ⎪
C: Plinii Epistolæ, rec: Boxhornii, ... 1653 ⎬ 12:^mo
Senecæ Epistolæ & Quæstiones, rec: Gronovii. . . . . Paris, 1658 ⎪ ap: Elzevirios.
Caesaris Commentar: rec: J: Scaligeri, ... 1661 ⎪
Plauti Comœdiæ . . . . 1652 ⎭
Testamentum Græcum Novum ⎫
Lucretii Opera ⎬ 12mo a Mattaire, Londini.
Justini Historia ⎭

Homeri Opera, cum Scholiis Didymi; cur: Schrevelio, 4:^to . . . 1656, ap: Elzevir: fol. 1vo

Euripidis Tragœdiæ, cur: Barnesii, cum Scholiis,

               L S D
 Fol: 1694 . . . . 1 . 12 . 0 . . Cantabrigiæ.
Horatii Opera, cum not: Dacerii, & translat: Gallicâ, 10 Vol: 12:^mo 1691 Parisiis.
Longini Opera, cum not: Tollii, &c: 4:^to . . . . 1694 . Ultrajecti

Virgilii Op: . cum schol: Servii, 1620, 4to . . . . Colon: Allobrogum.
Sophoclis Tragœdiæ, 2 vol: cur: Johnsoni, 8vo . 9^S . 1705 . . . . . . Oxoniæ
Juvenalis & Persii Satyræ, cur: Prateo, 1727, Londini. ⎫
Virgilii Opera, cur: Ruæo, 1723, Hagæ.   ⎬ 8vo In us: Delphini
Ciceronis Orationes Selectæ, cur: Merovillio, Londini, 1692. ⎪
Ovidii Metamorphoses, cur: Crispini, Oxoniæ.   ⎭
Macrobii Saturnalia, cur: Jac: Gronovii, 8vo . 4^S . 1694 . . . . . . Londini
Dionysii Periegesis, cur: Hill, cum Schol: Eustathii. 8vo, 1688 . . . . . Londini
Xenophontis Apomneumata, cur: Leunclavio, . 1720 . 8vo . . . . . Londini
Anacreontis Opera . cum not: Daceriæ, 12mo, 1699. . . . . Amstelædami
Statii Opera . . . . 1624 ⎫
Prudentii Opera . . . . 1624 ⎬
Catulli, &c. Opera . . . . 1640 ⎬ 16:^mo ap: Jansenium.
Claudiani Opera . . . . 1638 ⎭
Terentii Comœdiæ, cum not: Daceriæ, 12:^mo 3 vol: 1691 . . . . . Amstelædami
Plauti Comœdiæ tres, cum not: Daceriæ, 12:^mo 1691 . . . . Amstel:
Aristophanis Plutus & Nubes, cum Scholiis, 8vo, 1695 . . . . Londini
Cebetis Tabula, 8vo, cur: Johnsoni, . . . 1720 . . . . Londini
Isocratis Opera . cur: Wolfii, 8vo . . . 1621 . . . . . Col: Allobrogum
Apuleii Asinus aureus, cur: Beroaldi, . 8vo . 1560 . . . . Basileæ
Theocriti Opera, cum scholiis, 8vo . . . 1729 . . . . Londini
Ovidii Opera . . 2 Vol: 12mo . . . . 1649 . . . . ap: Blavium
Sophocles, rec: Camerarii . . 12mo . . . 1534 . . . . Hagenoæ
Xenophontis Cyropædia . . . 8vo . . . . 1613 . . . . Etonæ
Demosthenes & Æschines de Coronâ, . . . 8vo . 1695 . . . . Oxoniæ
Ciceronis Officia, &c: cur: Grævii, 12ma . 1691 . . . . Amstelæd:
Herodiani, & Zosimi Historiæ, cur: H: Stephani, 4to, 1581 . . . . Parisiis
Æliani Opera, rec: Tanagri: Fabri, 12mo, . . 1668 . . . . Salmuriæ
Caesaris Commentarii, 16mo . . . 1578 . . . . ap: C: Plantinum
Taciti Opera, 16mo . . . 1551 . . . . ap: S: Gryphium
M: Cicero de finibus, 8vo, cur: T: Bentleii . 1718 . . . . Cantabrigiæ

fol. 2ro

Juliani Cæsaris Opera, curâ Spanhemii, cum S: Cyrilli in eum libri
                             L   S   D
    decem, Folio, ... 1 . 4 . 0 . . 1696 . . . . Lipsiæ
Virgilii Opera, rec: Maasvicii . . 12mo . . 1730 . . . . .ap: Westen:
C: Taciti Opera, colla Traduzion Fiorentina di Bern: Davanzati, 4to maj: . . . .
    1^L . 0^S . . 1637 . . . . Florentiæ
A. Gellii Noctes Atticæ . 12mo . . . 2^S . . . . Elzevir: 1650.
Hesiodi, quæ extant, ex Recens: Clerici, cum Not: Variorum . . 1701 . . 8vo
    . . . . Amsterdam.

[¾ page left empty]

fol. 3ro

Grammarians, Antiquaries, &c:

Harris's Lexicon Technicum . fol: 1st Edit:^n . . . .
Scapulæ Lexicon Græc: Lat: Fol: . . . . Leyden
Thesaurus Geographicus . 4to . . . . London
Heylin's Cosmography . . Fol: . . . . London

Potter's Antiquities of Greece, 2 Vol: 8:^{vo} . 10^S . . . . Oxford
Schrevelii Lexicon . . . . 8vo . . . . Leyden
Kennet's Antiquities of Rome . . 8vo . . 3^S . 6^D: . . . . Oxford
Sanctii Minerva . . 8vo . . . . Franeker
Boyer's French Dictionary abridged, 8vo . . . .
Busbey's Greek Grammar . . . . 8vo . . . .
Littleton's Dictionary . . . . 4to . . . .
Veneroni's Dictionary, Fr: & Ital: . . 4to . . . . Amsterdam
Compendious Method for the languages, by Philips . 8vo . . . . . .
Index ad Homerum . . . . 8vo . . . . ap: Commelin:
Veneroni's Italian Grammer . . . . 12mo . . . .
Tallent's Chronological Tables . . . . Fol: . . . .
Cluveri Geographia . . 12mo . . . 2^S . 6^D: . . . . ap: Wetsten:
Jul: Scaliger de causis linguæ Latinæ, 8vo, 1623 . . . . ap: Commelin:
Sturmius de amissâ dicendi ratione, 12mo, 1542 . . . . ap: Gryphium
Vigerus de Græcis Idiotismis, 12mo . . 1^S . 6^D . 12ma Edit: 1678 . . . . London
Laurentius Valla de Elegantiis Ling: Lat: . . 1688 . . . . Cambridge
Gordon's Geography . . . .

[last 1/3 3ro and all of 3vo empty]

fol. 4ro

Respublicæ	Gallica, a Joan: de Laet,	1629	apud Elzevirios
	Persica, ab eodem	1633	
	Chinensis, a N: Trigaltio,	1639	
	Italicæ, a T: Segetho	1631	
	Anglica, a T: Smitho	1630	
	Veneta, a Donat: Jannotio	1631	
	Veneta, a Casp: Contareno,	1626	
	Romana, a Pomp: Læto, J: Lipsio, &c:,	1626	
	Constantinopolitana, a P: Gyllio,	1632	

Respublicæ	Atheniensis, a G: Postello.	1635	ap: Le Maire.
	Hebraïca, a P: Cunæo,	1666	ap: J: Janson:
	Hanseaticæ, a Werdenhagen,	1631	ap: Le Maire.

[2/3 4ro, all 4vo empty]

fol. 5ro

Moral & Natural Philosophy, Mathematicks, Logick, &c: in several Languages.
Lock on human Understanding . Fol: 2^d Edit: . 10^S . . . .
Lock, on the same . 8vo, 2 vol: . 6th Edit: . . . .
Religion of Nature delineated, by Wollaston, 4to, 6th Edit: . . . . . .
Enquiry into the Nature of the Soul, 8vo, 2 Vol: 2^d Edit: . . . .
Introductio ad Physicam, a Keil. 3^d Edit: 8:^{vo} . . . . Oxoniæ
Lectiones Astronomicæ, 8:^{vo} 1st Edit: . . . . Oxoniæ
Wisdom of God in the Creation, by Ray . . 8vo . . . .
Rohaulti Physica, Latiné versa a D: Clarke . 8vo . 2^S . 2^d Edit: . . . London
Burgersdicii Logica . . . . 12mo . . . . London
Tacquet's Geometry, by Whiston . . 8vo . . . . Cantabrigiæ
Pardie's Geometry . . . . 7th Edit: . 12mo . . . . London
Ward's Algebra abridged . . . 12mo . . . .
Wingate's Arithmetick . . . . . 8vo . . . .

Cocker's Arithmetick . . 12mo . . . .

Webster's Arithmetick . . 12mo . . . .

Watts's Logick . . . . 8vo . . . .

Whole duty of Man . . . . 12mo . . . .

Puffendorfi Officium Hominis . 12mo . 8th Edit: . . 1^S . . . . . Cantabrigiae

C: Hugenii Cosmotheoros . 4to . . . . Hagae Com:

Malbranche sur la Recherche de la Verite, 12:^{mo} . 2 Vol: 4th Edit: . Amsterdam

C: Huygens sur la Lumiere . 4to . . . . Leyden

Traité des Couleurs, par Mr Mariotte . . 12mo . . . . Paris

Schooteni exercitationes Mathemat: . 4to . . . . ap: Elzevir:

Sinclari Dialogi Philosophici . . . 4to . . . .

Sturmii Mathesis . 8vo, 2 Vol: . . . . Nuremburg.

Morals of Princes, 8vo . . from the Italian of Comazzi . . . .

[fol. 5vo empty]

fol. 6ro

Poetry, History, Travels, &c: &c:

Milton's Paradise lost . . . . 12mo . . . 9th Edit: . . . .

Homer's Iliad, by Pope . . 4to . . 6 Vol: . . . .

Waller's Poems . . . . 12mo . . . 9th Edit: . . . .

Ethic Epistles of Pope . Fol: . 1st Edit: . . . .

Virgil, by Dryden . . 8vo . 3 Vol: . . 3^d Edit: . . . .

Spectatours . . . 12mo . . 8 Vol: . . . . . 16^S . . . .

Tatlers . . 8vo . . 4 Vol: . . . . . 1^L . 0^S . . . .

Guardians 2 Vol: 12mo . . . .

Prior's Poems . . . . 12mo . . . .

History of the Royal Society, by Dr Sprat, 4to . . 7 ^S . . . . . .

S^r J: Davies on ye Immortal:^y of the Soul. 12mo . . . .

Plutarch's lives with Dacier's Notes . 8 Vol: 8vo . . 1 . 12 . 0 . . . .

Sandy's Travels to Egypt, the Levant, &c: fol: . . . .

Dryden's Miscellanies . 12mo . 6 Vol: . 5th Ed: . 16^S . . . .

Congreve's Plays . . . 12mo . . . .

Etheridge's Plays . . . .

Addison's Plays . . . .

Steel's Plays . . . .

Collection of Plays, 3 Vol: 4to,

Vol: 1: contains
- Rival Ladies
- Aurengzebe
- Don Sebastian } Dryden
- Conquest of Granada
- Amboyna . . . .
- Orphan
- Alcibiades } Otway
- D: Carlos
- Cambyses . . . Settle
- Oroonoko . . . Southern

Vol: 2^d contains
{
Rival Queens, C: Borgia, } Lee
Sophonisba, Mìthrìdates,   }
Earl of Essex, Cyrus, ... Banks
Ant: & Cleopatra . . . . Sedley
Tamerlane the Great . . . . . Sanders
Distres'd Innocence . . . . . . Settle
Rival Sisters . Gould . Libertine . Shadwell
}

fol. 6vo

Vol: 3^d contains
{
Macbeth   }
Hamlet   } Shakespear
Othello   }
Fatal Marriage . . . Southern
Indian Emperour }
All for Love   } Dryden
Oedipus   }
L: Junius Brutus }
Theodosius   } Lee
Nero   }
Circe . . . . Dr Davenant
Unnatural Brother . . . . . Filmer
}

Collect: of Plays . 4to containing, Double Gallant . Cibber . Busy Body .
  Centlivre . Love triumphant . Dryden . Victorious Love . Walker .
Collection of Poems, by Buckingham, Roscommon, Rochester, &c: . 8vo .
Collection of Voyages . . Fol: . containing . Navarette to China, Baumgarten
  to the Levant, Beauplan to Ukraine, Monk to Greenland, Merolla, Carli, &c:
  to Congo, Sr Tho: Roe's Journal .
Poems & Plays . 8vo . Gay's Pastorals, Thomson's Spring, Spartan Dame, .
  Southern, &c:
Don Quixote, 4 Vol: 12mo by Motteux . . . .
Persian Tales, 3 Vol: 12mo. . . . .
Turkish Tales, 12mo . . . .
Suetonius, by Hughes, 12mo . . . .
Account of the Italian Painting, Statues, &c: by Richardson, 8vo . . . . .
Richardson on Painting, 3 Vol: 8vo . . . .
The Intelligencer . . . 8vo . . . . Dublin
Leonidas, a Poem, by Glover, 4to . . . . . 1st Ed: . . . 4 . 6 . . . . .
Tale of a Tub, by Swift, 12mo . . . .
Poems by Rochester, Dorset, &c: . . 12mo . . . . 3^S . . . .
The Spleen, &c: by M: Green . . . 3^d Edit: . 12mo . . . .
Coll:ⁿ of Novels, (cont:^g) Prazimene, the Loving Revenge, Cynthia, &c: . . 12mo
Wonders of the Peak, by Cotton . . . 12mo . . . .
Milton's Juvenilia . 12mo . . . .
Scotch Songs . . 12mo . . . .
Coll: of Poems, contain:^g Philips's Cyder, Blenheim, Dryden's Absalom &
  Achitophel, &c:
The Dunciad, by Mr Pope, 4to . . . . 1729 . . . .
Le Comte's Account of China . 8vo . . 1738 . 4 . 6 . . . . London
Shakespear's Works, by Theobalds . 8 Vol: 12mo . 1741 . 1 . 1 . 0 . London

Conduct of Sarah, Dutchess of Marlborough . 8vo . 1742 . 3 . 6 . . London
Spencer's Works, by Hughes . . 12mo . 6 Vol: . . 1715 . 0 . 18 . 0
Observations on the Florid Song, from the Italian of P: Fr: Tosi .
          s
   1742 . . 2 . 6 . . . .
Dryden's Juvenal, & Persius . . . 3^d Ed: 1702 . . 8vo . . . .
Creech's Lucretius, & Manilius . . . 5th. Ed: 1700 . . 8vo . . . .

[rest of 7ro empty]

fol. 7vo

Architecture, Sculpture, Painting, & Antiquities, &c:

Le Antichitá di Roma, in 40 Tavole di Rame, dallo Scamozzi . 1633 . . Venetia
Vestigi di Roma, ritratti in perspettiva, da Stef: Duperac . 1575 . . . . Roma
Edifices de Rome, dessinés & mesurés par Desgodetz, Folio . 1695 . . . Paris
Statue Antiche, in 100 Rami, da Fr: Perrier . Folio . 1638 . . . . . . Roma
Pitture antiche del Sepolc: de Nasonii, intagliate da P: Santi Bartoli,
    colle note del Bellori . . . Folio . 1680 . . . . Roma
Sepolchri antichi, da P: Santi Bartoli, Folio, 1727 . . . . Roma
Lucerne antiche, dal medesimo, colle note del Bellori, 1691 . . . . Roma
Raccolta di Statue antich', e moderne in 163 rami, intagliate dal Dorigni,
    Poilly, Randon, Fr: Aquila, &c: da Dom:^{co} de' Rossi, Foglio, 1704 . Roma
Admiranda Roman: Antiquitatum, a P:S:Bartoli delineata, &c: 1693 . . Roma
Colonna Trajana intagliata da P:S:Bartoli, coll' esposizioni di Ciaccone, e
    Bellori . . . da Gio: Giacomo de' Rossi, Foglio, in 119 Rami . . . Roma
Columna Antoniniana, a P:S:Bartoli, cum not: Bellori . Foglio in ⎫
    75 Rami . cum picturis in Piramide C: Cestii . . . . ⎬ Roma
Nozze Aldobrandine, & un Fregio. del Polidoro in 9 Rami . . . . . ⎭
Palazzi di Roma, intagl: da G:B:Falda, e P: Ferrerio, in 100 rami . . . Roma
Insignium Templorum Prospectus, da' Rossi . 1684, in 72 rami, Foglio . Roma
Ornamenta Monocromata partim, partim opere plastico à Rafaele ⎫
    Urbinate elaborata in Pal: Vaticano, a P: S: Bartolo delineata . . ⎬ Roma
    in 73 tabulis . . . . ⎪
Battaglia de' Giganti, dipinta nel P: Té à Mantova, da G:^{lio} Romano ⎭
Ædes Barberinæ ab H: Tetio descriptæ, cum tab: C: Bloemart, &c:
    1647, Foglio, ... Roma
Claustro di S: Michele in Bosco dipinto da L: Caracci, Guido, &c: intagl:
    dal Giovannini in 18 rami . Folio, 1694 . . . . Bologna
Galleria di Psiche nel Pal: Farnese piccolo, dipinta da Rafaele, e da N:
    Dorigni intagliata, colla Galatéa . 1693 . in 12 Rami . . . . . Roma
Galleria Farnese maggiore, dipinta d' An: Caracci, intagl: da P: Aquila,
    col Gabinetto annesso, in 34 Rami, Foglio . . . . Roma
Discorso degl' amfiteatri antichi, del C: Scipion Maffei . 1728 . 12mo . Verona
Roma antica, di Fam: Nardini . 4to . 1704 . . . . Roma
                                  L   s
Vetus Latium, di Monsign: Corradini, 4to, 7 Vol: . . 1704 . 2 . 10 . . Roma
Vite de' Pittori, Scultori, &c: da G: Vasari, 4to, 3 Vol: . 1647 . 1^L . 1^S
   . . . . Bologna
                                s   D
Felsina Pittrice, del Conte Malvasia, 4to, 2 Vol: . . 1678 . . 12 . 6 . Bologna
                               s
Vite de' Pittori, &c: da G: Bellori, 4to . . 1728 . 6 . . . . Roma
Vite de' Pittori, scritte da G: Baglioni, 4to . 1733 . 6^S . . . . Napoli

Riposo del Borghini, . 4to . . 1730 . . . . Firenze
Vita del Cav: Bernini, scr: da F: Baldinucci . 4to . 1682 . . . . Firenze
Dialogo della Pittura, di M: Lud: Dolce . . 8vo . 1735 . . . . Firenze
fol. 8ro
Roma antica, e moderna, 2 Vol: 8vo . . 1739 . . . . Roma
Descrizion della Villa Borghese . 8vo . . . 1700 . . . . Roma
Ammaestramento di Pittura nelle chiese di Roma, dall' Ab: Titi, 12mo,
  1686 . . . . Roma
Guida di Napoli, da Mons: Sarnelli . . 12 . . 1713 . . . . Napoli
——— di Pozzuoli, Baia, &c: dall' istesso . 12 . . 1709 . . . . . . Napoli
Abecedario Pittorico d'Orlandi, 4to . . 1719 . . . . Bologna
Vite de' Pittori moderni, da L: Pascoli, 3 Vol: 4to . 1730 . . . . Roma
Vite d'alcuni celebri pittori, co' ritratti, dal Cav: Lioni, 1731, 4to, 6^{S} . . . Roma
Capricci di Salv: Rosa, intagl: da lui stesso, in 31 mez: foglii . . . . . . Roma
Galeria Verospi, dipinta dall' Albani, int: di Gir: Frezza . in 16 rami . . Roma
Soffitte, e Lunette di P: da Cortona nel Pal: Pitti à Firenze, int: da Corn:
  Bloemart, &c: in 25 rami . . . . Roma
Altri Capricci, & Istorie di Sal: Rosa in 8 mezzi fogli . . . . Roma
Storie grandi dello stesso in 4 foglii . . . . Roma
Spanhemius de præst: & usu Numismatum, 2 Vol: Foglio . 1717 . . . Amsterd:
Avanzi dell' antica Roma, opra dell' Overbeke, copiate da Giac: Amiconi,
  Foglio in 376 Rami . . . . . . 1739 . . . . Londra
Epilogazione del sudetto, 8vo . . . .
Bellezze di Firenze, da F: Bocchi, ampliate dal Cinelli . 8vo . 1677 . . Firenze
Ristretto delle cose notabili in Firenze, da Carlieri . 12 . 1733 . . . Firenze
Pitture di Bologna . . . . 1732 . . . . Bologna
Itinerario d' Italia, di F: Scotti . . . . 12 . . 1737 . . . . Roma
fol. 9ro

Books bought since I came to London.[1]
1760.
Folio.

	L	S	D
Dr Geo: Hickes's Antiqua Litteratura Septentrionalis, with Sr And: Fountaine's Numismata Sàxon: & Dano-Saxonica, & Humphr: Wanley's Catalogus Lib: Vett: Septentr:^{m}. 3 Vol: Ch: Max: Oxon: 1705	2	0	0
Willughby's Historia Piscium, sumpt: Soc: Regiæ recognovit Joannes Raius . . Oxon: 1686	1	1	0
Catalogue of the Harleian Manuscripts. 2 Vol: Lond: 1759	2	10	0
Life of Edward, Earl of Clarendon . Oxon: 1759	1	5	0
Armoiries des Connetables, Grand-Maitres, Chanceliers, &c: de France, par J: le Feron, augmenté par Claude Morel, 1628, Paris	0	1	6
Musæum Societatis Regalis, by Nehem: Grew, 1681. Lond:	0	4	9
Romanæ Urbis Topographia & Antiquitates, auctore J: Jacobo Boissardo, artificio Theod: de Bry. 1597. Leodii. 6 Tom: in 3 Vol:	1	5	0
Sigonius, de antiquo jure Populi Romani. Paris: . 1576	0	2	9
Matt: Westmonasteriensis Flores Historiarum . Francof: Typis Wechel: 1601 . cum Chron: Florentii Wigern:	0	5	0

[1] This section (to "Poetæ . . . recentiores," fol. 11vo) is in a later hand and obvi ously does not belong to what precedes and follows it.

Novus Orbis Regionum Vet: incognit, S: Grynæi. Basil: 1537 . . . 0 1 9
Raph: Volaterrani Commentarii Urbani. ap: Frobenium Basil: 1544 0 1 9
Pauli Jovii Vitæ illustrium Virorum, Tom: 2. Basil: 1578 ⎱ 0 2 6
—— Elogia illustrium Virorum, Florent: 1551. . . . . ⎰
Scipione Ammirato, Istorie Florentine, L:20 Firenze 1600 . . . . 0 1 0
*—— Delle Famiglie Nobili Fiorent: Parte 1ma, 1615 . . . . . . 0 1 6
*Louis Videl, Vie du Connetable de Lesdiguieres. Par: 1638 . . . . 0 1 0
Ligon's History of Barbadoes . . Lond: 1673 . . . . 0 3 3
Etienne Pasquier, Recherches de la France. Par: 1665 . . . . . . 0 4 0
Marg:t Dutchess of Newcastle, Life of the Duke. Lond: 1667 . . . 0 1 0
Fabyan's Chronicle . . . Lond: ap: W: Rastell. 1533 . . . . . . 0 2 6
Guillim's Display of Heraldrie . . 1638. Lond: 0 1 3
Chaucer's Works, by Speght. black letter. 1602. Lond: 0 2 6
Holland's Heroologia Anglica, with the cuts. 1620. Lond: 0 8 6
*Burton's Anatomy of Melancholy. 1676. Lond: 0 2 0
Matt: Paris, Historia Major, &c: ed: W: Watts, 1640 . . . . 0 5 6
*Claud: Menetraius, Symbolica Dianæ Ephesiæ Statua, with cuts.
Rom: 1688 . . . . 0 4 0

10 19 0

fol. 9vo

Hooker's Works . . . Lond: 1666. . . . . 0 2 0
Earl of Orrery, State-Letters publ:d by Morrice. Lond: 1742 . . . 0 5 6
Hacket's Life of Archb:p Williams. 1693. Lond: 0 2 6
Croniche di M: Giovan Villani. Venezia, 1537 . . . . 0 1 9
Broweri & Masenii Annales Trevirenses. Leodii, 1670, 2 V: . . . 0 3 9
Sr Thomas Roe's Letters, & Negotiations, 1740. Lond: 0 11 0
Stow's Survey of London, by Strype. 2 V: 1720 Lond: 0 13 0
Anthony Wood, Hist: & Antiquitates Oxon: . . 1674. Oxon: 2 V:
in one 0 5 0
Salmasii Exercitationes Plinianæ. 2 V: 1689, Utrecht cum Homon:
Hyles Jatricæ, de Manna & Saccharo. 0 5 6
Sallengre, Thesaurus Novus Antiq:m Rom:m, 3 V: 1716: Hag: . . 0 16 0
Milles's Catalogue of Honour 0 2 0
Dugdale's Baronage, (1st Vol:) 0 8 6
*Bizot, Histoire Metallique de Hollande. 1687. Paris: 0 4 6

[1/5 page left]

Quarto

Howel's Perlustration of London, with Melan's Frontispiece &
Hollar's View of ye City. 1657. Lond: 0 2 0
Fabricii Bibliotheca Græca, the 6 first Volumes. Hamburg: 1705 . 0 6 0
*Fil: Torre, Monumenta Vet: Antii. Rom: 1700 . . . . 0 1 0
Dr Gale's Antonini Iter Britanniarum. Lond: 1709 . cum Anon:
Ravennatis Chorographia Britann: 0 2 3
Chassot de Nantigny, Genealogies Historiques des Maisons Souve-
raines, &c: Paris, 1736. 2 first Volumes 0 4 0
Hai Ebn Yokdhan, sive Philosophus Autodidactus, Lat: Arab: ed:
Edward Pococke. . Oxon: 1671 . . . . 0 2 0
*P: Alexandre de Rhodes, Voyages en la Chine &c: Paris, 1666 . . 0 1 9

ADDENDA   159

P: Garasse, Doctrine curieuse. Paris, 1624 . . . . o   1   o
*Habert, Abbé de Cerisy, Vie du Cardinal Berulle, Paris, 1646 . . . o   1   o

                                                                    15   8   o

fol. 10ro
Gratiani, De Casibus Illustrium Virorum. Par: 1680 . . . . . . o   1   o
G: Bates, Vitæ select: aliquot Virorum. Lond: 1681 . . . . o   o   9
*Priorato, Istoria del Card: Mazarino (first Vol:) Bologna, 1677 . . o   o   6
*Histoire de Louis Treize. Paris, 1617 . . . . o   o   3
Godefroy, Ceremonial de France. Paris, 1619 . . . . o   1   o
Gibson's Chronicon Saxonicum. Sax: Lat: Oxon: 1692 . . . . . . o   2   9
Hesselii, Fragmenta Ennii. Amstel: 1707 . . . . o   3   3
Vaillant, Numismata præstantiora Imper: Romanorum a Julio
    Caesare ad Tyrannos. 2 V: Par: 1696 . . . . o   3   9
Rochefort, Histoire des Isles Antilles. Rotterd: 1681 . . . . o   2   3
Epistole di Franc: Redi. (4th Tom:) Firenze. 1724 . . . . . . o   o   9
Miscell: Tracts. Execution of Justice in England, by Wm Ld Bur-
    leigh. bl: letter, 1583. Lond:, Pair of Spectacles for the City,
    1648. Supplication to ye King's Majesty, 1604. Mythomystes &
    Tale of Narcissus, by H:R: Vox Cœli, 1624. English Spanish
    Pilgrim, by Wadsworth, 1630. Swedish Intelligencer, 1632. &c: o   3   o
Fabretti, de Aquæductibus Vet: Romæ. Rom: 1680 . . . . o   1   3
Boscha, De Origine & Statu Biblioth:cæ Ambrosianæ Mediolan: 1672 o   1   9
Imperiali, Illustrium Virorum Imagines. Venet: 1640 sive Musæum
    Historicum . . . . o   2   o
Brefe Chronycle of Sr John Oldcastle, by John ⎫
    Bale Lond: 1729 . . . . ⎪ These three   o   1   9
Collins, Life of Wm Cecil, Ld Burleigh. 1732. . . ⎬   are   o   1   3
Fraser's History of Nadir Shah. Lond: 1742 . . . ⎭ in Oct:vo   o   1   3
Amyrault, Vie de François de la Noue. Leyd: 1661 . . . . o   o   6
*Memoires de M: de Mornay. 2 first Vol: 1624 . . . . o   2   o
Workes of John Heiwood. 1550. black letter . . . . o   o   6
History of Graund-Amour & La Belle Pucelle, by Stephen Hawes.
    1555. black letter . . . . o   9   6
The thirteen Bookes of Aneïdos, translated by Tho: Phaer Esq: and
    Tho: Twyne M:D. black lett: 1607. Lond: . . . . o   o   6
Ovid's Metamorphosis, transl:d by Arthur Golding Gent:n black let-
    ter. 1587. Lond: . . . . o   o   6

                                                                    17   9   6

fol. 10vo
Person's (the Jesuit) Leicester's Commonwealth, 1641 . . . . . . o   1   o
Hyll(Tho:) Art of Gardening. Lond: 1593 . . . . o   1   o
Vaillant, Historia Regum Syriæ. Par: 1681 . . . . o   4   6
Norris, De Epochis Syro-Macedonum. Lips: 1696 . . . . o   1   o
Fabricius, De Augusti Imp: Genere, Temporibus & Scriptis. Ham-
    burg: 1727 . . . . o   1   o
Maffei, Istoria Diplomatica . . Mantova. 1727 . . . . o   3   6
                        [1/5 page space left]

Octavo, & infra.

Edmondes (Sʳ Thomas) Negotiations, with Sʳ Geo: Carew's Relation of France, by Dʳ Birch. 1749. Lond:	o	2	o
Birch's Life of Archb:ᵖ Tillotson. 1752. Lond:	o	2	3
Dᵒ. Life of Henry, Prince of Wales. 1760. Lond:	o	6	o
Hearne, Tit: Livii Vita Henrici 5ᵗⁱ. Oxon: 1716 . . cum Sylloge Epist: a variis Angliæ Princip:ˢ script:ᵃʳᵘᵐ	o	2	3
Beeckman's Voyage to Borneo. 1718. 8ᵛᵒ	o	1	6
Maichelius, de præcip: Bibliothecis Paris:ˢ, Cantab: 1721	o	o	6
Burnet's Life of Bᵖ Bedell. 1685. Lond:	o	o	6
Joutel, Journal du dernier Voyage de M: de la Sale. 1713. Par:	o	o	6
Pavillon, Oeuvres de . . . Hag: 1715	o	o	9
*Dierville, Voyage de l'Acadie. Amst: 1710	o	o	9
Du Maurier, Mem:ˢ pour servir a l'Hist:ʳᵉ de Hollande. 1687. Par:	o	o	6
Account of the Loss of yᵉ Wager &c: by an Officer of Adm: Anson's Squadron. 1744. Lond:	o	2	o
Ancient and present State of Portugal. 1706. Lond:	o	o	3
Dʳ Merret, Pinax rerum Natural:ᵐ Britannic:ᵐ. 1667. Lond:	o	2	o
*Relat:ⁿ of a Journey into England & Holland, by a Saxon Physician. 1711. from the Latin. Lond:	o	1	o
*Wotton, Conspectus Thesauri Septentr: Geo: Hickes. 1708. Lond:	o	1	3
Sam: Daniel's Poetical Works. 2 V: 1718. Lond:	o	2	o
Boke of spiritual Physick for dyvers diseases of the Nobility of England. black lett: 1555. (satyrical)	o	1	3
Aulicus Coquinariæ (in answer to Sʳ A: Weldon). 1650.	o	o	3
Celsus de Medicinâ, ab Almelooveen. 2 V: Lugd: 1730	o	2	9
*Bennet, Theatrum Tabidorum. 1714. Lugd: Bat:	o	o	5
Wepfer, de Apoplexiâ. Amst: 1724	o	o	3
Baglivi, Praxis Medica. 1699. Lyons.	o	o	4

fol. 11ʳᵒ

Musgrave, de Arthritide anomalâ, & R: Mead de imperio Solis & Lunæ . Amst: 1710	o	o	4
Sydenham, Opera Universa. 1726. Lugd: Bat:	o	o	5
Mead, Monita & Præcepta Medica. Lond: 1751.	o	1	9
Caii Opuscula, a S. Jebb, 1729. Lond: ch: max:	o	3	3
*Grotius, de Jure belli & pacis. 1651, Amst:	o	o	2
Fletcher of Saltoun's Political Works. 1737. Lond:	o	1	9
Riccoboni, Hist:ʳᵉ du Theatre Italien. Par: 1727	o	3	6
Sʳ Henry Wotton's Remains. 1685. Lond:	o	1	6
Winstanley's Lives of English Poets. 1687. Lond:	o	o	4
Langbaine's Lives of Eng: Dramatic Poets. 1699. Lond:	o	o	4
Dʳ Pope's Life of Seth Ward, Bᵖ of Salisbury. 1697. ib:	o	1	o
Dodonæus' Herbal, transl:ᵈ by H: Lyte Esq: bl: letter. 1586.	o	o	2
Life of Robert, Earl of Leicester. 1727. Lond:	o	1	o
Memoirs of Sʳ John Reresby. 1735. Lond:	o	1	3
Leland Comment:ⁱ de Scriptoribus Britannicis. Ox: 1709	o	4	o
*Herissaye, Contes d'Eutrapel. 2 V: 1732	o	1	6
*Santa-Cruz, Reflexions militaires. 4 V: Hag: 1735	o	1	6
*Reflexions sur les Ouvrages de Literature. 9 V: 1738. Par:	o	4	6

*Joncourt, Bibliotheque Britannique, 14 V: Hag: 1733 . . . . . . o 6 6
*Account of the Danish Mission in Malabar. 1718. Lond: . . . . o o o
Winstanley, England's Worthies. 1660. Lond: . . . . o 1 3
*Lister, Exercitat:ˢ Medicinales. 1697. Lond: . . . . o o 2
Merlin Cocaii, Macaronica. Ven: 1613 . . . . o o 9
Collection of Original Letters, publ:ᵈ by Mʳ Moore. 2 V: 1755 . . o 6 o
Mirabeau, Ami des Hommes. 3 V: 1758. Hague. . . . . o 7 6
Linnæus, Systema Naturæ, 2 Tom: Halmiæ 1758–9 . . . . o 15 o
Artedus, Opera omnia de Piscibus. Lugd: Bat: 1738 . . . . . . o 6 o
London & its Environs described, with cuts. 6 V: Lond: 1760 . . 1 10 o
Cambden's Remains, by J: Philpot, 7ᵗʰ Ed: Lond: 1674 . . . . . o 1 o

fol. 11ᵛᵒ

Poetae, Historici, &c: Latini recentiores.

Vidæ Poemata profana; ed: T: Tristram cum Icon: 2 vol: 4:ᵗᵒ . . . . . Oxoniæ
Casimiri Lyrica . 12ᵐᵒ min: . . . . Cantabrigiæ
Rapini Poemata . . 12ᵐᵒ . . . . Lugduni B:
Buchanani poemata . . 12ᵐᵒ . . . . ap: Wetsten:
Quilleti Callipœdia ⎫
Samarthani Pædotrophia ⎬ 12ᵐᵒ . . . . Londoni
Bonefonii Basia . 12ᵐᵒ . . . . a Mattaire
Fam: Stradæ Prolusiones . 12ᵐᵒ . . . . Goudæ
Historia Henrici Septimi, a Franc: Bacono . 12ᵐᵒ . 1662 . . . ap: D: Elzevir:
Sannazarii Poemata . . 8ᵛᵒ . . . 1719 . . . . Patavii
Leonardi Arretini Epistolæ, Pars prima . . 1741 . 8ᵛᵒ . . . . . . Florentiæ
Busbequii, Ad Suleimannum ab Imp: Ferdinando Legati, Epistolæ . .
1633 . . 16ᵐᵒ . . . . Elzevir
Huetii Poemata, cum ejusd: Notis ad Anthologiam . 12ᵐᵒ . 1700 . 1ˢ Utrecht
Huetius, de Rebus Suis . . . 12 . 1718 . 2ˢ . . . . Amstelæd:
Censura Celebriorum Authorum . (Sʳ Tho: Pope Blount) Fol: . . 1690
. . 18ˢ . . . . Londini
Polydori Virgilii de Rerum Inventoribus L:ᵇʳⁱ 8 . . 8ᵛᵒ . 1550 . . 1ˢ . Basileæ

[1/2 page left]

fol. 12ʳᵒ

Livres François, & Italiens, de Poesie, d'Histoire, de Critique, & de Plaisanterie, &c:
Oeuvres de Boileau, avec les annot: de Mʳ Brosset, 4 Vol: 12ᵐᵒ . 14ˢ . . . Haye
Oeuvres de Voiture, 2 Vol: 12ᵐᵒ . . . . Paris
                                    ˢ ᴰ
Telemaque . . . 12ᵐᵒ . . . 3 . 6 . . . . Rotterdam
Oeuvres de Racine, 2 Vol: 12ᵐᵒ . . . . Amsterdam
                                    ˢ ᴰ
La Gierusalemme Conquistata, di Tasso, 2 Vol: 16ᵐᵒ 3 . 6 . . . . . . Elzevir
L'Orlando Furioso, di L: Ariosto . . 4ᵗᵒ . . 1566 . . 15ˢ . . . . . Venetia
Sonetti di Petrarcha, ravisti da M: Lod: Dolce . . 16ᵐᵒ . . 2 Vol: 1560 Venetia
Caracteres du Siecle, par Bruyere, 2 Vol: 12:ᵐᵒ . . . . Amsterdam
Oeuvres Critiques du P: Rapin . . . 2 Vol: . . 12:ᵐᵒ . . . . . Amsterdam
Traité du poeme Epique, par Bossu . . . 12ᵐᵒ . . . . Paris
Lettres Persannes, de Montesquiou . . . 2 Vol: . . 16:ᵐᵒ . . . . Amsterdam
Pluralite des Mondes, par Fontenelle . . . 12:ᵐᵒ . . . . Paris
Reflexions Morales, de Rochefoucault . . . 12:ᵐᵒ . . . . Paris
                                    ˢ: ᴰ:
Contes de Fontaine, 16:ᵐᵒ . . . . . . 2 . 6 . . . . Hamburg

Fables du même, 16:ᵐᵒ . . . . Hamburg
Voyages de Cyrus, 12ᵐᵒ . . . . Amsterdam
Poemes de Clem: Marot: 16:ᵐᵒ 2 Vol: . . . 1538 . . . . Roan
Description de Siam, par Loubere, 12:ᵐᵒ 2 Vol: . . . . Amsterdam
Dialogues des Morts, par Fontenelle, 12:ᵐᵒ . . . . Haye
L'Oedipe de Sophocle & deux Comedies d'Aristofane, par Mad: Dacier,
    12ᵐᵒ . . . . Amsterdam
Rime di M: della Casa, col Galatéo . . 12ᵐᵒ . . 1572 . . . . Fiorenza
Fables de M: de la Motte . . 3ᵐᵉ Edit: . . 12ᵐᵒ . . . . Paris
Quinte Curce, de Vaugelas . . 12ᵐᵒ . . 1696 . . . . Haye
Maniere de bien penser, par le P: Bouhours . . 12:ᵐᵒ 2:ᵈᵉ Ed: . . . Amsterdam
Pensees Ingenieuses, du même . . . 12ᵐᵒ . . . . Paris
Pensees des Peres, du meme . . . 12ᵐᵒ . . . . Amsterdam
Entretiens d'Ariste & d'Eugene, par le même . . 12ᵐᵒ . . . . Paris
Pensees de Pascal . . . 12ᵐᵒ . . . . Paris
Considerations sur les Romaines, par Montesquiou . . 12ᵐᵒ . . . . Amsterdam
Dialoghi di Sper: Speroni . . . 4ᵗᵒ . . . 1596 . . . . Venetia
Fureteriana . . . 12ᵐᵒ . . . . Brusselle
Les Amours d'Henri le Grand . . 12ᵐᵒ . . . . Cologne
Contes d'Ouville . . . 12ᵐᵒ . . . .
Ambassades de M: le Comte d'Estrades en Italie, Angleterre, &c: 1718–12 Amsterd:
Vie de l'Empereur Julien . . . 12ᵐᵒ . . . 1735 . . . . Amsterd:

fol. 12ᵛᵒ

Lettres de Mad: de Sevigné à sa Fille, 6 Vol: 12ᵐᵒ . . . 1738 . . . . . Paris
Histoire du Card: Ximenes, par M: Flechier, 2 Vol: 12ᵐᵒ . 1694 . . . . . Paris
Reflexions Critiques sur la Poesie & la Peinture, 2 Vol: 12: 1719 . 5ˢ . . . Paris
Histoire de Theodose le Grand, par M: Flechier, 12 . . . 1714 . . . . . Paris
Description de Paris, 3 Vol: 12ᵐᵒ . . . .
Egaremens du Cœur & de l'Esprit, par M: Crebillon le Fils, 12ᵐᵒ . 4ˢ . . Paris
Dante, coll' Esposizioni di Cristoforo Landino, &c: 4ᵗᵒ maj: . 1578 .
    L   S   D
    1 . 5 . 0 . . . . Venetia
Petrarca, del Muratori, colle note d'Ales: Tassoni, &c: 8ᵛᵒ maj: 1711 . Modena
La Coltivazione di L: Alamanni, e le Api di G: Rucellai, 4ᵗᵒ . 7ˢ 6ᴰ . . Padova
Rime del Chiabrera, 3 Vol: 8ᵛᵒ . . . 1718 . . . . Roma
Pindaro, dell' Adimari . . . 4ᵗᵒ . . . 1631 . . . . 5ˢ . . . . Pisa
La Tebaïde, di Selvaggio Porpora . . 4ᵗᵒ . . 1729 . . . . Roma
Discorsi della Ragion Poetica da V: Gravina . . . 1731 . . . . . . Venetia
Lettere del Card: Bembo . . . . . . 8ᵛᵒ min: . . 1575 . . . . . Venetia
                                          L. S.
Opere di N: Machiavelli . . 4ᵗᵒ . . . 1550 . . . 1 . 15 . . . . . Geneva
                                          L. S.
Istoria di M: Caterino Davila, 2 Vol: Folio . . 1733 . . 2 . 0 . . . . Venetia
Istoria delle Guerre, dall' 1696 . all' 1725, del Conte Ottieri . 1728 . 4ᵗᵒ Roma
Satire di Salvator Rosa . . 12 . . . . Roma
Histoire de la Guerre, par Massuet . . 5 Vol: 12ᵐᵒ . . 1736 . . . . Amsterd:
Bibliotheque des Theatres . . . 8ᵛᵒ . . . 1733 . . . . Paris
Description des Etats du Gr: Mogol, par Bernier 2 Vol: 12ᵐᵒ 1709 4ˢ Amsterdam
[item crossed out: La Canapé Couleur de feu, par Crebillon 12ᵐᵒ . . . 1ˢ
    . . . . Amsterdam]

Le Sofa, Conte Morale, par Crebillon, le Fils, 2 Tomes, 12mo 1741 . 4 . .

L'Ecumoire, Histoire Japonoise, par Crebillon, le Fils, 2 Vol . 12mo . . .

   1735 . . 2^s . . . . Londres

Memoires du Marechal de Bassompierre, 2 Vol: 12mo 1666 . 2 . . . . Cologne

Cymbalum Mundi, par Bon: des Perriers . . 12mo . 1732 . 1 . 6 . Amsterdam

Catholicon d'Espagne, avec les Notes de M^r Du Puy, &c: 12mo 1699 . . .

   1 . 6 . . . . Ratisbon

2. NOTES ON LEARNED JOURNALS

January. 1744/5. Journal des Sçavans. 20 V: 12. par M: de Salo, l'Abbé Gallois, L'Abbé de la Roque, &c: 1665.

1666 [196] Transylvanians put the Christian Name after the Surname, as Betlem Gabor, Chimin Ianos (Gabriel Betlem, John Chimin. .Rer: Transylv: Libri 4. Joan: Betlenii. Amst: 1666 — [367] the Dalmatian Fragment of Petronius. its Authority disputed by Hadr: Valesius, & M: Vagenseil. the first discovers many Barbarisms in it. a Roman Lady with Neck-Handkerchief & Garters. his Opinion of the genuine Petronius, that he lived under M: Aurelius, wrote a bad Style — [455] Medal of Britannicus in the Cabinet of M: Seguin, exceeding rare, struck at Alabanda — [558] Simon Paulus, Phys:ᵃⁿ to the K: of Denmark, de Abusu Tabaci, & Herbae Theae — [585] J: Grant's Observations. 1666. Bills of Mortality introduced in the Plague-Time. from 1603 to 1625. that Distemper carried off near a 5ᵗʰ of the Inhabitants of London. he reckons that usually one Person in 40 die of a Fever, of Chron:ᶜᵃˡ Distempers as Dropsy, Consumption, &c: 70 in 239. of external Maladies, as Wounds, Cancers, &c: 1 in 60. in Child-Bed after Delivery 1 in 100. in Labour 1 in 200. of 229000 Persons dead within the last 20 Years in London, 71124, of Worms, Teeth, & Fits. 12210, of Small-Pox & Measles. some Distempers are perceived to decrease & others to Increase; of the Rickets in 1634, died 14, in 1660, 500. the Stone seems to have diminish'd. the Gout at a Stand, about one in 100 [1000] dieing of it. with Respect to different Ages there are 20 times more Children born in due time, than before it. of 100 born at the same Time 6 Years after there remain 64 alive, at 16 Years End, 40; at 26 Years, 25; at 36, 16; at 46, 10; at 56, 6; at 66, 3; at 76, 1. at 80, seldom any at all. he reckons in Town 14 Boys are born to 13 Girls: but more Men die, than Women. that in the Country usually for 52 that die, 63 Persons are born. in Town 12 Persons die for 11 that are born. that in those Years that many die so much fewer are born, & vice-versâ. that in London are 15000 Burials Yearly, of wch 5000 are Infants, & 12000 are Christen'd. he reckons in London 48000 Families at 8 Persons to each, wch makes 384000 Persons, & in the rest of England about 14 times as many or 6,000,000 of Souls. that 6000 Persons come every Year to London, & that in 20 Years that City has increased from 7 to 12, in 40 Years from 23 to 52. that one Marriage with another produces 4 Children, that of 7 sick Persons one dies – [606] Letter from M: de la Voye to M: Auzout, on certain Worms that feed on Stone. they are black about 2 Lines long, & 3/4 broad, liveing in little Societies enclosed in a small Cone the Size of a Barleycorn, at the sharp End is a Hole for their Excrements, at the other they put forth their Heads, & Legs, by wᶜʰ they adhere to the Stone. but they can quit this Case on Occasion. there is another kind feeding on old Mortar, &c –

V: 2   1667.

[59] Lettre du P: Pardies a M: Payen. a Source of Salt-Water at Sallies en Bearn, wᶜʰ twice a Week fills a Bason of 40 Ft Diam:ʳ the Rain-Water does not mix with it, but swims a-top, nor will an Egg sink in it. it is distributed to the Inhabitants, as often, who keep it in a large wooden Reservoir, & evaporateing the Liquid in a flat Vessel of Lead on the Fire a fine white Salt remains. &c: – [125] Petri Blesensis Opera. the Feast of Fools on New Year's Day, the Bishop of Fools celebrated

Mass, while the Rest in Masks danced, sung, eat, &c: in the Church; not quite abolish'd, till the 15th Century – [186] Dissert: of Ott:^{via} Falconieri on a Medal of the Emp: Philip struck at Apamea in Syria with Noah's Ark on the Reverse – [218] a Dog, (whose Thorax was open'd, the Diaphragm, & Pericardium taken out) preserved alive above an Hour by blowing into the Lungs – Cessation of Motion in that Part not fatal, but only the Want of fresh Air – [230] Dissection of a Lion, Head exceeding big from the Quantity of Flesh & Size of the Jawbones, no Sheaths to the Talons, Stiff Neck from the Hardness of the Ligaments. Roughness of the Tongue, Gilding of the Choroides. Nictitans Membrana, as in the Cat. Æsophagus not very large. huge Heart with capacious Ventricles. Thickness of the Skull. Strength of the Wind-Pipe, Quantity of Bile, Solidity of the Flesh, little Brain. [320] Lettre de M: J: Dennis. ten Ounces of Blood taken from a Mad-Man, & 6 of a Calve's Blood transfused, & 2 Days after a Pint more. a Sweat succeeded, & violet Evacuations both ways. then 10 Hours Sleep; he after made blackish Urine, bled much at the Nose, grew quiet & gradually recover'd his Senses – [379] Mem:^{res} de Deageant. . James 1^{st's} Intention to write to the Pope, & be reconciled to that Religion a little before he died – [382] Worms of an oval Form frequently found in Sheep's Livers – [410] Spicileg:^{um} Vet: Scriptorum a D: Luc: Dachery, chiefly Ecclesiastical. T:8. Par:4to. Treatise by Henry of Huntingdon on the Misfortunes of such as seem'd happiest in his Time – Harangue of Pius 2^d in answer to the French Embassadours on his giveing the Investit:^{ure} of Naples to Ferdinand. Of the Card: d'Albi in 1469 on the Fr: and Span: Nations – Chronicle of Nic: Traveth, a Dominican from 1136 to 1307 – [456] T: Bartholinus de Medicinâ Danorum domesticâ – Bread in Norway made of Barley & Oats, that keeps 40 Years. Food of the Danish Common-People, Stockfish, salted & smoked Flesh – Snow, a nourishing Food – Scurvy, Mulberries, a Specifick for it – In Iceland a periodical Small-Pox every 20 Years – only 3 Apothecaries in Copenhagen – [466] the Mss: of Petronius brought from Dalmatia to S: Grimaldi of Bologna, probably near 300 Years old – [551] Dissection of a Dromedary, &c: – Gibbus on the Back only a Tuft of Hair – 6 Knees (as Herodotus asserts) really so – [561] Erasmus condemn'd by the Theologians in 1526 at Paris, for writeing Paraclētus instead of Paraclitus. [619] Village call'd Bonnecourt on the R: d'Eure near Passy consumed at different Times by a spontaneous Fire of a blewish Colour & stinking Smell – *vid: infra. [Vol. 3 below.]

Vol: 4. 1675.

[150] Lettre de M: Perrault, of a Girl, aged 22, who had a daily & regular Vomiting of Worms, of the Shape & Size of small Leeches, but white, wch when exposed to the Sun's Warmth grew more lively. she was help'd by drinking iced Water – [183] Architecture Navale de N: Witsen. Fol: Amst: – Ancient Vessel found on the Coast of Africa in the Sea, under Pius' 2^d, supposed to be 1400 Years old – [195] T: Bartholini Acta Medica & Philos:^{ca} Fibres of the Torpedo, their Motion causes the Pain we feel – D: of Brunswick died of Worms caused by eating Fruit & Salades – 1676 [71] Lett: de M: Dodart. On a sort of distemper'd Rye, found in Sologne & Gatinois, the eating of wch causes Gangreens in the Nose, Fingers, &c: wch drop off. [172] Bibliotheca Hispana. Fol: Romæ. Account of all their Writers, the several Editions, &c

Vol: 5. 1677.

[30] The Fleur de Bluet with its Calix bruised, steep'd in Snow Water 24 Hours & distilled in a Sand-Heat. this Water excellent for Inflammations & all Dis-

tempers of the Eyes, a few Drops being instilled Morning & Evening. confirm'd
by M: Charras & the Journ: d'Allemagne – [83] T: Bartholinus de Peregrinatione
Medicâ Hafniæ – Fol:º Manna an Exsudation of the Calabrian Ash-Tree in June
& July. an inferiour Sort gather'd from Incisions made in the Bark. Coral gather'd
near Trapani in Sicily. Sugar cultivated & made there – [175] Telescopes invented
& described by J: Battista Porta in 1589. Microscopes by Fontana a Neapolitan
in 1618 – [201] Marquis de Langey A: 1653 accused of Impotence by his Wife
demands the Congress, wᶜʰ proves unsuccessful: they are separated, & both marry
again. he has 7 Children by his 2ᵈ Wife, & (as this Marriage was contrary to the
Prohibition of the Court) it is rehear'd by the Court at their Instance in 1675,
determined for them, & all future Congresses forbid. . [282] a Stone, on wᶜʰ
Nature had represented 16 Figures, among wᶜʰ were 2 Portraits of Lewis 14ᵗʰ,
the Emperour, the Pope, &c: – [352] Artificial Man, made by Reyselius, a
Physician, whose Viscera perform'd all their proper Motions, & Evacuations –

*Vol: 3. 1672.

[5] Invention of the Speaking Trumpet by Sʳ Samuel Morland – [7] Recherches
de M: Bocconi, Sicilien, 12ᵐᵒ.Par: – Account of the Eruption of M:Ætna in 1669,
wᶜʰ he saw – [14] A Male Child, born in the Mans, wᶜʰ at 1/2 a Year old had the
Head, Body, & Genitals as large as a Man of 30. it was cover'd in several Places
with flaxen Hair, had a Beard, &c, & was 3 Foot. it died at 3 & 1/2 old – [40] In
the Year 1670 the Number of Burials exceeded the Baptisms by 4651. in 1671 the
Baptisms surpassed the Burials by 1134, at Paris –[53] Egg found in the Matrix
of a Woman by M: Kerkering, after 3 or 4 Days Impregnation. it was of the Size
of a Black Cherry [grosse Guigne], & the Head & some Lineaments of a Fœtus
were perceptible. another after 15 Days & the Features of the Face, the Legs &
Arms appear'd. in 3 Weeks the Bones (like Cartilages as fine as Hairs) are
separable from the Flesh. the Eggs in the Ovary of Birds much larger than those
of Women & these than those of Cows – Hippocrates, Fallopius, Wharton, Harvey
&c: had some imperfect Idea of this before Kerkering – Ovary as large as a Goose-
Egg found in a Maid of 18, & in it an Egg of the Size of an Olive, wᶜʰ killed her
– Horn that grew out of the Knee of a Man at Florence near 70 Years of Age in
3 Years Time; Girl at Chieri born with 5 little Ram's Horns. another at Palermo
with Horns at every Joynt. [263] Observations de M: Redi, Proofs of the Serpent-
Stone, its Inefficacy – [265] Eyes of several Birds pricked so as to let out the
Humours, & restored of themselves in 24 Hours – [273] Pearl swallow'd by
Pigeons lose much of their Weight in 24 Hours – African Money found in the
Stomach of an Ostrich 8 Months after it came out of Barbary, little impair'd –
[291] Experiments of Borelli, &c: to shew that naturally the left Eye sees clearer
& more distinct than the right – [Conferences, 1673, 52] the Styptic Essence of M:
Dennis, wᶜʰ stops presently the Flux of Blood from an Artery – [67] Dissection of
a Child, who lived 9 Months without any Brain, the Skull being one solid Bone –
it died the Instant it was born, as tho' suffocated by the Air. [71] another born
with the Navel-String separated & no way joyn'd to the Afterbirth. it lived & did
well. –

Vol: 6.   1678.

[29] Dissection of a Kidney 4 Fᵗ 8 Inches in Circumference, that weigh'd 68
Pounds, & more. it had been growing 13 Years, & at length kill'd the Person –
[93] Bread made in Upper Lusatia with a Mixture of white Earth, but only in
Time of Want – [143] Alexandreïs of a Flemish Poet in the 12ᵗʰ Century call'd

Gualterus, borrowed from the very Words of Q: Curtius. that Historian probably wrote in Claudius' Time – [217] Arch of Triumph, served as a Gate to the City of Rheims, till it was buried in the Rampart of 1544. call'd Porte de Mars, a Roman Way led to it. probably of Julian's Age. it has 3 Arches with 2 Corinth: Columns between each. betwixt the Columns are square Reliefs with Pediments over them & Medaillons with Heads above, &c: on the Vaults & Sides are also Reliefs, in Compartments of Romulus & Remus, Leda & the Swan, the 12 Months, included in Borders of Arms thrown together, & a Victory writeing on a Shield at the Corners. the Workmanship indifferent – [305, with full-page illustration] Letter from M: Bayle at Toulouse. a Child, that continued in his Mother's Womb (Belly, for it was out of the Matrix.) 26 Years. she died aged 64, & it was then taken out, weighing [8 pounds of] 16 Ounces, & not corrupted. she fancied she felt it move for near 20 Years. its Teeth were full grown, the Skull broke in pieces, the Head downwards, & no appearance of Blood, except about the Heart – [308] Museo Cospiano, Fol: Bologna. 1678 – [324] Pope Silvester 2^d (Cæsius) accused of Magick on account of his Mathematical Knowledge – [426] Treatise on the Tarantula by Sanguerdius – [435] J: Kunkelius, Animadv: de Salibus fixis & volatilibus. Receipt for the Philosopher's Stone preserved in the Archives of the Electors of Saxony, with wch Christian 1st turn'd Mercury, Copper, &c: into Gold. Augustus, in 1590, did the same – [452, illustrated] Besnier, a Locksmith of Sablé, invented a machine to fly with –

[Omitted: scattering notes to 1700; and *Acta Eruditorum* for 1696.]

Hist: & Memoires de l'Academie des Sciences.

1692.

Observ:^{ns} of Cassini on the Parallel of Marseilles as observed by Pytheas 2000 Years ago – Strings of red Berries produced by a common Oak. they were smooth & spongy with no Signs of an Animal within – Burning Phosphorus invented by one Brandt, a Chymist at Hamburg in 1669. re-discover'd by M: Kunkel of Saxony, communicated to Homberg – it's uncommon Properties. Metallic Vegetations by Homberg – On the Longitude of East-China, by Cassini – Some Account of the Kingd:^{m} of Ava, by P: Duchatz who was made Prisoner in the Revolutions of Siam, & sent thither –

1693.

M: Charas, being bit by a Viper in the Finger, suck'd the Wound, then made a Ligature with Packthread above it immediately, & some time after another just below the Elbow. went to Bed 2 Hours after the Bite, & took 24 Gr:^{ns} of the Salt of Vipers, & 4 Hours after as much more w^{ch} (with drinking something warm) brought on a Sweat. in 2 Hours more he undid the Ligatures, wch were painful; & went to sleep. he felt nothing the next Day, only a Redness remaind about the Wound 3 Days, & the Skin peel'd off. in Case the Vol:^{le} Salt can not be had, he recommends the Head, Neck, Liver & Heart of a Viper a little broil'd – Dissect:^{n} of a Crocodile near 11 Feet long in Siam. the Hind-Feet web'd. Smallness of the Eyes, Membrana nictitans, 30 Teeth & upwards in each Jaw, all canine. the greatest Opening of the Jaws 15 Inches & 1/2. the Top of the Skull was Musket-proof. Upper Jaw falsely said to move. Æsophagus admitted a Cylinder above 7 Inches Diam:^{r}. Tongue lies closely fix'd to the lower Jaw – Information concerning Camels from the Persian Embass:^{dour} at Siam – the Breed with 2 Gibbus's on their Back, esteem'd for Carriage, & only found in Turquestan. the Gibbus of all Camels is a Substance of spongy Flesh & Fat, & not in the Bone. Water said to be found in their Stomach, false –

1699.

Burning Fountain near Grenoble (mention'd by S: Austin)Civ: Dei.L:11. C: 7. examined into. it is a lambent Flame on the Steep of a Mountain proceeding from a certain Spot of Ground, & smelling of Sulphur. it burns chiefly in Winter or moist Weather, & gradually diminishes dureing the Heats. – Snails, Slugs, Earth-Worms, Leeches, &c: observed to have both Sexes in themselves, by M: Poupart. Dissection by Tauvry, of a Young Man, who died by the Bite of a Mad Dog – Blood in the Arteries would not coagulate. Gall-Bladder full of a black Bile. Hot-Remedies (Sea-Salt excepted) bad for the Patient. Vomits gave much Ease. Hydroph:bia cured by binding a Person down & almost drowning them – Tourne-fort, Account of the Tamarind-tree, a Native of Africa, Arabia, & India, since transplanted to America. Serapion & the Arabs are the first that have mention'd it. one grew in 1689 at Granada on the Alhambra-Terrass, planted by the Moors. it is the Size of a large Walnut-tree, but more thick and shady. the Pulp is con-tained in Siliquæ of a reddish Colour. it is highly acid, of a Nature like Verjuice, giveing an essential Salt like Cream of Tarter – Angelus Palea & another Cordelier, who commented on Masue in 1543 first affirm'd that Manna was an Exudation of the Calabrian Ashe – Homberg, on the odd Copulation of the Demoiselle-Fly (the Blue Libellus) – Poupart, curious Account of the Scurvy at Paris, this Year re-sembleing the famous Plague of Athens, Ol2:87.2. in the spots on the Skin, the ulceration of the Mouth, fœtid Breath, continual Flux, extreme Dejection of Mind, &c: the Summer (contrary to the common Scurvy) heighten'd the Dis-order. the Pains of the Head, Stomach, Belly, Legs, &c: were violent, the Gums continually itch'd, a corrosive & putrid Water ran from their Nostrils, & other Parts; those, who could move, rather totter'd than walk'd, their Appetite was ravenous to the last Moment. large Abscesses broke out under the Arms, & in the Groin of many; some grew stupid, stareing Statues with their Mouths wide open; on moveing a crackleing sort of Noise of the Bones was heard; the Muscles grew hard as Wood, & blew Spots, the sure Signs of Death, appear'd all over them. in some old Persons a Flux of Blood not to be stop'd broke out by the Nose, or by Stool, wch destroyed them: many younger found extreme difficulty in breathing, & died instantly, as suffocated. some Corps's were so horrible, that he dare not open them: in dissecting several the Skin of his Hands & Face peel'd from the Corrosiveness of their Juices. he found that the Epiphyses were separated from the Bones, & these latter grown black swell'd & carious, the Ligaments corroded, & instead of the Oyl, that should moisten them, a green caustick Water remain'd: the Breast full of Pus. the Pericardium sticking to the Lungs, & these to the Pleura. in short the Surface of all the Viscera so ulcerated, that they form'd all-together one confused Mass. the Substance of the Liver & Spleen all rotte[n]. the Auricles of the Heart full of clotted Blood. the Brain alone remain'd unalter'd, & in good Condition — the Discourse on the Instit:on of the Academy by Fontenelle at the Beginning of this Vol: is excellent.

1700.

Account of the Grotto of N: Dame de la Balme near Grenoble, by Dieulamant – Amber found in the Clefts of barren Rocks in Provence – Vernage, a young Woman tap'd for a Dropsy, from whom was taken 14 Pints of a Substance like Milk each time. it was saltish & would not coagulate with Acids, but with Salt of Tartar. she died in a Year – Dodart, on the Formation of the Voice – Courtial, on a Woman who after a Fever & violent Pain in her Limbs for 19 Months, was found to have all her Bones (the Teeth excepted) as soft as Wax. (v: supra P:4, Art: 5) – S: Donat a[t] Sisteron, a Swelling as large as a Turky Egg extracted from the Testicle of a Young Man, in wch were some Rudiments of a Fœtus – Petrified Spleen in a Man 60 Years of Age –Du Verney. a Worm 4 Inches long found in the Superiour longitudinal Sinus of a Child's Brain, 5 Years old. it resembled an Earthworm, & lived 6 Hours – a Woman 20 Years old lost her Voice totally after an intermitting Fever, & recover'd it by a Decoction of Vulner-ary Herbs drank as Tea – Sauveur, on a Manner of fixing a Sound, as a Standard – Tournefort, on Marine Plants – Lemery, on fiery Earthquakes &c: Receipt to make an artificial one – Burlet, on Lime-Water. first used internally by Dr Willis. it should be Stone-Lime new made, in large Lumps & kept dry. the Water, Rain warmed (8 Pounds of Water & one of Lime). Dysenteries & Asthmas cured by it. it is a powerful Alterative Alkaline. produces almost always a Sickness & Disgust in the Stomach(wch is conquer'd by Alicant or Wormwood Wine) most success-ful in Holland, where Beer, Butter, Fish, &c: are much used, & the Air is moist. best mix'd with Milk, or some Pectoral Infusion, 4 or 5 Ounces at a Time. given twice a Day – Couplet, Fils – his Voyage to Brasil, shipwreck'd in his Return on the Coast of Picardy & all his Papers lost – the Serpent call'd by the Portuguese (tho falsely) the double-headed, about 2 Foot long; the Author, (tho' fore-warn'd by the Natives) on flaying a dead one, was seized with a Sort of Itch in reddish Pustules, that lasted 3 Months – another Serpent shot in the Woods 15 F^t long & 18 Inches round, wch Kind is eaten by the Brasilians – Dodart, on the human Voice, (v: supra)

1701.

Homberg, on the Army of Pismires in Surinam – Geoffroy, the Black shineing Sand of Italy, a Mixture of Iron-Dust, & Falk – the Sand of Pesaro, an Assemblage of small pretious Stones – Story of 3 Persons & a Dog suffocated in an old Well, as in the Grotta del Cane – Gaetano Giulio Zumbo of Siracusa, his curious Works in Wax, presents a Head to the Academy –

1702.

Geoffroy, return'd from Italy. his Account of the Tarantula & its Bite – Manner of makeing Alumn at Civita-Vecchia & Solfatara – Mollart, keeps a Cheese-Mite between the Glasses of a Microscope, wch lived 7 Months, then went into a Chrysa-lis, & came out a Fly – Lemery; a Man of 45 Years old, robust & cover'd with black Hair, on takeing a Purge from an Empirick, looses all his Hair, wch grows again, but thin & flaxen – Cassini, on compareing the Distance from Nemausus to Narbo, mark'd by Strabo (88 M:) & that from Bononia to Mutina in the Itinerary & Peutinger's Tables (25 M:) an ancient Mile is found to be 767 Toises of Paris; & a Foot Roman equal to 11 Inches 1/25 of Paris – Boutier & Delisle, on the Canal of Communication between the Nile & Redsea: a Part of it still visible. Elmacin says that the Calife Amr made such a Canal (that is probably, clear'd the old one) A: D: 635 in order to convey Corn from Egypt to Arabia, & that Almansor in 775 stop'd it up toward the Sea – Cassini – ancient Measures (as above) applied. Distance between Narbo & the Temple of Venus Pirenæa mark'd by Strabo 63 Miles does not answer to the modern Port-Vendre near Colioure but (within 21 Toises) to la Selve, a large Port N: of Cap-Creux (the Aphroditic or Pirenæan Promontory) – Distance between the Mouth of the Var & the Venus Pirenæa, in Strabo 277 Miles, that is 2600 (or 2800 according to some) Stadii. 9 Stadii at least ought to be reckon'd to an ancient Mile. a Stad: 85 Toises or 510 Feet

of Paris. Herodotus reckons 600 Greek feet to a Stad:ᵐ, a Gr: Foot is then to a
Paris F:ᵗ as 51 to 60. Herod:ᵗᵘˢ makes the Side of the Great Pyramid 800 Fᵗ (a
Stad: & 1/3) that is 680 Paris Feet. Chazelles measured it & found 690 Fᵗ (but
subtracting something for the Inequality of Ground, this agrees nearly to the
former) P: Fulgence, a Capucin of Tours (as Gemelli reports) in 1693 found it
682 Fr: Feet, wᶜʰ corresponds to the Measures of M: de Nointel. Greaves differs
vastly; he makes it $\frac{693.}{683}$ English Fᵗ, wᶜʰ is 723 French (here seems some Mistake
the Fr: Foot being longer than ours by 68/1000). Du-Verney, le jeune – wonderful Cure of an Arm gangrened after a Wound by a Woman's Oyntment, not
alone the unsound Flesh, but the Bone separated of itself – Tournefort, Description of the Labyrinth of Candia, & on the Vegetation of Stones –

1703.

La Hire – Account of the Pucerons, that live on the Backside of Peach & Nectarine
Leaves, &c: they are transform'd from a creeping to a flying Animal without any in-
termediate Chrysalis-State – the Pismires eat them – Felibien, a young Man deaf from
his Birth on a sudden begins to hear, & 4 Months after to speak. his Account of himself, & the State of his Mind dureing his Deafness – Account of the Mountain
call'd inaccessible in Dauphiné 9 Leagues S: of Grenoble. Fictions reported of it –
Du Verney le jeune – an Ox in good Case (haveing broke loose 4 Times before
it was knocked down) is found to have the Brain almost entirely petrified, hard
as a Flint. a similar Case reported by Bartholini, Centur:ᵃᵉ Anat.ᶜᵃᵉ, L: 6, Hist: 91.
but the Animal was lean, & always drooping its Head – the Chev: Colbert at the
battle of Walcourt had his left Eye (by a Stone) drove quite into his Brain, & a
Part of its Substance work'd out of the Wound. yet (except the first Minutes,
when he lost his Senses) for 7 Days that he lived after it, his Judgement & Facul-
ties remain'd unalter'd – A Girl 7 Years old after a Fever loses both her Arms, wᶜʰ
wither & drop off of themselves – Eloge of Viviani, the Florentine Mathematician –

1704.

Maraldi – Several Alterations made by the Earthquakes in the Abruzzo, & else-
where in 1702 & 3 – Eloge of the Marquis de l'Hôpital – Sarrasin – Dissection &
Way of Life of the Bever – Poupart, of the Formica Leo – its Manner of preying on
Animals by a Pit-fall, wᶜʰ it digs in the Sand. its Transformation into the grey
Demoiselle Fly – Pʳᵉ Truchet – the various Combinations of 2 Squares, diagonally
divided into 2 Colours, with Plates of them –

1705.

Dodart – Letter from M: Lippi, a Physician, who attended M: du Roule into
Æthiopia. Discovery of a Bee-Hive not entirely petrified on the Mountains of Siout
in Upper Egypt – Bonnac, Fossile Amber found near Dantzick – a sort of it found
on Mount Bugarach (27600 Toises distant from the Sea) in Languedoc. the Inhabitants burn it in their Lamps, for it is soft & resinous – Littre, Account of a
young Man condemn'd to be broke on the Wheel, who run with his Head against
the Prison Walls, & died instantly without a Groan: on opening the Head no
Contusion or Fracture could be found. Lemery. .Account of Camphire – Delisle,
his Theatre Historique, being a large Map of the Roman Empire & Countries
adjoining, about the Year of Xᵗ 400, where Sanson's Faults are corrected – Eloge
of James Bernoulli, of Bâsle – of M: Amontons – Poupart, on the Froth found on

Plants in the Spring (Cuckow-Spittle) or the Generation of Grasshoppers –
Tournefort on the China Pink. The same, on the Maladies of Plants, & the Capri-
fication still used in the Levant –

1706. P: 1.

A Danish Bitch, big with young, being shut up in a Room & forgot for 41 Days,
was found alive on a Matrass, part of wch she had gnawed, but reduced to extreme
Weakness. there was no Appearance of her Puppies, nor Excrements; she was
likely to recover – Du-Hamel, another confined 6 Weeks (with nothing but Water,
& the Straw out of a Chair) which also recover'd – Lemery, a strong Scent of
Musk observed to result from Bitumen, Galbanum, Sagapenum, & Opoponax
laid by Chance together in Parcels – Poupart; another small Worm, wch lives like
the Formica-Leo, & turns into a kind of large Gnat – Animal with 80 Legs, that
seems to have two Heads & moves alike backwards or forwards – La Hire, on
Cataracts in the Eye – Dissection of a Woman, who died of drinking Wine &
Brandy, at 45 Years of Age; the Blood was black & clotted, being full of Tartre,
the Liver & Lungs schirrous, & several Glands petrified – a Young Woman over-
turn'd in a Cart – had a Part of it enter'd into the Skull, tore the Dura & Pia
Mater, so that the Substance of the Brain issued out. she walk'd after the Accident
15 or 20 Paces, & then lost her Senses for 4 Hours, & she was entirely cured at
length – Eloge of J:B:Du Hamel – Poupart, on Muscles & other Shell-fish – their
progressive Motion, their fluttering a-top of the Water, their Distempers – Dodart,
on the human Voice & its Mechanism –

1706. P: 2.

Lemery, Chymical Analysis of Honey. that of Corbiere near Narbonne highly
esteem'd in France: it is white. that of Champagne, wch is yellow, excellent. that
of Normandy worst of all – Cassini, Account of the lambent Flame seen on the
Apennine at Pietra Mala. Combustible Substances, thrown on that Spot of Ground
take Fire instantly. Snow thrown on melts; but the Flame burns more lively than
before. there arises thereabouts a fragrant Odour, as of Aloes-Wood consumeing
– Dodart, as above, & on the ancient Musick – La Hire, on the Invention of the
Barometer –

1707. P: 1.

A Musician of Note cured of a violent Frenzy by Musick in 10 Days – Homberg.
Europæans who go to Batavia not able to suckle their Children, their Milk is so
salt. so that the Black Slaves give Suck there – Eloge of M: Regis – Of the Marshal
de Vauban – Of the Abbé Gallois – Of M: Dodart – Lemery, On the Virtues of
Cow's-Piss; long in Use in Germany. the Animal must be young, at Grass, &
without the Bull, in Springtime, or Autumn; 2 or 3 Glasses fasting for 10 Days.
it purges both Ways. good for the Rheumatism, Gout, Dropsy beginning, Jaundice,
Asthma, Hystericks – Tournefort, On the Cultivation of Mushrooms.

1707. P: 2.

Homberg, on 6 Species of Spiders; the House-Spider, wch sheds its Skin every
Year, lives 4 Years & upwards, is apt in hot Countries to grow scaly & lousy;
the Garden-Spider of different Colours, spinning a large thin Web in the Centre
of wch it commonly dwells. Oyl of Turpentine destroys it instantly. the Black
Cellar-Spider wch has a large belly & short legs, will kill a Wasp, & bites the
Instrument that lays hold of it. it is long-lived, & continues alive more than 40

Hours, after its belly is pierced thro'. the Wanderer, wch makes no Web, but runs after it's Prey. this is of several Colours & has two Feelers, like Plumes of Feathers. the Carter or Long-leggs, & the Tarantula, wch has 8 yellow Eyes. the other kinds (except the black, wch has but 6) have 8 Eyes apiece, but differently situated in each Species – On the Effect of Gunpowder in Mines, by M: Chevalier – Lemery, on the several Kinds of Vitriol –

1708.

Letter to the French Embassadour at Constant:^ple from P:^re Bourgnon at Santorini (Thera) giveing an Account of the wonderful Production of a new Island, that rose from the bottom of the Sea near it with a horrible Noise & Burning in 1707, from May 23 to Nov: 20. like Appearances have happen'd there in 726, 1427, & 1573, & 1650 – La Hire, Burning Glasses known to the Ancients, shown from Aristophanes in the Clouds. Sc:1.Act:2, & the Scholiast. Plin: L: 36.37. Lactantius de Ira Dei – Eloge of M: Tournefort – Reneaume, On the Manner of preserving Corn. some in the Citadel of Metz reposited in 1578 of wch good Bread was made in 1707 – the Ζειὰ of the Greeks, Far, Triticum rufum grano maximo, Lat: Spelt, Germ: Espeautre, Blance, Fr: the Husk not separable from the Grain without parching. it is much used in some Parts of Germany, where there are Mills contrived on purpose – Delisle, on the Island Meroë. Strabo & others assure that it is form'd by the Conflux of the Nile, the Astaboras & Astapus, that it is 5000 Stad: from Syene South, (wch is about 16 Deg: & 1/2 N: Latitude) Pliny & Ptolemy confirm this. Diodorus & Strabo give it 3000 Stad: (120 Leagues) in Length & 1000 Stad: (40 Leagues) in breadth. Strabo assures, the regular Rains are first met with in this Country; that it is in form like a Buckler. Pliny, that Plants & Trees are first seen here, as you travel from Egypt South, & Elephants caught. now as to Islands strictly speaking there are none approaching these Dimensions in the Nile. but there is a Peninsula enclosed by the Nile, the Tacaze (still call'd by the Scheiks of Nubia, Atbara) & the Dender. its N: Bounds are in 17 Deg: 1/2 Lat: the Jesuits have made the same Observations as to the Rains, the Plants, the Elephants, & the Fertility of the Country with the Authors abovemention'd. the City of Guerri is seated on the Nile, nearly where Strabo & Pliny place the Capital of Meroë.

[A drawing of the region described follows.]
*   *   1712.

Eloge of J: Domenico Cassini, the great Astronomer – Reaumur, on the Motion of some Shell-fish of a kind of Starr-fish, & the Sea-Urchin – the latter walks by means of its Prickles, wch it has often to the Number of 2100, & from their Roots it exerts occasionally 1300 Horns, like those of Snails, by means of wch it fixes itself to any Body it pleases. these it so contracts, that they are no longer visible, when it is out of the Water: the numerous Holes with wch the Skeleton of an Urchin is all over embroider'd, are made to admit & to thrust out these Horns, wch are moveable in all Directions, as are their Prickles also – Homberg, Art of copying graved Gems in colour'd Glass – Geoffroi jun: on the Bezoar & its Production – on the Pearl found in the Pinna marina on the Coast of Provence – of the Byssus, or Filaments spun by this Shell-fish. the Pinnophylax (a small Crab often found in the other's Shell) ancient Storys about it false – the Castor-Stone, found in the Pouch of the Bever – on the Choice of Castor. that from the Levant best; next, that of Dantzic. (some taken in the Rhone, not inferior in Goodness) the worst, that of Canada – Reaumur, on Crabs, Craw-fish, Lobsters, wch if you break off either of their great Claws, produce another, or (if a Part only be lost) just so much as is wanting. but the Part from whence a new Claw grows with greatest Ease is between the 3ᵈ & 4ᵗʰ Joynt from the Extremity; the Horns also & little Legs grow again, but slower. (as do the Tails of Lizards) they lie in Holes & eat nothing near 8 Months in the Year all the cold Weather. in Summer between May & September they cast their whole Shell (their entire outward Covering, even of the Eyes, & also the Cartilages in the midst of the Flesh of yᵉ great Claws) from wᶜʰ by repeated Efforts they disengage themselves, & that about the Claws being most difficult to quit, they often leave Claw & all behind them. the new Membrane comes to its hardness in two or three Days: at the same time a new Stomach is produced in them, within wᶜʰ the Remains of the old one is by degress digested — Maraldi – Curious Account of Bees & their Manners –

1713.

Reaumur, on the Ductility of Gold &c: an Ounce beat into Leaves cover'd 146 square Feet & 1/2. the Wire-Drawer makes the same Quantity cover 1190 Feet square – of Glass, & the Matter contain'd in Spider & Silk-Worms – Jussieu, History of Caffee-Tree of the Jessamine-Kind, Leaves like Laurel, Flower like the Spanish Jasmine but all white, very sweet, Fruit like a Heart-Cherry, red & when ripe, dark brown; each contains 2 Kernels, wᶜʰ is the Coffee. in Arabia grows 40 Feet high, trunk not 6 Inches in Diam:ʳ. the Seed soon loses its vegetative faculty, if not directly put into the Ground, when gather'd. the only Place, that produces it in any Quantity, is the Kingdom of Yeman in Arabia. the small green Berry brought to Cairo by the Mecca Caravan is finer than that from Moka, wᶜʰ is bigger & whiter: Vessels of glazed Earth are best to roast it in; when it approaches a deep violet Colour it is done enough.

1714.

Geoffroy, on Gum-Lac, 'tis the Work of an Insect, form'd on the small Twigs of Trees, chiefly in Pegu, & all its colour comes from the Remains of these Animals, left in the Nest or little Comb, for it is a waxy Substance. it is used for the finest red Dye in the East, & the matter that remains afterwards makes Sealing-Wax with other Ingredients. the Kermes is formed (like the Gall) [see Nisson at the End of this Volume] on the Flex aculeata cocci-glandifera, & serves as a Case to a small Insect; it is produced in Languedoc & elsewhere, very little used at present in Dyeing, but only in Medicine. the Cochineal of Poland is an Insect, wᶜʰ forms itself a Case about the Root of the Knavel or Alchimilla gramineo folio, once used for the true Cochineal in Holland. the true kind breeds on the Opuntia major (or Indian Fig) & serves for the finest Scarlet Dye. Carmine also, & Lake for Painting are made from it with Alumn &c: – Delisle, on the Roman Mensuration. 75 Rom: Miles are a Degree of Latitude. Distance of Rome & Florence (before the Observ:ⁿˢ of the Academy) in the Maps 20 Min: Lat: too little & 45 Min: Long:ᵗᵘᵈᵉ too much. Cluver mistaken in makeing the ancient & Modern Ital: Mile the same: these last differ in different Parts of Italy. 60 are reckon'd to a Degree of Latitude. Modern Maps make 90 Leagues to Carthage, & 60 to Prom: Mercurii from Lilybæum in Sicily, wᶜʰ are 2 thirds too much. they give twice the real Distance between Otranto & Sasina; the true one is 400 Stad: or 50 Rom: M: (about 12 Sea-Leagues). Greece is actually less, than that Part of Italy call'd Magna Græcia – Reaumur, on the Torpedo (Torpilla) ou Tremble) it is a kind of Scate, or Ray. it is often handled without exerting this Power, wᶜʰ feels like a sudden Shock on the Elbow, a numbing Pain, reaching even to the Head, &

takeing away the Use of the Arm for a few Moments. it seems caused by the Action of 2 Muscles in the Back, by w^ch (before the Stroke, haveing made its back gradually flat, or even a little concave) it restores it in one Instant to its natural Convexity. he put a Duck & a Torpedo into a Vessel together cover'd, & in an Hour the Duck was dead. The Fishermen eat this Fish (wch is insipid enough) but the Liver is better. . . La Hire, Roman Foot, compared with that of Paris, is eleven Inches of it, the Greek 11 & 1/2.

1715.

Part of the M: Diableret in the Valais, fell down at Noon-Day in fine Weather, 1714, & destroy'd 55 Cottages, 15 Persons, & above 100 Cattle. its Ruins cover'd a League square. the Root or Base of it was probably weaken'd & rotted by Time – Petroleum, best in Europe rises near Monte-Sestino in a barren Valley 12 Miles from Modena. there are Sources of 3 different Kinds. the first almost as clear & fluid as Water, of a pierceing & not disagreeable Scent: this is the finest, & very rarely exported. the 2^d is thicker & of a clear yellow; this they sell, but mix'd with the 3^d Kind or adulterated with Oyl of Turpentine. the 3^d is of a black-red, & smells of Bitumen. Boulduc procured some of the first. it catches Fire, if warm'd, from a Candle held at some Feet distance, & continues burning under Water. it swims on all Liquors, even rectified Spirit of Wine, & never freezes. Eloge of Morin, the Botanist; N: Lemery, Chymist, & of G: Homberg. of P: Malebranche – Reaumur, on the Turquoises of Simore in the lower Languedoc. they find them always in the Form of Arm or Leg-Bones, or Jaw-Teeth. the first often of 15 Pounds Weight, & the latter as big as one's Fist. they are moist & crumble usually to Pieces in takeing out of ye Mine. they are white; but being disposed in Furnaces of a particular Structure & gradually heated, they assume their blue Colour. if kept too long there, they lose it again; as they likewise do in distilld Vinegar, and Time (as it does by all other Sorts of Turquoise) reduces them to a pale Green. the Mines of Oriental Turquoise are both in Chorassan, a Province of Persia. the old Rock (as it is call'd) at Necabourg is dug only for the King's Use. the old Jewellers esteem a perfect Turquoise equal to the finest Emerald, wch thy rank with the Diamond. – Geoffroy, on the Oyl of Aspic (or Monpelier-Lavender) used in Japanning & Enamelling. they adulterate it with Spirit of Wine, wch is known by mixing Water with it. the Spirit (in Time) will unite with the Water, & the Oyl swim atop. it is also mix'd with Oyl of Turpentine, wch is known by the great Smoke it makes, if you burn a little in a Spoon.

Fabricii Bibliotheca Graeca. Vol: 1.

[One and a quarter pages listing contents more or less in detail, with references.]

Memoires de l'Academie des Inscriptions & des Belles-Lettres. 4to. Par: 1733.
beginning with Vol: 8th. from 1726 to 1730 inclus:^ve

[Five and a quarter pages of notes, mostly historical, from ancient and medieval times.]

REGISTER OF GRAY AUTOGRAPH MANUSCRIPTS [1]

I.   Commonplace Book. Three vols. folio, 7″ x 11″, containing poems, numerous articles, notes on reading, and (on flyleaves and inside covers) miscellaneous notes. Pagination continuous: vol. I (1–461), II (462–932), III (933–1096). III, 1097 ff., has some additional notes in Mason's hand taken from Gray's pocketbooks and stray papers, but most of vol. III is blank. Probably begun *c.* 1736 and abandoned *c.* 1759, although additions and corrections were made as late as 1768. Several articles were published (with corrections) by T. J. Mathias, *Works,* 1814, vol. II (reprinted in part by Gosse, *Works,* vol. IV), but most of it remains unpublished. Martin, *Chronologie,* gives a table of the chief articles and prints excerpts, including the entire article, "Cambri." Gray bequeathed it, along with other papers, to Mason, who left it to Stonhewer, who in turn gave it to the master and fellows of Pembroke College, Cambridge, in whose special care it now remains.

II. Quarto notebooks, mostly 6″ x 8″. All except No. 3 and No. 8 are now in the Pierpont Morgan Library, New York City, where they are kept in a box together with a copy of Gray's will.

  1. Catalogue of books, arranged by classes. Probably an early list of Gray's own library, begun *c.* 1734 and abandoned *c.* 1742. Contains also itemized list in later hand: "Books bought since I came to London, 1760." Printed, for the first time, in this volume, pp. 151–163.

  2. Catalogue of books, arranged alphabetically. Not a catalogue of Gray's library as usually described, but a bibliographical notebook kept for reference. Probably begun *c.* 1744, certainly before 1746, and abandoned presumably *c.* 1750. See discussion, pp. 42 ff.

  3. Miscellaneous, mostly travels of Shaw and Pococke. 1744–1745.
     (a) 1–3. "Nov: 1744. Mabillon's Musæum Italicum. Paris, 1687."
     (b) 3–17. "Travels by Dr. Shaw, Fellow of Queen's College, Oxford, and for 12 Years Chaplain to the Factory at Algiers. Ox: Fol: 1738. Dec: 6: 1744."
     (c) 17. "Ducatiana, 2 V: 12ᵐᵒ. Amst: 1783. x Dec: 6: 1744."
     (d) 18–22. "April: 25, 1745. Dʳ Pococke's Description of the East. Vol: 2d. P: 1. of his Travels." Recently (1930) in possession of Mr. Geoffrey Howard, Castle Howard, Yorkshire.

  4. Notes on learned journals. January 1744/5.
     (a) 1–4. *Journal des Sçavans.* 1666–1697.
     (b) 4. *Acta Eruditorum* (6 lines).
     (c) 5–9, 12. *Histoire et Mémoires de l'Académie des Sciences.* 1692–1715.
     (d) 10–11. Fabricii *Bibliotheca Graeca.*
     (e) 13–17. *Mémoires de l'Académie des Inscriptions et des Belles Lettres.* Vols. VIII–XV.

---

[1] This list does not include letters or poems. For letters, see Whibley, "List of Letters," prefixed to each volume of the correspondence. Autographs of the poems are mostly in the letters or in the Commonplace Book. Most of Gray's autographs included in the 1851 sale at Sotheby's were sold in one lot for £500.

5. Three classical notebooks, undated but probably 1745–1746.
   (a) Sophocles – notes only on *Ajax* and *Electra*.
   (b) Plutarch.
   (c) Thucydides (abandoned after five lines), Xenophon (1–11), and (bound in) fragments of extensive study of Diodorus Siculus (11–18). See VI. 7. g.
6. Notes on Greek philosophy and antiquities.
   (a) 1–8. Diogenes Laertius. Nov. 20, 1746.
   (b) Athenaeus. Jan. 4, 1747.
7. Notes on Greek orators.
   (a) Lysias. March 20, 1747.
   (b) Isocrates. Dec. 26, 1747. Finished March 1, 1747/8.
8. Notes on Greek poetry. British Museum Add. 36817.
   (a) fol. 1vo – 3ro. Tables of Greek royal families.
   (b) 4ro – 6ro. Notes on Pindar, mostly metrical.
   (c) 6vo – 19ro. Notes on Aristophanes (Mathias, II, 132 ff.).
9. Notes on Xenophon, mostly the *Cyropaedia*. March 1, 1748.

III. Pocketbooks for travel and field trips, about 4″ x 6″, all belonging to Sir John Murray, 50 Albemarle St., London. The account of the journey to the Lakes is a rough draft, with interpolated information on roads and with occasional corrections. The other notes, a few on architecture but most of them on natural history, are roughly done, in pencil gone over with ink or in many kinds of ink. Numerous corrections show the care Gray took with his observations on natural history.

1. Journey to France and Italy. Detailed account that extends only to Florence at the end of 1739.
2. Suffolk, 1761; Southampton, 1764; Old Park and Hartlepool, 1765.
3. Scotland, 1765; Bishoprick, Old Park, &c; Cumberland, 1769.
4. London and Kent, 1766 – 1768.
5. Journey to the Lakes (continuation of 3).
6. Not Gray. Mason on Gray and West.

IV. Diary pocketbooks kept by Gray. (The descriptions, except for 1755 and 1760, are taken from Mason's notes in CPB, III, 1097 ff.)

1754. Quotations and chronological memoranda relative to " the old modern Poetry." Gray also kept a journal with " most careful meteorological and botanical observations made daily from March 1 to Sept. 30," general observations on days in which flowers first bloom, and remarks on health. See below, V. 2.
1755. Now in Pembroke Library. Memoranda of books and articles on poetics, early English literature, and geography. Expense accounts; London, April 28 and Oct. 30; Stoke, June – October, with visits to the Vine and Twickenham. Notes on health printed in full, Martin, *Chronologie*, pp. 151 ff.
1756. " Nothing of any consequence."
1760. Now in Pembroke Library. Mostly expense accounts in London. Cambridge, July 29 – October 6. Thoughts published in Tovey, *Gray and His Friends*, pp. 270 f.

1761. "Too poor for a bribe," etc. "Some memoranda which may be of consequence relative to Harleian MSS. and the numbers referred to."

1762, 1763. "Nothing of any consequence."

1764. "Memoranda of rise of different rivers in Scotland. Mr. Gray was this year at Southampton. Some memoranda of natural history."

1765. "Memoranda of Places he saw in Scotland when on a visit to Lord Strathmore at Glamis in August to 8 of October. Memoranda also of Scotch words, &c." Very interesting extracts in Mitford MSS. (III¹, 112 ff.). Part of the notes are amplified in Gray's letter to Wharton from Glamis, September 1765 (Tovey, III, 82–93). Mitford's extracts deal mainly with return journey from Glamis by way of Crieff, Stirling, Falkirk, Lindithgow, Edinburgh, Musselburgh, Tranent, Dunbar, and Berwick (where was a bridge "325 of my paces (which makes 975 feet) in length"). They contain also a few observations on Scottish superstitions and language, as well as a long list of geographical terms used in Scottish place-names with meanings and examples. Expense account in London from October 30 to December 2, when he returned to Cambridge.

1766. "Catalogue of Hyacinths proper to blow in water. One or two notes of Natural History."

1767. "Memoranda in West of Yorkshire, Derbyshire, Cumberland, Durham, &c. but almost merely of his route."

1768. "Memoranda of Journey into Kent. Settled with Mrs. Oliffe this year and sold the Houses in the city."

1769. "Memoranda of journey Cambridge to Old Park, Hartlepool, back by Keswick through Craven to Aston to Cambridge – latter end of this year in Town."

1770. "Journey into Wales, &c."

V. Notes on natural history (see also Group III).

1. Leaves in copy of Linnaeus, *Systema naturae*. Harvard College Library. Facsimile reproductions of selections in C. E. Norton, *The Poet Gray as a Naturalist*, Boston, 1903.

2. Journal for 1754, March – September, four columns (date, wind, weather, remarks on health) and on opposite page detailed notes on growth and flowering of plants. Fifteen and one-half pages sm. 4to. Described in Hodgson catalogue, May 6, 1915.

3. Seven leaves, 7" x 11", mostly on insects, with seven drawings and notes on experiments, written in English. Also contains rough description of specimens observed at Cambridge. Harvard University, Library of Museum of Comparative Zoölogy.

4. Naturalist's journal. Entries from January 1, 1767 to May 18, 1771. Records minutely journeys as well as natural history. Described in 1851 catalogue (Lot 97) and sold to Maddon for eight guineas.

5. Loose leaves.

(a) Two leaves (two and one-half pages) in Gluck Collection, Buffalo (N. Y.) Public Library. Mainly birds. January 28, 1771.

(b) Two pages, 6" x 8", on insects. W. S. Lewis, Farmington, Conn.

(c) Four small sheets (about 750 words) on bulbs. Four columns "listing the name of the bulbs, the time of planting, the time of blooming, and the various colors and shapes of the flowers." Roderick Terry Sale, Anderson's, May 2, 1934. Sold to Brick Row Bookshop.

(d) Leaf from a botanical notebook and half-page description of a bird called the Bohemian Chatterer. See *Autograph Prices Current*, IV, 71 f.

VI. Miscellaneous papers (rough chronological arrangement).

1. 1730? Original drawings. "This Book contains a few attempts in Drawing by Mr. Gray, when a Boy; they prove him to have an accurate eye, which might have carried him much farther in the Art, had he pursued it," W. M(ason). Only in Evans sale, 1845.

2. 1734? Classical extracts, mostly poetical. Fifteen pages. Now in York Minster Library (given by Mrs. Dixon, widow of Mason's nephew). Cf. *Times Literary Supplement*, April 5, 1928.

3. 1739–41. MS. Collection of music. Cat. 1851, p. 21: "Gray has most carefully noted school of each composer, and the names of the Operas, &c. whence these selections have been made. In the volume which contains the compositions of Fini, there are two leaves in Gray's autograph, commencing 'Regole per l'Accompagnemente.'" Recently owned by H. E. Krehbiel, who described it in his *Music and Manners in the Classical Period* (New York, 1898), pp. 1–54. Cf. *Nation*, XI (1870), 10, and *Notes & Queries*, Nov. 7, 1885, 6th ser., XII, 368.

4. Travel notes on France and Italy. 1739–1741. These notes are on leaves which have been bound in an elaborate volume extra-illustrated with numerous engravings. They constitute a part of the John Morris Collection (marked also "John Dillon, 1863"), now in the Eton College Library. Published in full by Tovey, *Gray and His Friends* (Cambridge, 1890), pp. 204–260.

5. 1742. Loose leaf, 6″ x 8″, of random notes, W. S. Lewis, Farmington, Conn. Contains variant for *Ode on the Spring*: "Disclosed the breathing
flowers, & waked the purple Year."   infant
                          verdant
Also the following English lines: "Love of Business with some Men is but an excuse for Insipidity. Those, who have spent their Youth in the acquisition of what should be the Means of Pleasure, in their Age either know not or care not to apply it, & so it descends to a Race, who. . . ." Also notes on classics, with some Greek-Latin glosses and much on Greek military formations.

6. 1742–43. Notes on Roman Law, taken probably while reading for LL.B. Now in York Minster Library (from Mrs. Dixon). Cf. *Times Literary Supplement*, April 5, 1928.

7. 1746–50. Notes on Greek chronology, geography, northern words, and various miscellaneous papers, translations from the Greek, etc. Translations from the Greek, papers on chronology, modern history, etc. N.B. These papers, grouped in two lots (617, 619) in the 1845 sale at Evans's, seem to have been dispersed. The following miscellaneous items probably belonged to them:

(a) The chronological tables of Greek history, of which two leaves are now in the Harvard Library (in Mrs. J. T. Fields's copy of Gray's 1753 poems) and two fragments were recently owned by Dr. A. S. W. Rosenbach.

(b) Two leaves for sale by W. T. Spencer: 30 lines, containing 86 works of authors used in study of Oriental history, arranged alphabetically, and 22 lines on classical references concerning the laws governing marriage.

(c) Two leaves now owned by the Marquess of Crewe: "A Note on the Present State of India" and "Heads of the Treaty of the Peace of Versailles."

(d) Oriental history: four and one-half pages on Persia, half-page on Mesopotamia. *Autograph Prices Current,* I, 71.

(e) Loose leaves of classical notes, in Pembroke Library, in the possession of W. S. Lewis (genealogy of Appius Claudius & Fabius; "Ant: Augustinus de Legibus") and elsewhere (e.g., see the files of *Autograph Prices Current*).

(f) Notes on the invasion of Italy by the barbarians. Four pages 8vo. Now in Huntington Library, San Marino, Calif.

(g) Notes on Diodorus Siculus. Seven pages 4to. On the earlier books of the history, therefore obviously the part missing in the Morgan notebook (II. 5. c). Sold at Rains Galleries, New York City, Jan. 27, 1936.

8. The following miscellaneous notes of Gray from this period are listed by Mitford at various places in his MSS., but I have not been able to trace them:

(a) Notes on ancient authors. Strabo, Thucydides, Aeschylus. In list of "MSS. of Gray seen," Mitford MS. III^2, 131.

(b) Mitford MS. III^1, 60: "List of the Prints, Plates, Engravings of Antiquities, &c. (36) sent to Leghorn, the beginning of July 1740. At the back of the above is written: 'Bonducci, July 11 – every other day. Paid Berni for 3 months. Oct: 18 or 19: Oct: Begun with Prini Nov: 30. Wednesday. Paid Berti.' (I presume his Music Masters at Florence.)"

(c) "List of 168 Articles of Prints & Books of Prints in folio. 4 leaves."

(d) "University Library among the Pamphlets. Class. B."

(e) "Beauties and faults observed by Mr. Chambers in any of ye buildings in or near London." Extracts in Mitford MS. III^1, 62–64. One page (15 lines) for sale by W. T. Spencer.

(f) "Catalogues of Houses where are pictures, Statues, &c:"

N.B. Perhaps the above two items constitute what is described in the 1851 catalogue as "Copious and various MS. memoranda about Fine Arts."

(g) Miscellaneous classical extracts. Mitford MS. III^1, 69 (three pages from Dion: Halicarnass:); III^1, 82–85 (misc. extracts with some English lines); III^2, 115 (some parallels between Tibullus & Propertius and Greek dramatists).

N.B. These may be identical with two items offered for sale to Pembroke Library in 1928 by W. T. Spencer: (1) Notes on readings from the classics, 1750, 7 pp. 4to; and (2) Latin with some printed Latin verses, 3½ pp. 8vo.

(h) "Catalogue of his books & prints, both of them good & valuable."

(i) Latin essay, about twelve pages, beginning "Patria potestas Quiritium" and ending, "Nemo servus nascitur." Mitford MS. III^2, 131.

9. French verses, mostly *bergeries*. Luxuriously bound with translations and " note on the influence of French verse on Gray " by Samuel Clegg. Recently owned by Dr. A. S. W. Rosenbach. Mitford MS. III[1], 101–108.

10. June, 1752. Various Papers: political, historical, and biographical. Curious narrative *re* Duke of Richelieu. . . "Idee de la Personne, de la Maniere de Vivre, et de la Cour du Roi de Prusse."

11. Metaphysical papers, especially strictures on Lord Bolingbroke's writings. First published by Mason, 1775.

12. Welsh poem. One stanza in Welsh with literal translation of rest. Printed from Mitford MS. III[1], 88–90, by Tovey, *Gray and His Friends*, pp. 275 f. See *Autograph Prices Current*, I, 71.

13. Miscellaneous notes on English poetry and romances. Now at the end of first volume of Gray – Mason MSS. owned by A. Thomas Loyd, of Lockinge, Wantage, Berks.
    (a) Outline sketch of History of English Poetry, virtually same as that sent to Thomas Warton, followed by two other drafts with some variations.
    (b) Notes on Samuel Daniel, first printed in *Athenaeum*, July 29, 1854, pp. 941 f.
    (c) Notes on early romances and other books, list of "Writers of Poetry after 1600," and list of books. Two pages in all.
    (d) Long note on origin and date of *Amadis de Gaul*. Described by Toynbee, *Modern Language Review*, XXVII (1932), 60 f.

14. Transcripts of history or literature:
    (a) Alfonso de la Cueva, Relatione di Venetia (1619) from a MS. Forty-five folio pages, imperfect. B.M. Add. MS. 36818 (Stonhewer-Mathias-Samuel Rogers).
    (b) Other transcripts from MSS. in British Museum, mentioned by Gray in his letters.
    (c) George II's will. Mitford MS. III[2], 135.

15. 1764. Journey into Scotland, from Rose-Castle in Cumberland. Aug. 1764. Bp. of Carlisle. Printed by Tovey, *Gray and His Friends*, pp. 260–264, where it is erroneously described as a journal of Gray's own trip. Now in Morris Collection in Eton College Library.

16. Sketch of inaugural lecture in history (Latin). Two pages. Extracts in Mitford MS. III[2], 97–100.

17. Proposal for Professor of Modern History at Cambridge. B.M. Add. MS. 38334 (Liverpool Papers, CXLV), fol. 152. Printed in *Times Literary Supplement*, March 4, 1926, p. 163.

18. Descriptive catalogue of folio books. Three folio pages. Purpose unknown. Probably abandoned, third page unfinished and verso blank except for figures. Now in Cambridge University Library, Add. MS. 5994 ("found among H. Bradshaw's papers, 15 June, 1917").

19. Numerous papers (not in Gray's autograph but found with his MSS.):
    (a) Latin poem, Alcaic ode, signed "Antrobus." Mitford MS. III[1], 108–110.
    (b) Latin versions of 84th Psalm, of Cinna, of Philips' Splendid Shilling. Mitford MS. III[1], 76, 110.

(c) "Brevi Regole della Poesia Italiana," seven pages closely written, attributed by later owners to Gray but not in his autograph. Appeared in recent catalogues of Thomas Thorp, 93 St. Martin's Lane, London.

(d) "Epitre de M. de Voltaire en arrivant dans sa terre pres du Lac Leman en Mai, 1775." Copy sent to Gray by Stonhewer.

(e) Verse to Mr. Lyttelton, at Soissons, from Oxford. Mitford MS. III¹, 93–95.

(f) Garrick's "To Mr. Gray on his Odes." Printed copy?

(g) Anecdote of a familiar spirit that haunted the house of Tullochgoram, with Gray's note: "Given me by Mr. Abercrombie."

(h) Roll "of the names of certain Knights that dwelt in the County of Durham inter Tyne et Tease at the Battle of Lews."

(i) Mason's copy of "dialogue of books." Cf. Tovey, I, 93 f.

(j) Inscriptions and memoranda relating to Gray and Antrobus families (some in Gray's autograph). Mitford MS. III¹, 61, 66.

(k) Translation of Ugolino Episode from Dante's *Inferno* (Canto 33), 84 lines on two quarto sheets. Note in same hand: "It is uncertain when Mr. Gray translated the following story from Dante but most probably very early, and when he was making himself master of the Italian language." Now owned by the Marquess of Crewe.

20. Miscellaneous autographs bound with other material.

(a) Gray's own copy of his 1757 Odes contains: Verses on Miss Speed (corrections in second stanza and natural history notes on back); letter to Miss Speed (heraldic notes on back); and an epitaph on a child. Now in the Morgan Library.

(b) Gray's own copy of his 1753 poems with designs by Bentley, containing "Ode to Poesy" and other things. See *Book Prices Current*, XV (1901), 434.

(c) Works relating to Gray, with two pages from poet's notebook, autograph letters, and a MS. index by W. Cole. See *Book Prices Current*, XVII (1903), 465. Sold at Anderson's, January 25, 1904.

(d) H. Paul, *Queen Anne*, Asnieres, 1906, with rough draft of Latin verses on insects. Now in the Morgan Library.

Grand Tour, 6, 71
Grande Chartreuse, 6, 8, 51, 71
Gray, Dorothy (mother), 4, 9, 11, 14, 27, 33 n., 71
Gray, James C., 134 n.
Gray, Philip (father), 4, 8
Gray, Thomas
general and biographical: aesthetic nature, 28, 30, 36, 72, 126, 142 f., 147, 178; antiquarian tendencies, 16 f. 33 f., 38, 44–47, 53, 56 f., 110–117, 120; boredom, 3, 7, 8 f., 11, 16 f., 20, 37; character, 3, 11 f., 22–28, 142, 146 f.; curiosities, love of, 46 f., 57, 61 f.; fastidiousness, 5, 23 f., 28; food, love of, 18, 57, 128 f., 139; health, 17–19, 110, 118; history, theory of, 53, 55, 69, 74, 109 f., 115 f., 121, 123; humor and satire, 11, 17, 31 f., 36 f., 56, 71 f.; philosophy of life, 12 f., 20, 27 f., 60, 67 n., 68; publication, aversion to, 12, 13, 14, 16, 21, 28; romantic qualities, 6, 15, 37, 46 f., 51, 62, 70 f., 75 f., 93, 99; sterility, 12 f., 29, 146 f.
library, books from Gray's, 16, 21, 32–34, 36, 42, 81, 93, 96 n., 106 n., 116, 119, 122, 128 f., 181
literary output: criticism, 59–61, 62 f., 64, 65 f., 67 f., 69 n., 104, 143 f.; letters (quoted), 7, 8, 10 n., 11, 13 f., 16 f., 20, 22, 23, 34, 35 n., 36, 37, 41 n., 50, 51, 52, 54, 55, 56, 62, 69 n., 110, 112, 114, 118, 119, 120, 126 f., 128 n., 140, 143, 145, 147; Latin poems, 8, 12, 30 f., 49–53; *Ode to Spring*, 8, 52 n., 126, 178; *Alliance of Education and Government*, 13, 59 f.; other early poems in English, 13, 32, 51, 56, 126; *Elegy*, vii, 3, 8, 12–14, 15, 16, 22, 28, 92, 115, 136, 145, 146, 147; Pindaric odes (1757), 3, 16, 18, 64 f., 107, 146; *The Bard*, 15 f., 92–94, 98, 99, 100, 102, 145; *The Progress of Poesy*, 15, 81, 84, 93; Welsh poems, 16, 99; Norse poems, 16, 94 n., 99, 101–105; collected poems, 3, 14, 16, 64, 93, 102, 104, 144; translations, 31, 35, 49, 50, 51 f.
manuscripts: Commonplace Book, description, 39–41; articles described: architecture, 111–115; early English history, 110 f.; English poetry, 10 n., 85–90; allusions to food, etc., in classical literature, 57; Gothi, 100–103;

Greek cities, 56; heraldry, 116; Oriental history and geography, 73 f., 76–78, 85 n.; Plato, 66–68, 85 n.; Wales, 90–99, 91 n.
Linnaeus, interleaved, 126, 128 f., 131–133, 141
marginalia, 16, 21, 81, 93, 94 n., 116 f., 122, 128 f., 136 f., 140, 181
quarto notebooks, 175–177; bibliographical, 42–44, 53, 69 n., 79 n.; early catalogue of library, 32–35, 151–163; Greek writers, 54–66; learned journals, 46 f., 164–174; Oriental travel, 74–76
pocket notebooks, 18, 23, 80 n., 81 n., 84, 89, 96, 113 n., 123 n., 127 f., 137–140
scholarship: dating, 32 n., 39–41, 44 n., 61, 66, 73 f., 76, 80 f., 84 f., 94, 99, 100 f., 107, 110 f., 132, 137–140; general nature, 3, 28 f., 30, 48, 68 f., 105–107, 142 f., 145–147; influence on poems, 15, 59 f., 64 f., 70, 81, 84, 92 f., 94 n., 101–103, 126; methods, 38–45, 48, 74, 81, 115–117, 126–129, 132 ff.; subjects treated: architecture, 16, 19, 111–115, 117; bibliography, 34, 41–46, 79 n., 80 n.; chronological tables, 34, 44, 55 f., 69, 109, 110; classical literature, 30 f., 34 f., 39 f., 41, 43, 49–69; contemporary history, 43, 110, 111, 118, 121 f.; contemporary literature, 8, 31–33, 37; English history, 19 f., 21, 41, 107, 108–124; French, 19, 31, 34, 35, 51, 110, 118, 121; Greek civilization, 12, 38, 40 n., 54–68, 72 f., 109, 144; heraldry, 19, 112, 115–117; Italian, 5, 15, 31, 34, 35, 39, 110, 144; learned journals, 10 n., 38 f., 43, 45–47; Oriental history, 12, 73–80, 145; philology, 40 n., 72 n., 73, 87, 97 f., 100 f., 106, 128; poetics, 15, 41, 64 f., 84–107 *passim*, 119 f., 144 f.; science, 21, 40 f., 46 f., 57, 81, 125–141, 145; travel books, 12, 33, 39, 40, 41, 43, 47 n., 56, 61 f., 71–83
Greaves, John, 79
Gronovius, 36, 54
Grynæus, Simon, 80 f.
Guarini, G. B., 39
Guidebooks, English, 16, 82 f., 110 f.
Guillim, John, 116
Gunther, R. T., 129 n.

Ray, John, 36, 129 f.
Réaumur, R. A. de, 133
Reggio (Italy), 7, 50, 51
Restoration comedy, 31, 33
Rheims, 6 f.
Rhyme, origins of, 90 f., 94 f.
Rhys, J. D., 91 f., 95, 98, 106
Robert of Rheims, 77
Robertson, William, 118 n.
Robinson, William, 25 f., 136, 137
Rochefort, Charles de, 81
Rochester Cathedral, 113
Roe, Thomas, 78
Rogers, Mrs. Jonathan, 118
Romances, 31 f., 33, 37
Rome, 6 f., 36, 49, 72
Rowland, Henry, 89
Rowlandson, Thomas, 82
Royal Society, 45, 47 n., 129
Rumphius, G. E., 133
Rymer, Thomas, 110, 111 n.

St. Asaph's Cathedral, 114
St. David's Cathedral, 114
St. Paul's Cathedral, 114
Sale, George, 73, 78
Salisbury Cathedral, 113, 123 n.
Sandys, J. E., 68 n.
Sansovino, Francesco, 78
Saracens, 76, 77, 78
Scaliger, Joseph, 55
Scaliger, Julius, 89
Scholarship, Gray's, see Gray, Thomas
Scopoli, G. A., 133
Scotland, 21, 23 f., 25, 82, 116, 123 n., 136, 137, 138, 139
Selden, John, 73 n.
Seneca, 49
Sévigné, Madame de, 35, 36
Shaftesbury, Anthony Ashley, 3rd Earl of, 125
Shakespeare, 24, 27, 31 f., 33, 70, 84, 143
Shaw, Thomas, 73, 74 f., 109
Shepard, Odell, 8 n.
Silius Italicus, 49, 50, 109
Sloane, Sir Hans, 130
Snyder, E. D., 91, 94 n., 96 n.
Socrates, 62, 65, 67
Somner, William, 87
Sophocles, 34, 65 f.
Southampton, 21, 137, 138
Spain, 72, 77
Sparta, 59
Speed, Henrietta, 13, 19, 27
Spelman, Henry, 120

Spence, Joseph, 69 n.
Spenser, Edmund, 33, 70, 84, 89, 143
Spon, Jacob, 78
Statius, 31, 49
Steele, Richard, 33
Stephanus, 54, 58, 61, 65 n., 66, 68
Stillingfleet, Benjamin, 127 f., 130, 141
Stoke Poges, ix, 9, 11, 14, 18, 25, 53, 117 n., 126 f.
Stonhewer, Richard, viii, 9, 108, 146
Stow, John, 110, 112
Strabo, 24, 36, 40, 53, 61 f., 66, 72–80 passim, 109
Strathmore, John Lyon, 9th Earl of, 25, 136, 138, 139
Strawberry Hill, 3, 16, 25, 112, 121 n.
Struvius, B. G., 45 n.
Strype, John, 110, 111 n.
Stukeley, William, 118
Suetonius, 33
Suffolk, 123 n., 136
Suidas, 54
Sweden, 125, 127, 128, 137
Swift, Jonathan, 36
Switzerland, 22
Syria, 73, 75, 76, 77, 79, 109

Tacitus, 49, 51, 55, 109, 144
Tallents, Francis, 34
Tanner, Thomas, 85, 95
Tasso, 35, 39
Tatars, 79, 80, 109, 123
Tavernier, J. B., 79, 80
Temple, W. J., vii, 3, 24
Templeman, W. D., 49 n., 83 n.
Thebes, 56, 59
Theocritus, 37, 52
Thessaly, 59
Thévenot, Jean de, 79, 80
Thévenot, Melchisedech de, 79, 80
Thomson, James, 70, 125
Thorney, Abbey, 114
Thorpe, C. D., 71 n.
Thuanus, 77, 78
Thucydides, 34, 51, 62, 65 n., 66, 109, 144
Thwaites, Edward, 104 n.
Torfæus, 100, 102, 103 n.
Tovey, Duncan C., viii, notes passim
Toynbee, Paget, x, 55 n., 123 n.
Translations used by Gray, 33, 41, 58, 65 n., 68, 78 f., 98, 101, 106
Travel books, collections and editions used, 33, 77–81; burlesque of, 71 f.; influence on English literature, 70, 82 f.

Trollope, William, 66
Turner, Shallett, 108
Tyrwhitt, Thomas, 87
Tyson, Michael, 21, 24, 131, 141

Urry, John, 84 n., 86 f.

Vaillant, Jean Foy, 78
Valkyries, 102
Valle, Pietro della, 78, 79, 80
Van Hook, LaRue, 65 n.
Venice, 7, 78 n.
Vergil, 30 f., 33 f., 34, 39, 50, 52, 68, 143
Vine, the (Hampshire), 11, 18, 25
Vogt, J., 45 n.
Voltaire, 3
Voyages, collections of, to America, 80 f.;
    to the Levant, 33, 77 f., 79; to the Orient,
    33, 79 f.

Wakefield, Gilbert, 144
Waller, Edmund, 33
Walpole, Horace, 5–8, 10 n., 11, 20, 22,
    32, 35 f., 49–51, 71 f., 99, 112, 114,
    119–123, 142
Wanley, Humfrey, 101 n., 105, 119
Warburton, William, 84, 85 n.
Warton, Thomas, 86, 107, 180
Wells Cathedral, 113
Welsh bards, 15, 95 f., 99, 109; history,
    96 f.; language, 92 f., 97 f., 106 f.;
    prosody, 15, 91–95; translation from, 99

West, Richard, 5–9, 31, 34, 35, 36, 50–52,
    71, 126, 142, 147
Westminster Abbey, 114
Wharton, Dr. Thomas, 9–11, 14, 16, 19,
    20, 22 f., 38, 43, 53–56, 62, 71, 82, 110,
    112, 119 f., 126–128, 136, 137, 138,
    141, 147
Wheeler, Sir George, 56, 78, 109
Whibley, Leonard, x, 7 n., 9 n., 12 n., 30 n.,
    103 n., 108 n., 123 n.
White, Benjamin, 128
Whithed, Francis, 11
William of Malmesbury, 89 n.
Willis, Browne, 118
Willughby, Francis, 130
Winchester Cathedral, 113
Wingfield (Suffolk), 123 n.
Winstanley, D. A., 123 n.
Wood, Anthony, 111 n.
Worcester Cathedral, 113
Wordsworth, William, 82, 126
Wormius, 104
Wotton, William, 95 n., 106
Wright, J. K., 79 n.
Wyatt, Sir Thomas, 119, 121 n.
Wynn, Sir John, 96
Wynne, William, 97

Xenophon, 54, 61–63, 66, 72, 76, 109

York, 112 f., 126
Yorkshire, 127, 137